# OECD Energy Investment Policy Review of Ukraine

OECD
BETTER POLICIES FOR BETTER LIVES

**Please cite this publication as:**
OECD (2021), *OECD Energy Investment Policy Review of Ukraine*, OECD Publishing, Paris, *https://doi.org/10.1787/6e6e58c6-en*.

ISBN 978-92-64-72997-1 (print)
ISBN 978-92-64-67973-3 (pdf)

**Photo credits:** Cover © biDaala studio/Shutterstock.com.

Corrigenda to publications may be found on line at: *www.oecd.org/about/publishing/corrigenda.htm*.

# Foreword

Scaling up investment in energy is critical to successfully implementing Ukraine's Energy Strategy as well as the 2015 Paris Agreement on climate change and the country's 2050 Green Energy Transition Concept (Ukraine Green Deal), which was launched in 2020. Despite the implementation of important reforms to date by Ukraine, a great deal remains to be done to underpin and ensure effective energy sector reforms. The energy sector represents 12.6% of the country's GDP, yet issues regarding governance, pricing policy, bid-rigging, management and security of energy assets have continued to present obstacles to its development. Key challenges for further investment in Ukraine's energy sector include improving energy security, reducing fossil-fuel consumption and imports, the closure of coal mines, improving market functioning, addressing corrupt practices and justice system weaknesses.

The OECD *Energy Investment Policy Review of Ukraine* provides analysis and recommendations to help policy makers strengthen the enabling conditions for investment in Ukraine's energy sector. It assesses Ukraine's investment climate *vis-à-vis* the country's energy sector reforms and discusses challenges and opportunities in this context. Capitalising on the OECD *Policy Framework for Investment* as well as on the OECD *Policy Guidance for Investment in the Clean Energy Investment Infrastructure*, the *Review* takes a broad approach to investment climate challenges facing Ukraine's energy sector, with chapters assessing investment trends in the sector, reviewing Ukraine's current policy and regulatory framework for investment in the energy sector (including key policy reforms implemented to date to support such investment), the legal and institutional framework for investment protection, investment promotion and facilitation, public governance, energy infrastructure and policies to promote and enable responsible business conduct (RBC).

This *Review* is a response to Ukraine's request to the OECD to undertake a sector-specific investment policy review in the framework of a broader OECD project aimed at supporting energy sector reforms in Ukraine. The project is carried out in the context of the OECD-Ukraine Action Plan, in line with the Memorandum of Understanding between the Government of Ukraine and the OECD, and encompasses a mix of analytical and capacity-building activities to ensure relevance and support to Ukrainian institutions in reforming the energy sector. The Government of Norway has been funding this project.

Building on previous OECD Investment Policy Reviews (IPRs) of Ukraine, including the 2016 IPR conducted in the context of Ukraine's application to adhere to the OECD *Declaration on International Investment and Multinational Enterprises*, the OECD *Energy Investment Policy Review of Ukraine* assesses specific aspects of the regulatory environment with implications for energy investments, as well as the overall quality of the country's investment climate for attracting investors in the energy sector.

The *Review* was developed by the OECD Investment Division and OECD Centre for Responsible Conduct, both of the OECD Directorate for Financial and Enterprises Affairs, in co-operation with Gabriela Miranda, Head of Unit, and Peline Atamer, Deputy Head of Unit, OECD Global Relations Secretariat (GRS). It was prepared under the overall guidance of Ana Novik, Head of the Investment Division, and Stephen Thomsen, Deputy Head of the Investment Division, in coordination with a team led by Dr. Frédéric Wehrlé (OECD Investment Division and OECD Centre on Responsible Business Conduct) comprising Boryana

Kiskinova and Baxter Roberts (OECD Investment Division); Coralie Martin (OECD Centre on Responsible Business Conduct); and Silvia Carolina Rocha, senior consultant at the Investment Division.

The *Review* benefitted from valuable comments received from Ukrainian officials, representatives from donor agencies and private and civil society stakeholders, including: The European Bank for Reconstruction and Development (EBRD), the Delegation of the European Union to Ukraine, the International Financial Cooperation (IFC), the Gesellschaft für Internationale Zusammenarbeit (GIZ), the Extractive Industries Transparency Initiative (EITI) and Dixi Group. It also benefitted from inputs by the OECD Secretariat, including the Global Relations Secretariat, the Corporate Governance and Corporate Finance Division, the OECD Centre for Responsible Business Conduct, the OECD Competition Division and the Anti-Corruption Division, all within the Directorate for Financial and Enterprise Affairs. The Review also builds on the experience of the Secretariat of the OECD Investment Committee in helping countries improve their domestic investment environment.

The *Review* was produced with the financial assistance of Norway. The views expressed herein can in no way be taken to reflect the official opinion of Norway.

The information in this *Review* is current as of 1 October 2021.

# Table of contents

## FIGURES



## TABLES

# Acronyms and abbreviations

| | |
|---|---|
| **BCM** | Billion cubic metres |
| **BEPS** | Base Erosion and Profit Shifting |
| **CEB** | Council of Europe Development Bank |
| **CGAP** | Corporate Governance Action Plan |
| **CGPA** | Corporate Governance Professional Association |
| **CHP** | Combined Heat And Power Plants |
| **CMU** | Cabinet of Ministers of Ukraine |
| **CoST** | Infrastructure Transparency Initiative |
| **CPCU** | Civil Procedural Code of Ukraine |
| **CPP** | Coal power plant |
| **DAM** | Day-ahead market |
| **DCFTA** | Deep and Comprehensive Free Trade Agreement |
| **DH** | District heater |
| **DHC** | District Heating Company |
| **DSO** | Distribution System Operator |
| **EBA** | European Business Association |
| **E&P** | Exploration and Production |
| **E5P** | Eastern Europe Energy Efficiency and Environment Partnership |
| **EBRD** | European Bank for Reconstruction and Development |
| **EC** | European Commission |
| **EEI** | Energy efficiency indicator |
| **EIA** | Environmental Impact Assessment |
| **EIB** | European Investment Bank |
| **EITI** | Ensuring Transparency in Extractive Industries |
| **ENTSO-E** | European Network of Transmission System Operators for Electricity |
| **ENTSO-G** | European Network of Transmission System Operators for Gas |
| **ESU** | Energy Strategy of Ukraine |
| **ETSO** | Energy Transmission System Operator |
| **EU** | European Union |
| **EUR** | Euro |

| | |
|---|---|
| **FATF** | Financial Action Task Force |
| **FDI** | Foreign Direct Investment |
| **FIT** | Feed-in tariff |
| **FPU** | Federation of Trade Unions of Ukraine |
| **HJC** | High Council of Justice |
| **HQCJ** | High Qualification Commission of Judges |
| **GCPF** | Global Climate Partnership Fund |
| **GDP** | Gross Domestic Product |
| **GTSO** | Gas Transmission System Operator |
| **GTSOU** | Gas Transmission System Operator of Ukraine |
| **HACC** | High Anti-Corruption Court |
| **HCJ** | High Council of Justice |
| **HPP** | Hydropower Plants |
| **HQCJ** | High Qualification Commission of Judges |
| **HUS** | Housing and Utilities Subsidies |
| **IBRD** | International Bank for Reconstruction and Development |
| **ICA** | International Commercial Arbitration |
| **IDM** | Intra-day market |
| **IFC** | International Finance Corporation |
| **IFI** | International Financing Institutions |
| **ILO** | International Labour Organisation |
| **ILO MNE Declaration** | ILO Tripartite Declaration of Principles concerning Multinational Enterprises and Social Policy |
| **IP** | Intellectual Property |
| **IPR** | Investment Policy Review |
| **IPS** | Independent Power Supplier |
| **JRC** | Judicial Reform Council |
| **JSRAP** | Justice Sector Reform Strategy and Action Plan |
| **km** | Kilometre |
| **ktoe** | Kilo tonne of oil equivalent |
| **MDB** | Multilateral development bank |
| **MEPR** | Ministry of Environmental Protection and Natural Resources of Ukraine |
| **MoU** | Memorandum of Understanding |
| **Mt** | Million tonnes |
| **Mtoe** | Million tonnes of oil equivalent |
| **NABU** | National Anti-Corruption Bureau of Ukraine |
| **NAPC** | National Agency for the Prevention of Corruption |
| **NBU** | National Bank of Ukraine |
| **NEFCO** | Nordic Environment Finance Corporation |

| | |
|---|---|
| **NEURC** | National Energy and Utilities Regulatory Commission |
| **NGO** | Non-Governmental Organisation |
| **NIB** | Nordic Investment Bank |
| **NMRS** | National Mediation and Reconciliation Service |
| **NPGU** | Independent Trade Union of Miners of Ukraine |
| **NPP** | Nuclear Power Plant |
| **OPP** | Odessa Portside Plant |
| **PEC** | Production Enhancement Contract |
| **PEO** | Private Enforcement Officers |
| **PPA** | Power Purchase Agreement |
| **PPP** | Public-Private Partnership |
| **PSA** | Production sharing agreements |
| **PSO** | Public Service Obligations |
| **PTP** | Power transmission project |
| **RBC** | Responsible Business Conduct |
| **RES** | Renewable energy source |
| **SAEE** | State Agency on Energy Efficiency and Energy Saving |
| **SAPO** | Special Anti-Corruption Prosecutor's Office |
| **SEO** | State Enforcement Officers |
| **SOE** | State-Owned Enterprise |
| **SPFU** | State Property Fund |
| **SPP** | Solar Power Plants |
| **SSGS** | State Service of Geology and Subsoil |
| **STEM** | Science, Technology, Engineering and Mathematics |
| **TCM** | Trillion cubic meters |
| **TPES** | Total Primary Energy Supply |
| **TPP** | Thermo Power Plants |
| **TRIPS** | Trade-Related Aspects of Intellectual Property Rights |
| **TSO** | Transmission System Operator |
| **UAH** | Ukrainian hryvnia |
| **UGV** | Ukrgasvydobuvannya |
| **USD** | U.S. dollar |
| **WB** | World Bank |
| **WIPO** | World Intellectual Property Organisation |
| **WPP** | Wind Power Plants |
| **WTO** | World Trade Organisation |

# Executive summary

This *Energy Investment Policy Review of Ukraine* is the fruit of a two-year inclusive work that was undertaken within the wider context of the OECD project *Supporting Energy Sector Reform in Ukraine*, which was launched in 2019 with the financial support of the Government of Norway. The work is carried out within the framework of the OECD *Memorandum of Understanding for Strengthening Co-operation with the Government of Ukraine*, which was signed in 2014 to support Ukraine in its efforts to carry out its reform agenda in line with international standards.

The *Review* assesses regulations and measures specifically affecting the sector and provides recommendations that can help Ukraine deliver on its sectoral objectives, which notably include ensuring energy security, and transitioning to a cleaner, more competitive, and more attractive energy sector. Along with efficiency, security, competitiveness, and integration with the EU energy community, attracting investment and further improving the country's institutional framework are key government priorities, as is evidenced by strategic documents such as "The Energy Strategy of Ukraine 2035", which was adopted by the government in 2017. In the aftermath of the Euromaidan revolution of 2013-2014, the Government of Ukraine has been seeking to improve the national energy sector's business environment by implementing a series of structural and institutional reforms.

On the one hand, Ukraine has taken important strides in providing adequate levels of investment protection in the energy sector and in general. Ukraine's investment legislation includes the principle of non-discrimination against foreign investment and general provisions on foreign investment protection. Efforts have also been made to create an open and transparent environment for foreign investment in the energy sector by adopting new laws reinforcing and simplifying the protection of businesses operating in the energy sector. To further encourage investment, Ukraine has also introduced significant reforms to modernise SOEs, improve transparency in public procurement, while opening the sector to private companies.

On the other hand, Ukraine's low score in several international rankings and the low trust levels of businesses in the judiciary are a cause of concern for both domestic and foreign investors. Despite substantial and structural reforms having been made to reduce corruption and mitigate its effects on the energy sector, corruption and favouritism remain widespread. According to a survey by the American Chamber of Ukraine on Ukraine's investment climate in September 2021, 93% of businesses stated that implementation of real and effective judicial reform, the rule of law, fair justice, and the eradication of corruption should be the government's primary objectives in order to deliver economic growth, improve the business climate, and attract investment. A strong judiciary is also lacking, which is essential for winning investors' trust not only in Ukraine's energy sector but also in the country overall.

The *Energy Investment Policy Review* also analyses Ukraine's track record in promoting responsible business conduct (RBC) in the energy sector. While Ukraine has been an Adherent to the OECD *Declaration on International Investment and Multinational Enterprises* since 2017, and has sought to create an enabling environment for RBC, further efforts are needed to enhance responsible conduct across energy sub-sectors and strengthen environmental, human and labour rights protection, anti-corruption measures, and transparency and disclosure practices.

Raising investment further requires a comprehensive and coherent policy package. This OECD *Energy Investment Policy Review* of Ukraine looks at challenges and opportunities for attracting more and better energy investment.

# 1 Assessment and Recommendations

This chapter provides an overview of the main findings in the publication and lists the accompanying policy recommendations.

## Stocktaking of Ukraine's policy framework for investment in the energy sector

Ukraine has a large endowment of gas and mid-stream infrastructure that offer investment opportunities in Europe. The country is rich in fossil fuel resources, including coal and natural gas, while developing low-carbon sources, including hydro, biofuels and other renewables. However, structural problems, such as lack of legal certainty and major financial imbalances in the energy sector, and the presence of vested interests undermine the energy potential of Ukraine. Despite the reforms implemented from 2014 to 2021, the sector is still destabilised by two issues that were already identified in the OECD Investment Policy Reviews of Ukraine of 2011 and 2016. Firstly, in some energy sub-sectors, SOEs and privately-owned companies do not operate on an equal footing. Secondly, energy prices are regulated with price levels that are below production costs and subject to cross-subsidisation within various sub-sectors and among different consumers.

The trajectory of energy reforms in Ukraine has been constant since the signing of the Association Agreement with the European Union (EU). As such, the country has deepened its energy inter-connectivity with Europe, increased energy efficiency and set a path towards a low carbon economy. However, the reforms implemented in different energy sub-sectors vary widely and reflect the political dynamics around each subsector. The Energy Strategy of Ukraine until 2035, approved by the Cabinet of Ministers of Ukraine on August 2017, addresses the most critical issues for achieving a sectoral transformation, and is aimed at improving the country's energy efficiency, security, competitiveness and integration with the EU energy community.

The reforms implemented in the energy sector by Ukraine have secured the participation of private companies in a wide range of contracts and structures. The government has also increased the in-flow of capital into the energy sector by privatising state assets, both large and small, and by reforming public procurement. These changes have led to growing interest from national and international corporations in the Ukrainian hydrocarbon and renewable energy sectors.

The outbreak of COVID-19 has affected investments in energy sectors both worldwide and in Ukraine. Long-awaited reforms, such as the cancellation of cross-subsidisation, have been postponed. Furthermore, restrictive measures on persons and goods put in place during the first wave of the pandemic have affected the electricity, hydrocarbon and renewables markets in Ukraine. However, by adequately implementing Ukraine's Energy Strategy until 2035 and the Energy Security Strategy, the latest approved in August 2021, the Government of Ukraine could be able to secure sustainable investments in the energy sector, going beyond corporate profitability and generating economic, social and environmental development.

## Policy framework for investment

Since Euromaidan in 2013-2014, attracting investment in Ukraine's energy sector has been a top priority of the government, as is evidenced by the Energy Strategy of Ukraine (ESU 2035). To improve the attractiveness of its energy sector, Ukraine has made continuous efforts to reform the regulatory framework in line with European legislation and other international standards.

As was already identified in the OECD 2016 *Investment Policy Review of Ukraine*, there are no generalised screening or approval mechanisms for new investments or established companies in Ukraine. Ukraine does not impose limits on access to local finance and incentives or government purchasing markets for foreign-controlled enterprises incorporated in the country. National treatment of foreign investors in the post-establishment phase is guaranteed, which means that foreign investors, when incorporated and headquartered in Ukraine, are considered to be domestic legal entities, with all the rights and obligations that apply to domestic investors. Exceptions to national treatment relevant to Ukraine's energy sector include the acquisition of farm land and some aspects of access to privatisation. In addition, only natural monopolies, which are regulated by the Law on Natural Monopolies, can carry out certain types of business activities such as transport of oil and oil products by oil pipelines, transport of natural and oil gas by pipelines, distribution of natural gas by pipelines, and electricity transmission.

## The protection of investment in Ukraine

Ukraine has established a legal framework containing domestic provisions aimed at promoting and protecting investments. Creating a level playing field for energy sector investors has been seen by Ukraine as important for fostering investments. The country has implemented several legislative reforms to ensure the supremacy of law and combat corruption. That being said, there is room for further improvement. To achieve a more holistic reform, Ukraine should further strengthen institutional co-operation between existing anti-corruption bodies, ensure equal access to justice, firmly uphold the rule of law and provide efficient protection of ownership rights through the use of alternative dispute resolution mechanisms.

Ukraine's governance challenges are among the most important impediments to improving growth prospects and unlocking the private sector's contribution to the development of the energy sector. While addressing these challenges requires fundamental institutional change that will take time and yield broad-based improvements only in the long term, progress in specific areas can have important impacts on strengthening transparency and accountability in the short and medium term. Therefore, it is important to sustain ongoing actions in key areas such as effective implementation of anti-corruption laws, implementation of reforms in the judiciary system, and strengthening of regulation enforcement.

Investor protection granted under Ukraine's investment treaties is another important part of the legal framework that is relevant for investment in the energy sector. Ukraine has over 60 investment treaties in force today. These treaties grant protections to certain investors in addition to and independently from protections available under domestic law to all investors. Most of these treaties apply to investments across the entire economy, including the energy sector, while some apply specifically to the energy sector. Like treaties that are signed by many other countries, Ukraine's investment treaties typically protect investments made by treaty-covered investors against expropriation, discrimination and unfair or unequitable treatment. They also give covered investors access to investor-state dispute settlement (ISDS) procedures, including international arbitration, in cases where they claim that the government has infringed these protections.

A significant number of Ukraine's investment treaties have rather vague investment protections and ISDS provisions that may create unintended consequences in ISDS cases and ultimately undermine the goals of such treaties – a situation that Ukraine shares with many other countries. Many governments now recognise that it would be desirable to reform some older investment treaties so that they include specific design approaches commonly used in newer investment treaties. Updating existing treaties remains a separate challenge to negotiating new treaties, with time, cost and resource allocation constraints. Reform options for older treaties may also need to take account of new needs and priorities for such treaties today, including the growing urgency of tackling the climate crisis and creating the necessary incentives for the transition to low-carbon, renewable energy sources. Recommendations to reconsider several aspects of the government's approach to investment treaties in this context are set out in chapter 4 of this *Review*.

Whatever approach the government takes towards investment treaty-making, these treaties should not be seen as a substitute for long-term improvements in the domestic business environment, including through measures to improve the capacity, efficiency and independence of the domestic court system, the quality of the legal framework, and the strength of national institutions responsible for enforcing such legislation.

## Energy infrastructure in Ukraine

Ukraine remains far behind developed countries in terms of building efficient and innovative energy infrastructure. Chronic underfunding from the state budget and inefficient state property management are two important factors for explaining the current condition of infrastructure. The government is aware that one way to enhance infrastructure is by attracting private investors to the country. Besides, the Ministry of Infrastructure has recognised seven necessary conditions that would aid in successfully implementing energy infrastructure in the country: i) political will and support by the state and society; ii) reliable legal framework and strong institutions; iii) flexible financing through equity and debt; iv) transparent and impartial tenders; v) reliable feasibility studies; vi) fair risk allocation between partners; and vii) rate of return expected by private partners remunerating adequately the level of risk.

Ukraine has the opportunity of generating policies that will enable energy infrastructure projects to advance the country's commitments to achieve a carbon-neutral economy and integrate with the EU market. For instance, strengthening policies that regulate electricity ancillary services will enable investments to upgrade transmission and distribution infrastructure by private sector participants. For Ukraine to comply with its National Determined Contributions under the Paris Agreement, it is essential that the government provides legal certainty to investors developing renewable energy generation projects. Ukraine should consider the importance of resolving the issue of fiscal arrears due to renewable energy companies. This could help improve the investment climate in the renewable energy sector and attract additional foreign capital.

1. Ukraine should establish principles to improve regulatory and administrative predictability not only during the preparation and construction of energy infrastructure projects but also during the operation, as less risk and uncertainty over infrastructure projects can increase the flows of investments in the country. Additionally, to decrease the high per capita consumption of electricity and heating, it is necessary to advance infrastructure projects that foster energy efficiency.

## Investment promotion and facilitation

In the context of reforming the energy sector and transforming it into a clean, green, decarbonised sector of the economy, one of the main challenges for Ukraine is the need to leverage significant investment flows. Targeted investment promotion and facilitation efforts, along with effective and quality policy-making relative to the overall investment climate are crucial for modernising Ukraine's energy industry.

Recent initiatives have aimed to promote Ukraine as an attractive destination for foreign investments in all sectors of the economy, including in the energy sector in line with the Energy Strategy of Ukraine until 2035. These initiatives are part of the liberalisation efforts in the electricity, oil and gas markets, and due to the potential of renewable energy generation in Ukraine. As a result, Ukraine, supported by international partners such as the OECD, the EU, EBRD and the IMF, has been exploring ways to develop a greener energy sector, notably through solar and wind power, and ultimately through a green hydrogen industry in the country.

Ukraine's investment promotion agency (IPA), UkraineInvest, has played a central role in investment promotion and facilitation activities since its creation in 2016, while government actions aim to enhance the regulatory and institutional framework surrounding foreign investment. Investment facilitation also stems from administrative simplification efforts that have been implemented over recent years. Despite Ukraine's improvement with respect to international rankings assessing its business climate (OECD FDI Regulatory Restrictiveness Index, World Bank Doing Business), the institutional environment remains challenging for investors and harmful for Ukraine's competitiveness. Further efforts are needed to improve investors' perception of Ukraine's business climate as this *Review* highlights, particularly in the energy sector, where the historical prevalence of monopolistic and state-owned enterprises has been viewed by business and international organisations as a feature that hinders investments.

## Public governance in Ukraine's energy sector

Since the Revolution of Dignity in February 2014, Ukraine has strengthened its anti-corruption policies by adopting reforms such as the 2014 Law on prevention of corruption (in force since April 2015) and reforms of the judicial system. A weak judiciary and corruption nevertheless remain outstanding issues despite important reforms. According to a survey on Ukraine's investment climate released in September 2021 by the American Chamber of Ukraine, 93% of surveyed businesses stated that implementation of real and effective judicial reform, the rule of law, fair justice, and the eradication of corruption should be the government's primary objectives in order to deliver economic growth, improve the business climate, and attract FDI

Public procurement has substantially improved, although numerous amendments to the law on public procurement have provided a challenge for businesses, as they have affected legal certainty. The enforcement of the Law on prevention of corruption and the work of Ukraine's anti-corruption agencies have also faced challenges, as evidenced by the 2020 Constitutional Court's controversial rulings. Strengthening judicial capacity is also crucial not only for the success of Ukraine's energy transformation but also for the country's development overall. There are also long-standing risks related to political interference in Ukraine's energy sector, which corruption continues to plague.

## RBC in Ukraine's energy sector

Promoting and enabling responsible business conduct (RBC) is of central interest to policymakers to attract quality investment and to ensure that business activity in their country contributes to broader value creation and sustainable development. RBC principles and standards set out an expectation that all businesses should avoid and address negative impacts stemming from their operations, while contributing to sustainable development where they operate.

Although Ukraine has been an Adherent to the OECD *Declaration on International Investment and Multinational Enterprises* since 2017, more work needs to be done to ensure that a comprehensive regulatory framework creates an enabling environment for the promotion and implementation of RBC principles in the upstream, midstream and downstream activities in the energy sector. Further to streamlining the existing RBC-related policies and legal and regulatory frameworks, further efforts are needed to strengthen environmental, human and labour rights protections, anti-corruption efforts, and transparency and disclosure practices.

## Box 1.1. Policy recommendations

**General recommendations**

- Progressively move from feed-in tariffs to more competitive support mechanisms. In addition to the feed-in tariffs, Ukraine's renewable energy market offers the possibility of auctions and the introduction of corporate power purchase agreements that will play an important role in energy transition efforts. Ukraine may wish to consider putting in place awareness campaigns highlighting the benefits of renewable energy.
- Advance the implementation of regulations on the development of bioenergy potential of Ukraine related to the development of solid biofuels market, development of liquid biofuels market, development of bio methane market, development of energy crops on marginal lands, reduction of the tax burden on bioenergy facilities running on biofuels by setting a zero rate of C02 emissions tax for them.
- Move forward with the implementation of regulations that promote competition in the electricity sector, while placing a special emphasis on the Auctions Law.
- Assess electricity and gas tariff schemes for consumer households, abolish cross-subsidies and provide targeted subsidies to benefit the poorest households. In this regard, ensure that tariff and pricing policies reflect the costs of production, transmission, and distribution and allow for a profit for investors. In addition, gradually reduce public service obligations and ensure that those applicable in the country are in line with the EU acquis.
- Develop a regulatory framework and action programmes that advance the economic switch from hydrocarbons to renewable energy sources at a faster rate by strengthening the national and regional efforts to phase out coal power plants and eradicating policy support mechanisms for the consumption of fossil fuels.
- Continue implementing policies and programmes that pursue the integration of Ukraine's power and gas system with the EU through synchronisation with the ENTSO-E and the ENTSO-G, including integration measures such as reinforcements of the transmission network, realisation of frequency regulation reserves, establishment of a telecommunication network, and studies on future grid stability.
- Establish a mandatory condition for power quotas for entities generating electricity from renewable energy investors, according to which they must simultaneously provide highly manoeuvrable generation, efficient balancing capacities or Energy Storage-type systems. Incite policy investments that allow RES producers to use the grid to store surplus generated power for a long time and to consume it later.
- Adopt a progressive regulatory framework to bring the players with new technologies, such as battery energy storage systems, demand response technologies, and green hydrogen to the energy markets. This step will encourage the implementation of many investment projects with these technologies.
- Ensure that public procurement and privatisation processes in the whole energy sector are transparent, open to quality private investors, free of corruption and continue using public procurement e-platforms such ProZorro and ProZorro.Sales, Continue providing training for public officials, both at the central and local levels of governments, on the use of ProZorro and ProZorro.Sales.
- Take additional actions to ensure that state-owned enterprises active in the energy sector observe high standards of transparency and are subject to the same high quality accounting,

disclosure, compliance and auditing standards as listed companies as recommended in the OECD 2021 *Review of the Corporate Governance of State-Owned Enterprises: Ukraine*.

**National treatment of investment**

- Further liberalise sectors that remain relatively closed to foreign investment as already noted in the OECD *2016 Investment Policy Review of Ukraine*.
- Finalise the pending land reform and evaluate the restriction on foreign companies purchasing agricultural land, especially if Ukraine wishes to activate the biofuel industry.
- Continue strengthening the competition law regime, notably in the areas highlighted in the 2016 OECD *Review of Competition Law and Policy in Ukraine* such as improving the impartial and transparent functioning of the Anti-Monopoly Committee of Ukraine, and ensuring that privatisation encourages more competition in previously monopolistic sectors instead of merely replacing public with private monopolies.

**Investment protection**

- Increase the number of IP rights-trained judges as well as judges with expertise in other key areas such as competition and economic regulation. An increase in the number of judges is likely to improve the quality and efficiency of IP dispute consideration. It will contribute to the Ukrainian court system and the state in general as the solution to the jurisdiction problem by boosting the effectiveness of decision, creating an opportunity to set special court procedures and practice generalisations to enhance efficiency and accuracy, serving as a basis for the consistency and predictability of case outcomes and the source of progressive development and dynamism in IP cases.
- Expedite the examination for green technology IP applications. As part of the strategy to enhance the protection of IP rights of green technologies, various national IP offices offer expedited examination for green technology patent applications. In the United Kingdom, the Green Channel platform is open to all patent applications that can make a reasonable assertion of having an environmental benefit.
- Strengthen international co-operation to nurture innovation. To stimulate the breakthroughs necessary to advance renewable energy investments, existing platforms designed to foster international collaboration should be prioritised at a national level. This allows countries to share ideas, pool resources and capital, and co-develop programmes that support common interests.
- Ensure independent, integral and rigorous work of the HACC towards adjudication of corruption without political interference and other undue influence. As mandated by the Law, the HACC must keep its independence and respect the separation of powers but it must solve the cases brought by NABU and SAPO against designated high-level officials (including ministers, deputies, members of parliament, agency leaders, judges, prosecutors, and heads of state-owned enterprises) for a specified set of corruption-related crimes that entail damage in excess of a monetary threshold (at the time of writing of this *Review*, NABU was conducting a pre-trial investigation into corruption offenses which incurred damages excessing UAH 1 189 500, roughly equivalent to USD 44 500). It is of the utmost importance that this final element in the specialised anti-corruption criminal justice system functions effectively and with integrity. The backlog of cases from NABU and SAPO should be eliminated to ensure fair and transparent judgements in corruption cases. This should help to strengthen trust in the judiciary, including on behalf of investors.
- Adopt a comprehensive legislative package that sets a complete systemic enforcement framework. Ukraine should incorporate a comprehensive problem-solving mechanism for a genuine enforcement reform. The proposed framework should involve an open discussion with representatives of the legal community, businesses and other service users, professional associations, and scholars, as well as international experts. The final enforcement framework

must ensure institutional independence of the enforcement service from state intervention and deliver significant results of judgment enforcements.

- Implement mediation and ADR mechanism legislation. It is recommended to further develop mediation and other ADRs in all types of process, which would have positive impact on the court's workload (the workload of the courts of first instance would be affected directly, while agreements reached through ADR mechanism could prevent appeals, thus reducing the workload of appeal courts). Compulsory pre-litigation settlement attempts in certain categories of cases (mandatory pre-requisite for taking legal action) should also be considered.
- Continue to reassess and update the government's priorities with respect to investment treaty policy. An important issue in this regard is an evaluation of the appropriate balance between investor protections and the government's right to regulate, and how to achieve that balance in practice. Many of Ukraine's older investment treaties do not contain the clarifications and more specific design approaches to key clauses used in many newer investment treaties. A clearer specification of these provisions would likely help to reflect government intent and ensure policy space for government regulation, as well as providing greater predictability for covered investors, including in the energy sector. The interface between investment treaties and broader priorities for Ukraine and many other governments – such as tackling climate change, promoting responsible business conduct and fostering sustainable development – are also important considerations. It has proven difficult for governments to update older treaties to reflect updated priorities but some multilateral reform initiatives are underway. Aside from multilateral action, it may be possible to clarify language through joint interpretations agreed with treaty partners or treaty amendments, depending on whether the parties wish to clarify original intent or revise a provision. Replacement of older investment treaties by consent may also be an appropriate option in some cases (as Ukraine appears to have done with Israel, Finland, Turkey and Slovakia).
- Continue to participate actively in and follow closely government and other actions on investment treaty reforms at the OECD, UNCITRAL and for the ECT. Consideration of reforms and policy discussions on frequently-invoked provisions in ISDS cases and whether investment treaties are achieving their intended purposes are of particular importance in current investment treaty policy. The government should prioritise its engagement in these various inter-governmental initiatives.
- Continue to improve ISDS dispute prevention and case management tools. The government may wish to consider drawing on examples of institutional frameworks in other countries for the prevention of investment disputes and policy-setting activities. It may also wish to consider ways to promote awareness-raising and inter-ministerial co-operation regarding the government's investment treaty policy and the significance of investment treaty obligations for the day-to-day functions of line agencies. Whatever approach the government adopts towards international investment agreements, complementary measures can help to ensure that treaties are consistent with domestic priorities and reduce the risk of disputes leading to international arbitration.

**Energy infrastructure in Ukraine**

- Improve market conditions for commercial banks to finance a higher share of energy infrastructure by adopting policies that enable competition between commercial and state-owned banks. Reinforce projects' screening by lenders to avoid the very high proportion of non-performing loans that in turn increase banks' profitability and widen access to affordable credit.
- Foster the development of green and climate financial products, such as green bonds, that comply with best environmental, social and governance standards and practices.

- Strengthen institutional capacity of the governmental agencies that participate in PPPs by providing training to officers and develop awareness-raising tools directed at investors.
- Establish prioritisation of PPP projects by the government in order to send clear signals to investors and outline long-term relevant goals in the PPP area. In addition, Ukraine should evaluate the possibility of allowing PPPs with SOEs that are in the process of being privatised to mobilise private capital in energy infrastructure.
- Finalise the pending reform on land and evaluate the restrictions on foreign companies to acquiring agricultural land, especially if Ukraine would like to activate the biofuel industry.
- Keep implementing measures to enhance transparency and tackle corruption in the energy sector by using technological tools in infrastructure energy projects such as CoST, and align citizen participation and information disclosure with the Open Contracting and Open Data Standards.
- Advance the efforts to upgrade district heating and open investment opportunities to private companies by scaling up the capital available for energy efficiency and DH modernisation projects with further potential to attract FDI.
- Transpose the EU Regulation 347/2013 through the Law on Projects of Highest National Priority in the Field of Energy.
- In collaboration with IFIs or development agencies, create and offer continuous trainings to officials involved in PPPs, covering topics from project selection criteria, contract management, prioritisation in infrastructure development and fiscal impacts of infrastructure projects, focusing on energy efficiency and renewable energy.

**Investment promotion and facilitation**

- Further align the promotion and attraction of investment efforts with Ukraine's international commitments on decarbonisation and reduction of greenhouse gas emissions. Ukraine has the opportunity to foster the attraction of green and renewable energy sources, as well as energy efficiency companies, to consolidate its pathway as a green economy and to attract investors that generate positive environmental impacts to the country.
- National image-building should strike a balance between promoting Ukraine's attractiveness and addressing foreign investors' needs and expectations through realistic targets and a pragmatic agenda of reforms.
- Implement a CRM system allowing customer feedback and regular evaluation. These services should be offered to foreign investors as part of aftercare activities as they would enable UkraineInvest to gather information on the success and shortcomings of its investment promotion and facilitation actions. Such information would then help to improve foreign investors' satisfaction with regards to the services that UkraineInvest provides.
- Ensure predictability and certainty of government actions by maintaining the conditions offered to investors throughout time. A history of honouring long-term government commitments, such as feed-in tariffs, special economic zones, without alteration of initial conditions would lower investors' perception of risks and encourage an increase of FDI flows into the country.
- Evaluate the incorporation of a one-stop-shop investment platform for renewable energy and energy efficiency projects that encompasses all the information and procedures to de-risk projects and scale up investments in the sector.

**Public governance**

- Continue ongoing reforms to prevent and combat corruption, with a special focus on high-level corruption.

- Ensure the independence of the anti-corruption agencies, NABU, SAPO, and the High Anti-Corruption Court, while also ensuring that these agencies are sufficiently resourced, staffed, and empowered to conduct investigations, as well as being shielded from political and other improper interferences.
- Pursue a holistic approach for reforming Ukraine's judiciary in line with international standards and good practices. Continue judicial reforms to strengthen the independence and effectiveness of the judiciary and increase public confidence, while addressing inconsistencies in legal and regulatory frameworks.
- Continue actions to simplify and enhance the transparency of public procurement proceedings in line with the findings of the forthcoming OECD *Typology of Corruption Schemes in the Energy Sector in Ukraine*, including ensuring clear and accessible policies on procurement in SOEs and encouraging the establishment of specialised board committees on procurement when appropriate. Given that the public procurement system in Ukraine still suffers from low levels of trust by businesses and citizens alike, the country could make further use of the OECD *Recommendation on Fighting Bid Rigging in Public Procurement* and of the OECD *Recommendation on Public Procurement*. Ukraine should also continue to seek international assistance to provide capacity-building training focusing on the fight against corruption and conflicts of interest in the procurement system.

**Responsible business conduct in Ukraine's energy sector**

- Further streamline the existing policy frameworks on RBC and ensure applicability to Ukraine's energy sector. Over the years, Ukraine has adopted RBC-related policies, including the Concept on CSR and the National Strategy on Human Rights, which introduced provisions related to business and human rights. However, further steps are needed to streamline these policies and ensure alignment with the OECD Guidelines for Multinational Enterprises and related guidance, while continuing efforts to develop a national action plan on business and human rights. Moreover, RBC policies should be translated within legal and regulatory frameworks applicable to Ukraine's energy sector and efforts should be made to ensure their implementation.
- Ensure protections and enforcement to prevent RBC-related infringements in the energy sector. This includes strengthening human and labour rights protections, particularly in addressing challenges in the state-owned coal sector, preventing discrimination against women and vulnerable groups, and encouraging just transition. Further efforts are needed to improve environmental protection, paying attention to air pollution and emissions, and low energy efficiency, as well as engaging in climate action. Furthermore, moratoria on inspections should be removed.
- Encourage energy companies to carry out due diligence to address and mitigate RBC-related risks throughout their operations, as well as in their supply chains and business relationships. Although a number of companies have started embedding RBC due diligence frameworks, practices should be encouraged on a broader scale. In particular, efforts should be made to align with the OECD *Due Diligence Guidance for Responsible Supply Chains of Minerals from Conflict-Affected and High-Risk Areas* for companies operating or engaged in the coal sector.
- Strengthen anti-corruption efforts in the energy sector. In particular, Ukraine should ensure that anti-corruption institutions, such as SAPO, NABU and the High Anti-Corruption Court are sufficiently empowered, staffed and resourced to carry out investigations. In parallel, anti-corruption regulations and requirements should be further streamlined to avoid potential conflicts and ensure enforcement. In parallel, both state-owned and private companies should be expected to implement high standards of disclosure and transparency, and develop risk management systems, while improving internal controls, ethics and compliance measures.

- Enforce transparency and disclosure in the energy sector, and strengthen non-financial reporting requirements so that companies disclose information on human rights, environment protection, labour rights and risk mitigation, among other areas. Further efforts are needed to implement laws and regulations, and ensure compliance with EITI requirements.
- Strengthen the role of Ukraine's National Contact Point. The NCP can play a key role in promoting the OECD MNE Guidelines and in raising awareness among energy companies, civil society organisations and trade unions to promote RBC practices. The NCP can also act as an effective non-judicial grievance mechanism with which stakeholders in the energy sector can engage.

# 2 Stocktaking of Ukraine's Policy Framework for Investment in the Energy Sector

This chapter reviews Ukraine's current policy and regulatory framework for investment in the energy sector, including key policy reforms implemented to support the country's integration with Europe's energy markets. The chapter assesses the laws, regulations and incentive schemes that the government has adopted to operationalise the Energy Strategy of Ukraine until 2035 and to improve the country's energy efficiency, security and competitiveness. It evaluates the challenges faced by private investors in the upstream, midstream and downstream energy industries and provides recommendations to address them.

## Introduction

Ukraine has undertaken a wide range of institutional, economic and regulatory reforms to increase the role of market forces in the energy sector and advance its integration with the European Union. Some of these reforms have been based on the commitments that Ukraine acquired by becoming, in 2011, a Contracting Party to the Energy Community Treaty, namely the legislative frameworks that enable private participation in the electricity and gas sectors. Additionally, in 2017, the government launched the "Energy Strategy of Ukraine until 2035" (ESU 2035) as an overarching policy to increase the share of renewables in the energy mix, and to achieve energy efficiency, security, competitiveness and greater integration with the EU energy space.

Ukraine has worked hard to reform its power and gas sectors by opening the energy industry to private investments, but the transformation of the country's energy sector to a fully-fledged competitive energy market remains incomplete. Although the government has increased the participation of private investors and opened the electricity and gas markets, both industries remain largely distorted by a range of regulatory measures, including price caps, cross-subsidisation, non-transparent calculation of imbalances and heavy participation of state-owned enterprises. Ukraine has the capacity to reduce market distortions by reforming certain elements of the power and gas market designs that currently undermine competition, such as deregulating prices for households.

Ukraine is at a critical juncture in terms of advancing policies that will put the country on a path to achieve sustainable development and carbon neutrality. Ukraine's biggest challenges to unlocking the private investments to finance sustainable energy projects that will lead to sustainable development and carbon neutrality are the regulatory and financial uncertainty faced by renewable energy producers, along with direct subsidies for coal-fired power generation, which in 2019 reached EUR 476 million. The recent and rapid increase of renewable energy capacity due to generous feed-in tariffs created financial and operational challenges for the power sector, including fast accumulation of arrears and legal disputes that increased the perception of risk among investors. These issues notwithstanding, the government has an opportunity to transform the energy sector into a green and sustainable industry by advancing policies that foster investments in renewables, energy efficiency and disruptive energy technologies. Specifically, Ukraine should strengthen policies and regulations that promote the use of auctions for renewable energy, the adoption of incentives that allow higher flexibility in the energy market, the introduction of new technologies like green hydrogen, bio methane or battery storage, the enhancement of ancillary services; the reduction of its dependence on coal, and the synchronisation of Ukraine's electricity and gas systems with European markets by 2023. The adoption of these policies would enable the full synchronisation of Ukraine's energy sector with the EU and imply the adherence to the objectives of the European Green Deal, which seeks to make Europe the first carbon-neutral continent.

The policies that Ukraine designs and implements to attract private investments should consider the impacts of the COVID-19 crisis on the energy sector. Utilities and Transmission System Operators (TSO) of electricity and gas, which were already burdened by incomplete sectoral reforms prior to the pandemic, have faced revenue shortfalls due to falling demand, price caps and reduced collections from residential and commercial users. Hence, receiving technical support, both in terms of policy design and implementation, as well as financing from the European Union, IFIs and other bilateral partners will be key for advancing essential reforms that could help to foster investments in Ukraine's energy sector.

## Energy Profile of Ukraine

### *Investment in Ukraine's energy sector takes an important place in the country's FDI*

FDI has been playing a prominent role in Ukraine's economic development. According to the most recent World Bank data on FDI, in 2019, net FDI inflows amounted to USD 5.8 billion, equivalent to approximately 3.8% of the country's GDP.[1] In addition, the energy sector is one of the most attractive sectors for investment. For instance, in the 2020 World Investment Report, the main sectors attracting FDI in Ukraine in 2019 were mining, electricity, and gas along with real estate, finance, and information and communication technologies. In addition, in 2017, approximately USD 250 million were invested in Ukraine in solar energy, which is almost double the solar energy investment for 2016.[2]

### *Energy production and consumption*

Ukraine's energy sector boasts abundant coal, natural gas and produces all fossil fuels. In 2018, the country produced 14.4 million tonnes of oil equivalent (Mtoe) of coal, 16.5 Mtoe of natural gas and 2.3 Mtoe of crude oil. The country's total primary energy supply (TPES) was dominated by four energy resources: coal (30%), natural gas (28%), nuclear (24%) and oil (14%) (Figure 2.1) (International Energy Agency, 2020[1]).

Ukraine's national energy production covers 65% of the country's total energy demand. This notwithstanding, the country still needs to meet most of its oil and derivative demands through imports. Ukraine heavily depends on imports for around 83% of its oil consumption, 33% of its natural gas and 50% of its coal for industrial and coking usage. In 2018, Ukraine imported 8.5 Mtoe of natural gas, 13.8 Mtoe of coal and 10.4 of oil products (International Energy Agency, 2020[1]).

**Figure 2.1. Total Primary Energy Supply (TPES) mix in Ukraine (2018)**

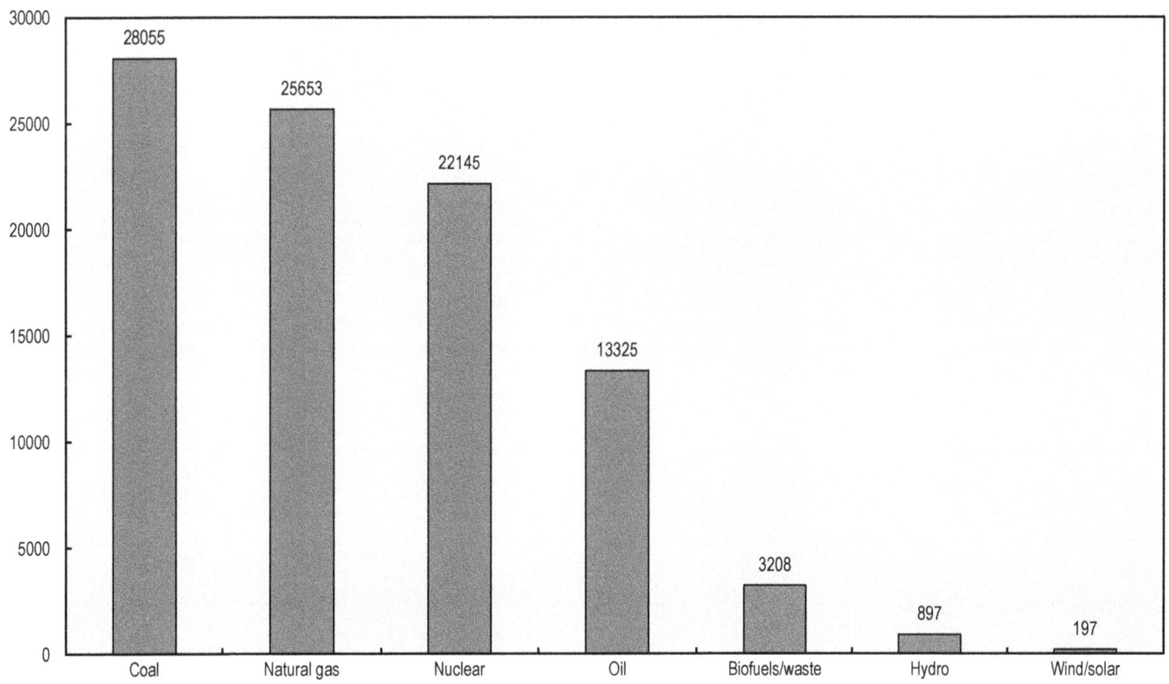


Source: (IEA, 2019[2])

Ukraine possesses substantial conventional and unconventional hydrocarbon resources. Proven reserves of natural gas equate to 1.1 trillion cubic meters (tcm), more than 400 million tonnes (Mt) of gas condensate and 850 Mt of oil reserves. Hydrocarbon resources in Ukraine are concentrated in three regions: the Carpathian region in the west, the Dnieper-Donetsk region in the east and the Black Sea-Sea of Azov region in the south (International Energy Agency, 2020[1]).The Dnieper-Donetsk region accounts for 80% of proven reserves and approximately 90% of gas production, while the Carpathian region has 13% of proven reserves and 6% of production. The remaining 6% of proven reserves are in the southern region, where production is conducted both onshore and offshore on the shallow shelves of the Black and Azov Seas (International Energy Agency, 2020[1]).

In 2019, the overall trend in oil production in the country remained negative and Ukraine continued to rely on oil imports to cover its national demand. The most important oil companies in Ukraine, Ukrnafta and Ukrgasvydobuvannya, are both part of Naftogaz Group and extract 90% of the total national share of production, however, they are characterised as having limited investment resources (Naftogaz, 2019[3]).

The Ukrainian petroleum market is heavily dependent on imports. In 2019, 75% of the domestic demand was met by petroleum imported primarily from Belarus and Lithuania. Since the petroleum market is import dependent, the price of petroleum fluctuates with the exchange rate and quotations for oil products on international exchanges (Naftogaz, 2019[3]).

In 2019, Ukraine was the fourth largest producer of gas among European countries (Naftogaz, 2019[3]). The country's gross gas production amounted to 20.7 billion cubic metres (bcm). Ukrgasvydobuvannya, the main gas production company in the Naftogaz group, produced 13.6 bcm, Ukrnafta produced 1.2 bcm and private companies operating in the country reached a production of up to 4.6 bcm. While Ukraine is a major producer of gas, its national production does not meet the national consumption. Thus, 14.2 bcm of gas was imported exclusively from the European market, of which Naftogaz imported 50.2% and roughly fifty private companies imported 48.9% in 2019 (Naftogaz, 2019[3]).

## Figure 2.2. Gross natural gas production in Ukraine in 2016-2019

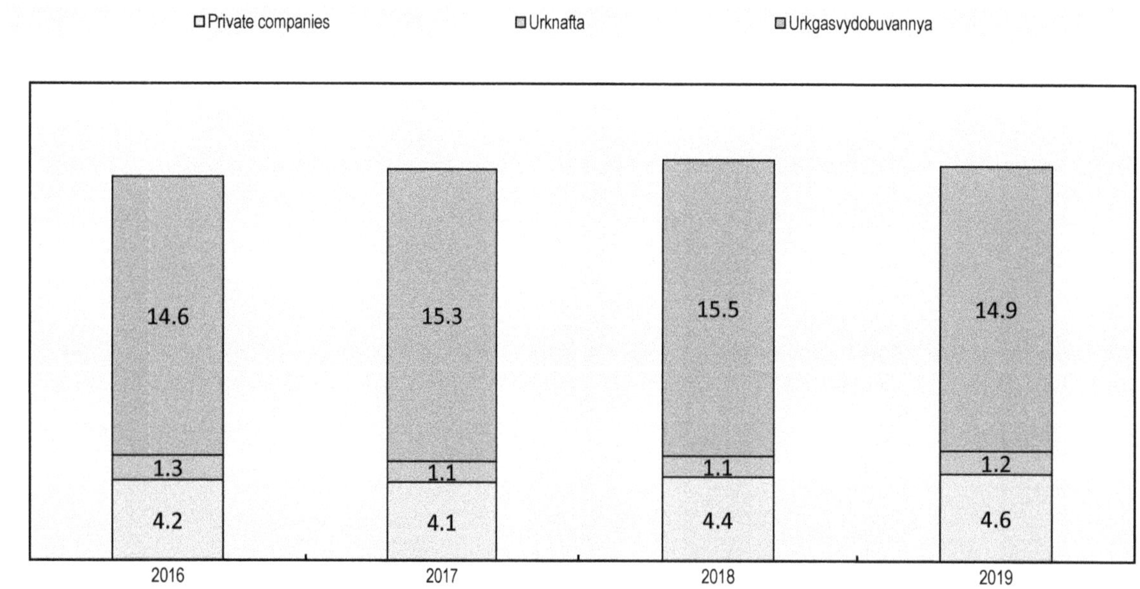


Source: (Naftogaz, 2019[4])

Ukraine has the largest gas transit infrastructure in the world (International Energy Agency, 2020[1]). Historically, 40% of Russia's gas supply to the EU has been supplied through Ukraine. In 2019, the transit volume in Ukraine was 89.6 bcm, which is 2.8bcm more than in 2018. However, there have been reductions in gas transit volumes since Gazprom decreased the annual amount of gas transit through Ukraine, from 90 bcm to 65 bcm (Naftogaz, 2019[3]). This decreasing trend will be exacerbated after the Nord Stream 2 and TurkStream pipelines are put into operation. These new pipelines pose risks for Ukraine's energy sector as they divert traditional gas supply routes where Ukraine occupies a central position as transit corridor between Russia and Europe, although Germany has committed to support Ukraine's energy transition as a remedy (Financial Times, 2021[5]). Ukraine has the second largest gas storage capacity in Europe (European Business Association, 2020[6]). The 13 underground storage facilities have a total working capacity of 30.9 bcm per year and Ukrtransgaz operates 12 of these facilities (Naftogaz, 2019[3]).

Ukraine's abundant coal reserves account for more than 90% of their total fossil fuel reserves. However, a number of coal mines are currently in nongovernment-controlled areas (NGCA) and the government has no oversight or control over those assets. Reserves of anthracite and bituminous coal are estimated at 32 giga tons (GT), ranking Ukraine sixth in the world for hard coal reserves (International Energy Agency, 2020[1]). Most of the coal in Ukraine is produced in the Donbass region – Donetsk Coal Basin – located in eastern Ukraine, in the regions of Donetsk, Luhansk and Dnipro. However, intensive mining for more than a century in the Donbass region has exhausted the best deposits (CMS, 2020[7]).

Traditionally, the mix in the electricity sector in Ukraine consisted of coal, nuclear, and hydropower, but a rapid increase in the share of renewable energy has taken place in recent years. Of the total installed power generation capacity, estimated at 54.3 GW, about half (27.9 GW) consists of thermal power plants (TPPs), with coal-fired power plants accounting for 90% of the TPPs. Nuclear power plants (NPPs) account for 26.7% (13.8 GW) of the installed capacity, while hydro power plants (HPPs), including pumped storage HPPs, represent 12% (6.3 GW) of the total installed capacity. Overall electricity production in 2019 was 154.0 TWh, of which 150.2 TWh was consumed domestically while electricity exports and imports were 6.5 TWh and 2.7 TWh, respectively. Four nuclear power stations comprising 15 reactors supply more than half of Ukraine's total electricity. The remaining electricity comes from coal fired TPPs (30%), natural gas fired combined heat and power (CHP) plants (8%), and HPPs (7%) (World Bank, 2020[8]).

## Regulatory analysis of Ukraine's energy subsectors

### *Upstream Oil and Gas sector*

Ukraine's Law on Oil and Gas provides the legal conditions for companies to participate in the oil and gas industry, as well as defining the regulatory basis of oil and gas exploration, production, transport, storage and the use of oil and its derivatives. The Law mandates that corporations should govern their upstream activities in accordance with the Subsoil Code of Ukraine and the Law on Production Sharing Agreements (Government of Ukraine, 2004[9]).

The Law on Oil and Gas establishes that companies holding permits to extract oil and gas have the right to search and explore new deposits within the subsoil area allocated in the permit. These explore and production (E&P) permits shall be granted through an auction process by the State Service for Geology and Subsoil of Ukraine (SSGS). It is possible to be denied a permit if the SSGS determines that the company does not meet the requirements of the tender, however, the E&P permits can only be deemed invalid if declared so by a competent court. Suspension and revocation of E&P permits are determined by the SSGS under a series of longstanding provisions. If a suspension or revocation action is enforced, affected companies have the legal right to challenge the authority's act in court (Government of Ukraine, 2004[9]).

In March 2018, the Parliament of Ukraine, Verkhovna Rada, passed a Law on Deregulating the Oil and Gas Industry (Government of Ukraine, 2018[10]). This law simplifies the regulatory procedures in the country's oil and gas sector, unlocking private investments and increasing the production of hydrocarbons, so that Ukraine can achieve energy security. It streamlines permits for the extraction of oil and gas, simplifies land allocation by introducing a new type of easement for the construction of oil and gas extraction facilities and cancels certain fees for the extension or reissuance of special permits for subsoil use.

Although some reforms have been implemented in the oil sector, the country still lacks legislation on stockpiling oil, as is required by the Energy Community Treaty. Ukraine relies heavily on oil imports from neighbouring countries to meet its national demand. Crude oil imports, sourced increasingly from Azerbaijan and Kazakhstan, supply the country's sole operating refinery, the Kremenchug facility (US Energy Information Administration, n.d.[11]). Considering that Ukraine only has a small stockpile of oil, a limited production of oil barrels per day and the fact that it imports 90% of its oil consumption (International Energy Agency, 2020[1]), it is imperative to approve stockpiling regulations. The availability of oil reserves will help create a stable and efficient internal market of oil and its derivatives. Additionally, it will regulate the use of strategic oil stockpiles in case of a supply disruption or any mandates enforced by the State Reserve Agency.

### *Natural Gas Market*

In 2015, the Law on Natural Gas Market was enacted with the objective of harmonising Ukraine's gas sector with the EU principles (EU Neighbours, 2018[12]). The participants in the natural gas market in Ukraine, in accordance with the law, are the gas transmission system operator (GTSOU), gas distribution system operator, gas storage facilities operator, LNG installation operator, wholesaler, wholesale buyer, supplier and consumers (Government of Ukraine, 2015[13]).

The law sets the regulatory basis for the unbundling of storage, LNG terminals and distribution system operators, if they were part of a vertically integrated undertaking. Moreover, the law creates private sector access to gas transmission, distribution and supply networks. Allowing private companies to sell gas to any consumer, including households (Government of Ukraine, 2015[13]). The Law on Natural Gas Market ensures equal rights to access gas transmission and distribution systems, LNG installations and gas storage facilities, ultimately allowing private companies to participate in the wholesale and supply markets (Government of Ukraine, 2015[13]). This law requires companies to obtain a licence from NEURC if they want to perform economic activities related to transport, distribution, storage, supply and management of LNG installation services. The only activity that does not require a licence is wholesaling and purchasing gas. It also mandates companies willing to participate in exploration and production activities to obtain licences, permits or a production sharing agreement (PSA).

In order to operationalise their gas transmission system, gas distribution system and gas storage codes, which set the basis for standard natural gas transmission, distribution and storage contracts, Ukraine adopted new reforms in 2015 (Government of Ukraine, 2015[14]) (Government of Ukraine, 2015[15]). Additionally, to effectively liberalise the gas market, the Ukrainian National Energy and Utilities Regulatory Commission (NEURC) set competitive transit, storage and distribution gas tariffs, which are comparable to those in Western and Central Europe.

In March 2019, NEURC successfully implemented one of the key reforms in the gas industry of Ukraine, as the natural gas market switched from monthly to daily balancing. To increase transparency, GTSOU launched an online information exchange platform to enable daily balancing. This makes it possible to determine the differences between gas input and output, to and from the transmission system (Energy Community Secretariat, 2019[16]). Daily balancing incentivises gas companies to self-regulate their own imbalances, which has a positive impact on the development of the wholesale gas market, thus, increasing the attractiveness of Ukraine's gas industry to investors (NEURC, 2019[17]).

In January 2020, after five years of constant reforms, the unbundling of the gas sector was completed. From this date, natural gas transportation activities were no longer performed by the SOE Naftogaz. The Ukrainian transport system is now operated by a new state-owned company, Gas Transmission System Operator of Ukraine (GTSOU), which was unbundled from Ukrtransgaz in line with EU market principles. GTSOU is a wholly owned subsidiary of JSC Main Gas Pipelines of Ukraine, which is owned by the Ministry of Finance. With the unbundling, Ukrtransgaz is the gas storage facilities operator and GTSOU is only engaged in natural gas transmission.

GTSOU and Naftogaz confirmed that private companies are able to book transit capacity in the pipelines (US-Ukraine Business Council, 2020[18]). Moreover, the gas market reform has prompted the participation of private companies in Ukraine's mid and downstream gas activities. NEURC informed that, in 2019, 347 private companies were operating in the wholesale market, 408 companies in transmission activities and 449 corporations in storage (NEURC, 2019[17]).

Undoubtedly, one positive effect of the Law on Natural Gas Market is increased competition with the entry of new players, including foreign ones such as the German companies RWE and Uniper, Polish incumbent PGNiG and Swiss trading companies Axpo and DXT Commodities (Atlantic Council, 2020[19]).

### *Coal Extraction*

The 1999 Law on Mining allows private and public companies to operate coal mines by obtaining a special permit (licence) for subsoil use, which is issued in accordance with the Subsoil Code. In addition, the Law on Mining foresees the possibility of privatising mining assets at the request of the State Property Fund and the approval of the Cabinet of Ministers (Government of Ukraine, 1999[20]).

Restructuring Ukraine's coal industry has been more difficult and politicised compared with other energy sub-sectors. In the past two decades, the government has managed to close several highly uneconomic coal mines, but more actions are necessary to transform the country from a coal-based economy to a carbon neutral one. According to the Energy Strategy of Ukraine until 2035, Ukraine envisaged reforming the coal sector by closing unprofitable mines, doing transparent and competitive privatisation, and establishing coal markets. Unfortunately, this has not happened at the planned time (Energy Community, 2020[21]). As a consequence, of the 300 mines that Ukraine possesses, profitable ones in the past have been either privatised or transferred to long-run concessions, predominantly to DTEK. The remaining mines are owned by SOEs whose operations are subsidised by the state of Ukraine (International Energy Agency, 2020[1]).

### *Electricity Generation and Transmission*

Power generation and transmission in Ukraine have a strong participation of state-owned enterprises. Regarding electricity generation, Ukraine owns and manages all Nuclear Power Plants (NPPs), which are operated by the state-owned company Energoatom. Similarly, all major Hydro Power Plants belong to the fully state-owned joint-stock company UkrHydroenergo. Thermal Power Plants (TPPs) are grouped into five regional companies - Donbassenergo, Dniproenergo, Centrenergo, Zakhidenergo, and Skhidenergo. Only Centrenergo is still under state control, while a majority of the shares from the other four TPPs are owned by DTEK. Until 2018, renewable energy (RES) generated by private investors accounted for a small portion of the electricity produced, but generous Feed-In-Tariffs for RES with no capacity caps resulted in over 8 GW of RES capacity being installed by the end of 2020. Concerning electricity transmission, the national transmission network is owned by the state and operated by the state-owned Electricity Transmission System Operator (ETSO) Ukrenergo.

### *Wholesale Electricity Market*

Since the mid-1990s, the government has begun working towards the creation of a wholesale electricity market and to unbundle electricity generation, transmission and distribution (OECD, 2019[22]). In 2017, the Law on Electricity Market was adopted to further reform the power sector. This law was designed to comply with the EU's Third Energy Package and to integrate Ukraine's Electricity Transmission System Operator (ETSO) into the European Network of Transmission System Operators for Electricity (ENTSO-E).

The Law on Electricity Market sets the rules to assist in making the power market more competitive; through introducing contracts in the wholesale electricity market (WEM), adopting a market-based pricing structure, reinforcing unbundling, stressing the autonomy of regulators, securing the independence of the ETSO - Ukrenergo and promoting investment in infrastructure (Table 2.1). It legally replaces the single-buyer model, which had operated since 1996, with more competitive elements, including the establishment of bilateral contracts between market participants, along with day-ahead (DAM), intra-day (IDM) markets, balancing market, and ancillary service market, where participants can trade electricity freely. The law also stipulates the introduction of non-discriminatory tariff settings and free supplier choice (Government of Ukraine, 2017[23]). Although the Law on Electricity Market has set the regulatory basis for the new wholesale electricity market since 2017, it was not until July 2019 that Ukraine successfully switched from a single-buyer model to a new wholesale electricity market model.

**Table 2.1. New Wholesale Electricity Market (WEM) participants in Ukraine**

| Company | Main functions |
|---|---|
| **SOE Market Operator** | Involved in electricity market oversight, such as monitoring day ahead and intraday markets.<br>Organise the sale and purchase of electricity in the DAM and the IDM. |
| **SOE Guaranteed Buyer** | Responsible for increasing the electricity generation from renewable sources by buying from entities eligible to green feed in tariffs (FITs). |
| **Transmission System Operator SOE Ukrenergo** | Transmits and dispatches electricity through high voltage networks.<br>Operates balancing and ancillary service markets.<br>Registers auction results on bilateral agreements.<br>Serves as commercial metering and settlements administrator.<br>Ukrenergo's transmission tariff is used to found RES Public Service Obligation (PSO). |
| **Supply Companies** | Private suppliers serve non-regulated consumers and prices are set in agreements.<br>Universal suppliers serve residential and small non-residential consumers at regulated tariffs.<br>They are geographically restricted.<br>Supplier of last resort serves consumers with cancelled services. |
| **Distribution system Operators** | Distribution system operators<br>DISCOs are responsible for distribution of electricity to end users.<br>Manage low and medium voltage networks<br>Serve as commercial metering providers. |

Source: (OECD, 2020[24]) and (NEURC, 2019[17])

However, in June 2019, a judgment of the Constitutional Court declared several provisions of the Law to be unconstitutional, specifically those related to NEURC's institutional set up and its independence (Energy Community, 2020[25]). On December 2019, the Rada adopted a new "Law on Amendments to Some Legislative Acts of Ukraine to Ensure Constitutional Principles in the Fields of Energy and Utilities", transforming the energy regulator from an independent authority to a central executive body subordinated to the CMU. The amendments also transfer the rights to name NEURC's leadership to the CMU. Regarding the ability to select the leading representatives of NEURC, the CMU integrated a committee including members of the Rada and the Ministry of Energy on June 2020, breaking the principle of independence required by the mandates of the EU acquis.

After the 2019 legal changes, NEURC was defined as a collegial body that supervises and controls the activities of business entities in the energy and utilities sectors. While performing its functions and powers, NEURC shall be free of influence from central authorities, local governments, business enitities, political parties, public associations, trade unions or any other entities. If any actor contravenes this principle, they are subject to administrative and criminal liability (NEURC, 2019[17]).

### Figure 2.3. NEURC main duties and responsibilities on tariff and price settings

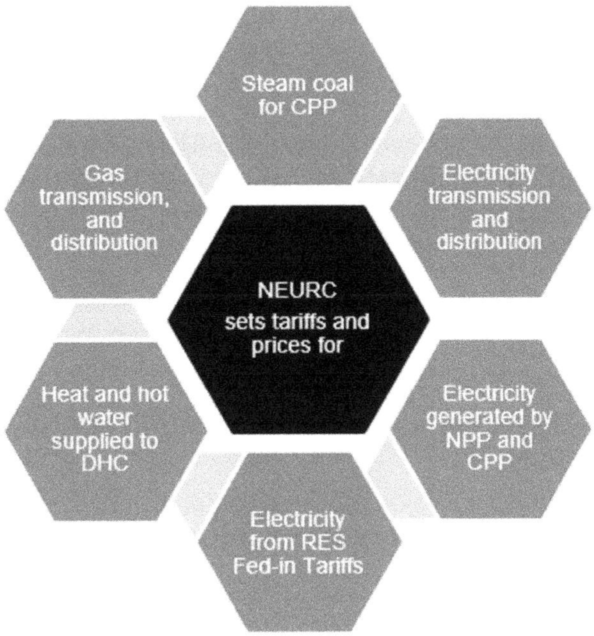


Source: OECD Snapshot on Energy Report (OECD, 2019[22])

The main tasks of NEURC are to ensure the effective functioning and development of markets in the energy and utilities sectors, to promote effective market opening in the energy sector to all suppliers and to ensure non-disciminatory access to networks and pipelines. Additionally, the NEURC promotes the integration of the electricity and natural gas markets of Ukraine with the European Union, which ensures the protection of consumers' rights to goods and services in the fields of energy, of adequate quality and at reasonable prices. NEURC is also responsibe for promoting cross-border trade in electricity and natural gas and for ensuring investment attractiveness for infrastructure development, implementing pricing and rate policy in the energy and utilities sectors, as well as promoting the implementation of energy efficiency measures through the increase of energy production from renewable sources. This helps to create favourable conditions for attracting investments in the development of energy markets, while simutaneously promoting competition in the overall energy market (NEURC, 2020[26]). At this time, one of the most crucial roles of NEURC is to improve the mechanism of control over functioning of wholesale energy market segments to avoid any manipulations and abuse of market power. In this regard, Ukraine is set to implement European rules on wholesale energy market integrity and transparency as outlined in EU Regulation No. 1227/2011, commonly known as REMIT, which will provide NEURC with additional power and functions to identify and penalise the specific offences in the wholesale electricity and gas markets (CMS, 2020[27]).

NEURC has legal power to assign licences to companies that perform economic activities in the power, district heating, oil and gas industries. As of January 2020, NEURC had registered 2 412 valid licences, of which 1 462 were for the electricity sector, 679 for the oil and gas sector and 171 for district heating. Once licences are granted, NEURC conducts scheduled and unscheduled on-site inspections to business entities participating in the energy sector. In 2019, NEURC carried out 500 verifications of compliance, of which, 342 were planned and 258 were unscheduled (NEURC, 2019[17]).

### Box 2.1. Authorities and their responsibilities in Ukraine's energy sector

Cabinet of Ministers of Ukraine: The ultimate decision-making body in Ukraine. It is responsible for policy co-ordination and oversight of state energy companies. It also sets the prices in the regulated markets of the energy sector. Energy policy is high on its political agenda, with the parliament and the president also involved in decision-making.

Ministry of Energy: Responsible for generating and implementing policies on the electricity, nuclear, coal, oil, and gas industries, as well as energy efficiency and renewable energy sources. The Ministry also exercises ownership rights in a number of energy SOEs, including, most recently, those of the transmission system operators – both electricity and gas.

Ministry of Environmental Protection and Natural Resources: Ensures the protection of natural resources, including the rational use of subsoil and the compliance with international commitments to preserve the environment.

Ministry of Finance: Responsible for taxation relevant to the energy sector and the ownership of certain SOE companies in the energy sector.

Ministry of Regional Development, Construction, Housing and Utilities Housing: Develops local-level policies and programmes on heating and is responsible for reporting estimated energy efficiency indicator (EEI) values to the SAEE.

Ministry of Economy: Creates programs and plans to achieve economic development, public-private partnerships, trade and investment that impact the energy sector.

State Agency on Energy Efficiency and Energy Saving: Under ME, is the central government body responsible for advancing energy efficiency and renewable energy developments, as well as promoting the deployment of energy-efficient and renewable energy technologies.

Anti-Monopoly Committee: Is a central body of executive power with special status responsible for protecting and promoting fair competition in the country's business activities and public procurement, which also cover the energy sector.

State Nuclear Regulatory Inspectorate: Has regulatory responsibility for the operation of nuclear facilities, including uranium mining, radioactive waste storage and decommissioning at Chernobyl.

State Property Fund: Implements state policy regarding the privatisation of state property. Also exercises ownership rights in SOEs slated for privatisation.

State Service of Geology and Subsoil: Responsible for issuing special permits, such as subsoil licences, monitoring their compliance with legislation and imposing sanctions for infringement of subsoil use terms.

Source: Authors' elaboration based on the OECD Snapshot on Energy Report (OECD, 2019[22])

## *Energy Pricing*

### Crude Oil and Gas Condensate

In accordance with Article 4 of the Law on Oil and Gas, companies extracting oil and gas condensate must sell crude oil and gas at exchange auctions, and selling prices should reflect global oil price trends.

### Natural gas

In compliance with the Third Energy Package, NEURC introduced the Methodology for Determining and Calculating Tariffs for Natural Gas Transport Services for Entry and Exit points for the regulatory period 2020-2024 applicable to the GTSO of Ukraine. This enabled the GTSO to sign new interconnection agreements with all neighbouring transmission system operators, thus increasing interoperability and enabling the smooth flow of gas along all routes (Energy Community, 2020[25]). The calculation of tariffs for services of pumping, storage and extraction of natural gas is carried out in accordance with the Methodology for Determining and Calculating Tariffs for Services of Storage (or pumping or extraction) of natural gas. This pertains to gas storage facilities and the regulated access regime is applied for these calculations (European Commission, 2019[28]).

Regarding the pricing of natural gas in the wholesale market, Ukraine divides it into two segments: the regulated segment of the wholesale market, which encompasses actors under the regime of Public Service Obligations (PSO), and the unregulated segment of the wholesale market, which operates with free pricing and covers the needs of industry and trade sectors, and the energy sector's own needs. The regulated wholesale price, in 2019, was UAH 207 per thousand cubic meters, or 4%, lower than the price in the unregulated segment of the wholesale natural gas market. Comparatively, in 2018, it was lower by UAH 3 353 per thousand cubic meters, or 39%. Thus, in 2019, the wholesale price in the regulated market segment began to approach the wholesale price in the free market, and at the end of the year the prices were almost at the same level (NEURC, 2019[17]).

Public Service Obligations limited the liberalisation of the wholesale and retail gas market because they required Naftogaz to buy volumes from local producers and sell them to household and district heating companies (DH) at regulated tariffs. It also prevented the state-owned gas company, Naftogaz, from selling gas directly to end users and forced it to provide gas to intermediaries (Atlantic Council, 2020[29]).

Naftogaz and private retail companies of gas had disagreements concerning retail market prices because certain retailers were making unauthorised offtakes of cheaper gas to producers. Ultimately, this involved paying a lower price due to a PSO but with the intention of selling the gas to non-regulated consumers at higher prices, including private manufacturing and steel companies. This practice has been blamed for distorting the daily balancing market, which is operated by GTSO (ICIS, 2020[30]).

Ukraine made headway in deregulating the gas sector, by unbundling its transmission systems and stimulating the establishment of a wholesale market. May 2020 was supposed to be the date when the natural gas market would take another step towards full liberalisation, as over 8 billion cubic meters of natural gas, representing 60% of the traded volume, would enter the free market. The government was expected to remove the PSO for protected consumers, such as households, religious establishments and district heating. Nevertheless, the CMU determined that the PSO for households would be extended until 1 August 2020 and for district heating until May 2021 (Ministry of Energy of Ukraine, 2020[31]).

**Box 2.2. Public Sector Obligations in the energy sector**

In the energy sector, regulators and policy makers strive to achieve three major energy goals: i) competitiveness of energy markets; ii) security of supply; and iii) environmental sustainability. The European Union acquis has recognised that Public Sector Obligations are sector-specific tools that shall be used, as an exemption not as a rule, to provide services of general economic interest. Moreover, the EU acquis determined that countries have wide discretion to define PSOs in line with the needs of end users. It is therefore the responsibility of the state to define public services or services of general economic interest provided that the rules of Article 3(2) of Directive 2009/72/EC12 are observed (Energy Community, 2020[25]).

Consequently, the State's discretion to define PSOs in line with national circumstances may be exercised only in full compliance with the acquis. Accordingly, while relatively free to define them, countries can use the public service obligations' provision only in exceptional and clearly defined circumstances, provided that they satisfy the criteria indicated in the European rules and case law (Energy Community Secretariat, 2018[32]). Therefore, PSOs that are prone to constituting an obstacle to the realisation of an operational internal market in energy, shall be an exception and not the rule, and they shall not be invoked to cover purposeful deviations from mandatory internal energy market rules.

According to the EU acquis on electricity[1] and gas[2], the national legislation of Contracting Parties may impose PSOs on energy undertakings if such obligations relate to security of supply, regularity and quality, price of supplies, customer protection, and environmental protection, including energy efficiency, energy from RES and climate protection. The case law has determined criteria for assessing PSOs, as they should pursue a general economic interest, comply with the principle of proportionality, i.e., impose PSO only in so far as is suitable and necessary to achieve their objectives in the general economic interest and, consequently, for a period that is necessarily limited in time, and are clearly defined, transparent, non-discriminatory, verifiable and guarantee equal access for energy undertakings of the Energy Community to national consumers.

In Ukraine's energy sector, PSOs are determined by the Ministry of Energy, according to the proposals of NEURC as the regulator, and submitted to the Cabinet of Ministers of Ukraine for approval.

Notes:
1. Electricity Directive 2009/72/EC, article 3 (2).
2 Gas Directive 2009/72/EC, article 3 (2).
Source: Energy Community Secretariat, *Ukraine – electricity Public Service Obligations Act 2020,* May 2020 at ECS_CN032020; Energy Community Secretariat, *Public Service Obligations: a black box case*, August 2019 at SS2019_D4_secretariat_public_service_obligations_a_black_box_case.

The termination of the PSO in August 2020 for households and religious organisations entails the deregulation of gas supply prices. It is expected that this reform will encourage more retailers to enter the market. So far, the retail gas sector had been dominated by the Firtash group, which controls 70% of the market (Atlantic Council, 2020[29]). Another benefit of the PSO termination is the clampdown on unauthorised off-take of natural gas. To further transition into a fully liberalised retail market, on July 2020, the competition committee of the Ministry of Energy selected Naftogaz as the supplier of last resort for the retail market.

Although the government removed the PSO for households in August 2020, it reversed this advancement by approving gas price caps for households in January 2021, arguing that it was a necessary temporary measure valid until April 2021, with the intentions of counterbalancing the effects of COVID-19 (Government of Ukraine, 2021[33]). This change means a return to subsidies and an intervention in the retail prices, in contradiction with the conditions imposed by the International Monetary Fund (IMF) for the disbursement of financial credits to Ukraine.

Ukraine recently lifted the gas PSO for district heating companies, however, this is still pending (and represents 25% of the annual consumption). The gas for district heating remains under regulated prices and are not offered on the wholesale gas market but the PSO ceased to be in force as of May 2021[3], and the Public Service Obligations were withdrawn from Naftogaz (Energy Community, 2020[25]). Summing up this challenge, on April 2020, the Rada adopted Law 553-IX on Modifications to the State Budget of Ukraine according to which heat producers, regardless of ownership, were exempted from fines and penalties by gas suppliers of electricity and natural gas for the period of quarantine or restrictive measures related to the COVID-19 pandemic.

### *Electricity*

The price at which generation companies sell their electricity varies depending on the source of production and is formed according to the Law on Electricity Market. In Ukraine, the price of electricity generated from Thermal Power Plants (TPP) includes the cost of fuels, fixed costs, profits and a surcharge. The price of electricity generated by Nuclear Power Plants (NPP) includes labour costs, fuel, repair costs, depreciation deductions, profits, administrative costs, operations and financial costs. The price of electricity generated at Combined Heat and Power Plants includes labour costs, fuel, production services, and depreciation charges (NEURC, 2019[17]).

Although noticeable advancements towards an efficient electricity market have been made, the Ukrainian wholesale power market is still limited by excessive Public Service Obligations and price regulations. For instance, price caps in all segments of trading, including IDM and DAM have been considered as generating price distortions (Energy Community, 2020[25]). Concerning the PSOs, as discussed earlier, two PSO mechanisms were introduced: (i) Household PSO to protect household consumers by keeping electricity tariffs below full cost recovery, and (ii) RES PSO to cover RES obligations under FITs which are significantly above the market price (see Box 2.2 and Box 2.3).

#### Box 2.3. Feed-in tariffs: A policy tool that encouraged the deployment of RES in Ukraine

Feed-in tariffs (FIT) are a policy mechanism used to encourage the deployment of renewable electricity technologies. A FIT program typically guarantees that producers who own a FIT-eligible renewable electricity generation facility will receive a set price for all the electricity they generate and provide to the grid. Typically, FIT will specify eligible technologies, rate and contract terms, system size and sector restrictions and program size limitations.

Historically, FITs have been associated with models in which the government mandates that power utilities enter into long-term contracts with generators at specified rates, typically well above the retail price of electricity. The premium level may depend on the underlying programme motivation and goals. For instance, in 2012, Japan implemented a new FIT with particularly high PV tariff rates as part of its post-Fukushima policy. However, without additional controls, generous FIT levels can lead to more investment than intended. One example is the experience of Spain, in which the government significantly reduced the tariff a year after its start, and suspended the FIT altogether in 2012, to contain costs that the government could not afford.

In 2008, the Government of Ukraine set a regulatory framework to promote investments for the generation of power through non-conventional sources of fuel, according to which, a model of differentiated feed-in tariffs would be paid to entities that generated electricity using non-fossil technologies. Ukraine agreed to grant the green FIT to investors until December 31, 2029. The regulations set green FITs in euros, passing the exchange risks to the government, at one of the highest levels in the world, with an annual decrease until 2030.

However, after a first period of fixed FITs for power plants commissioned until 2013, the green FITs in Ukraine started to be reduced gradually until 2017. Between 2017 and 2020 the FITs underwent a more significant reductions due to the increasingly burdensome payment obligations.

Notwithstanding the challenges that FIT generated in 2020, green feed-in tariffs substantially increased the installed capacity of RES from 2010 to 2019 in Ukraine. Since 2010, the share of RES (hydro, biofuels, waste, wind and solar) in the total primary energy has increased from 2.1% to 4.6% in 2018. In particular, solar capacities have been increasing significantly, reaching 4.9 GW in 2019. The wind capacities reached 1.1 GW in 2019. The general installed capacity of RES reached over 6 GW in 2019.

Source: (US Energy Information Administration, 2013[34])

The Household PSO imposed on SOEs requires 90% of the electricity produced by Energoatom and 35% of the electricity generated by Ukrhydroenergo to be sold in bilateral auctions to the SOE Guaranteed Buyer through 1 July 2022, as a mechanism to subsidise cheap electricity for households. Distortive PSOs imposed on SOEs should be eliminated gradually as the wholesale electricity market evolves. The electricity market should be effectively regulated and competition concerns addressed through effective enforcement of competition law. To mitigate any potential concerns about the price of electricity and vulnerable households, preference should be given to direct subsidy schemes that benefit these households.

Derived from the RES PSO, the biggest challenge that Ukraine currently faces in electricity pricing is related to the renewable energy segment. Since 2009, Ukraine has used green Feed-In Tariffs (FIT) when contracting with investors in solar power facilities, wind power plants, small hydro-power plants and biomass power plants. NEURC calculated the FIT based on the variety of alternative renewable energy sources (RES) used, with an additional premium for using equipment produced in Ukraine (European Commission, 2020[35]). Green FITs were applied to over 300 renewable projects and were expected to remain valid until 2030. The FIT scheme provided tariffs in the range of 4.35 to 24.56 US cents/kWh. for utility-scale solar and 10 to 11.4 US cents/kWh for wind, which is much higher than the average tariffs awarded in other countries. The FITs were regulated through a mandatory RES offtake by the SOE Guaranteed Buyer (GB).

From 2009 to 2016, when the single buyer model was operational, the SOE Energorynok used to control the wholesale electricity market. With the entry into force of the 2017 Electricity Market Law, the Guaranteed Buyer (an SOE constituted to increase the share of electricity generation from RES) absorbed the obligation to pay the FIT and to subsequently sell the RES electricity on the wholesale market. The Guaranteed Buyer receives the funds needed to cover the difference between the FIT levels paid out to generators and the usually lower electricity market prices from the TSO Ukrenergo, which finances these payments through its transmission tariff surcharges (European Commission, 2020[35]). The difference was supposed to cover the fees for the renewable producers. However, since the household tariffs have remained capped, due to PSOs, the Guaranteed Buyer could not recover the full amount to pay the renewable producers (OECD, 2020[36])

Since 2019, the Guaranteed Buyer has been unable to meet its payment obligations not only to RES producers but also to SOEs due to a lack of funds, mainly as a consequence of low electricity market prices and the inflexible design of the aforementioned levy system. The financial stability of state-owned companies, Ukrenergo and Energoatom, absorbed the largest burden of the PSO imposed by the government, primarily to cover expenses for below-cost electricity for household consumers and the cost of renewables. This situation has generated two major risks that affect the overall electricity market: a) lack of payment to the Guaranteed Buyer stalled compensation for green energy producers, including foreign investors, and b) a risk of corruption as a significant portion of domestic renewable electricity producers are affiliated to well-known businesspersons (OECD, 2020[37]). This situation also poses an overall disruption risk to the energy market in Ukraine. Under these circumstances, more predictable and transparent RES PSOs and accountable compensation schemes should be defined. In particular, PSOs for Ukrenergo should be determined in a transparent way and accounted for separately according to good practices.

The arrears to RES producers prompted the Rada to approve, in May 2019, the Law on Renewable Energy Auctions which amends the Laws of Ukraine on Alternative Energy Law on Electricity Market and the Law on the Regulation of Urban Development Activities. The Law on Auctions contains key provisions, such as terms of participation in auctions, size and allocation of support quotas for RES producers, availability of feed-in tariffs, a decreasing schedule of FITs, bank guarantee requirements, responsibility for imbalances and technical conditions for grid connection (Sayenko Kharenko, 2019[38]). Despite the Law on Auctions, the SOE Guaranteed Buyer was not able to fully pay its financial obligations to RES producers and the problem reached its peak in mid-2020 when the arrears reached EUR 500 million (European Commission, 2020[35]).

To reach a solution with RES companies, in January 2020, the Energy Community Dispute Resolution and Negotiation Centre hosted the first mediation sessions between representatives of the Ministry of Enmergy and two investor organisations, the European-Ukrainian Energy Agency (EUEA) and the Ukrainian Wind Energy Association (UWEA). The mediation activities aimed at agreeing on a stabilisation package, finding an amicable solution for the liquidity crisis threatening the SOE Guaranteed Buyer – offtaker of RES in Ukraine and proposing an adequate electricity market design (Energy Charter Secretariat, 2021[39]). On 10 June 2020, the parties signed a Memorandum of Understanding (MoU) "*Settlement of Problematic Issues in the Field of Renewable Energy*", by way of which producers of RES energy accepted the terms of voluntary restructuring of green FIT (Energy Community, 2020[40]). According to the Ministry of Energy, the MoU would reduce the financial burden on electricity market participants and the state would be able to save roughly EUR 2 billion by 2030, which is when the preferential green FIT would be applicable (Ministry of Energy of Ukraine, 2020[41]). RES producers agreed to reduce green feed-in-tariffs in exchange for a commitment by state authorities to repay the Guaranteed Buyer's outstanding receivables on renewables by the end of 2021, and resume regular payments for power production.

To maintain the reached consensus, the Memorandum was tranformed into binding legislation through Law 810-IX, which was signed by the President and began being implemented in July 2020 (Ministry of Energy of Ukraine, 2020[41]). Law 810-IX introduces a reduction of coefficient calculations for feed-in tariffs from RES, pertaining to wind and solar power plants. This Law also changes the upcoming green auction procedures, tightens the timeline for full imbalance responsibility and introduces regulations for compensating the RES producers for mandatory curtailments. The changes differ based on the type of energy source and commissioning date of power plants.

Additionally, in June 2020, the Rada adopted the Law 719-IX on Measures to Repay Debts Formed in the Wholesale Electricity Market, which aims to implement a set of measures to settle accounts payable and receivables that were accumulated as a result of the wholesale electricity market. These measures came into force on July 6, 2020, as did the termination of the activities of Energorynok. While the Law addresses old debts in the electricity market, a mechanism to stop the accumulation of the debts in the new market has not yet been established. Other structural problems in the market design, including market concentration, below-cost prices and tariffs, are yet to be addressed.

### *Heat*

The transition to cost reflective natural gas prices has presented significant challenges for the District Heating (DH) sector, since natural gas is by far the primary fuel and number one expenditure for DH in

Ukraine. Because of the gas tariff reform, District Heating Companies have been required to pass through much higher gas costs in their own tariffs. The required increase in heat tariffs has revealed the inefficiencies in DH operations and made consumers more sensitive to the demanding level of energy bills. Higher gas prices have also revealed the real economic cost of low energy efficiency in DH operations, in particular, regarding thermal losses in DH networks and with regards to boiler efficiency (NEURC, 2019[17]).

## The government's energy strategy and future energy investment requirements

Energy sector reforms almost always take place in the context of a wider national transformation process, and Ukraine prompted the reforms in the energy sector as part of a socioeconomic and political transition that followed the 2014 Euromaidan protests (World Bank, 2020[42]). Following the change in government in 2014, the country signed an Association Agreement with the European Union. The Agreement is a concrete path to enhancing EU-Ukraine relations, with a specific focus on supporting policy reforms in areas such as environment protection, taxation, mining and others intertwined within the energy sector. Additionally, it contemplates financial co-operation for sustainable development, which includes energy and environmental protection (European Union, 2016[43]).

Gas and coal-rich economies like Ukraine must go beyond simply replicating the standard model of energy reform and should adapt an integrated reform model to their unique context. An integrated model shall include policies that liberalise end user and wholesale prices, improve energy efficiency, adequately integrate renewables and eradicate the discriminatory treatment of private and public investors (International Energy Agency, 2019[44]). To this end, in August 2017, the government adopted the Energy Strategy of Ukraine (ESU) until 2035, which sought to promote a systematic and holistic approach to energy sector reform. It replaced a previous Energy Strategy that was initially supposed to be enacted until 2030, and was already outdated. The current 2035 Strategy envisions a sectoral transformation that will improve the country's energy efficiency, security, competitiveness and integration with the EU energy space. It outlines six headline objectives: a conscious and energy efficient society, energy independence, reliability and sustainable, market development, investment attractiveness, network integration and modern management system (Government of Ukraine, 2017[45]). Of the six objectives that the ESU foresees, market development, investment attractiveness, network integration and a modern management system play a key role in establishing a business environment that is attractive for local and foreign investors.

### Figure 2.4. Phases of the Energy Strategy of Ukraine until 2035

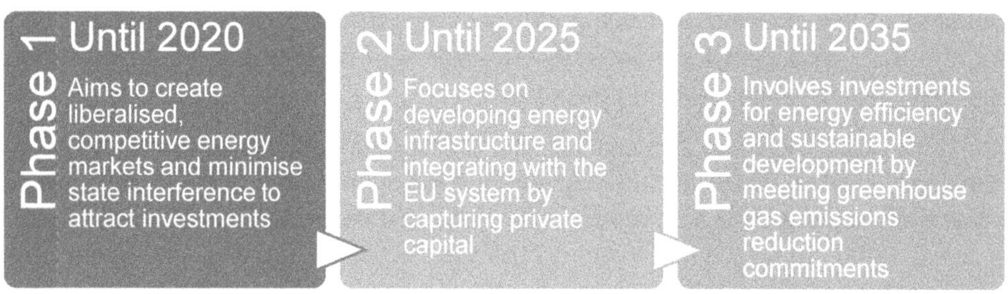


Source: ESU 2035, (The Government of Ukraine, 2017[46])

The Market Development objective is relevant to private investors as it aims to create competitive gas, electricity, heat, coal, and oil markets. A crucial component in achieving this goal is securing access to the grid for all energy producers. Market Development also aims to ensure the independence of NEURC and the Anti-Monopoly Committee of Ukraine.

The Investment Attractiveness objective mandates the implementation of the EU acquis in Ukrainian legislation, and supports a competitive environment that guarantees uninterrupted access to markets and to existing infrastructure. It aims for a stable and predictable investment attraction policy and to promote the entrance of international developers and investors in the domestic energy market.

The Network Integration objective aims to create fully functional natural gas and electricity markets that can enable Ukraine's integration into ENTSO-G, the European Network of Transmission System Operators for Gas, and ENTSO-E, the European Network of Transmission System Operators for Electricity (Government of Ukraine, 2018[47]). The objective envisions that European companies should be able to buy gas at the Eastern border of Ukraine. The Modern Management System objective foresees the introduction of public-private partnerships to advance the energy industry, develop resource management system in mining, and to enhance the flexibility of the energy infrastructure.

In order to support the implementation of ESU 2035 Phase 1, the 2020 Action Plan was approved by the CMU. It identified 186 actions to be completed by the end of 2020 and listed the plurality of stakeholders involved in their implementation (OECD, 2018[48]). The government published two reports on the implementation status of the Energy Strategy of Ukraine in March 2019 and May 2020 (Government of Ukraine, 2020[49]). The reports mentioned that 105 actions had been effectively implemented, 39 actions were being currently executed, and 37 actions had not been implemented. For five actions, no data were available (Razumkov Centre, 2019[50]).

## Figure 2.5. Evolution of Ukraine's energy mix

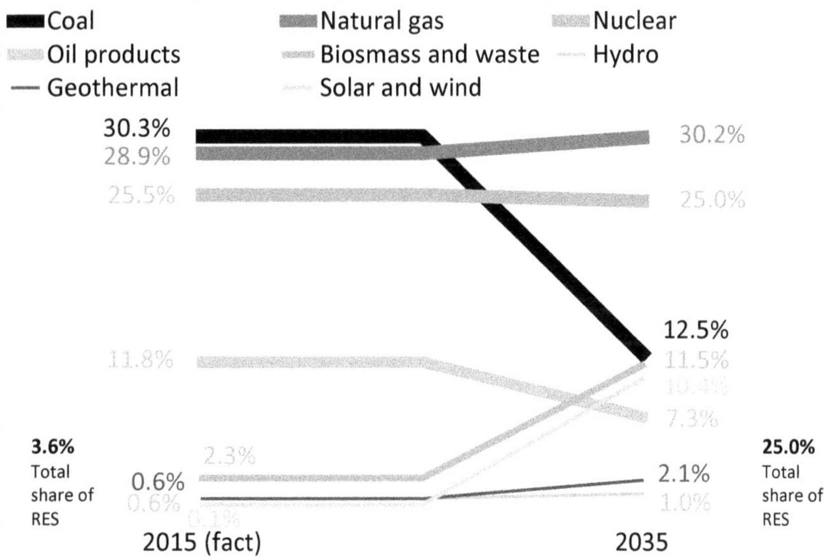


Source: Energy Strategy of Ukraine until 2035, (The Government of Ukraine, 2017[46])

According to forecast analysis that was prepared by the Wilson Centre, if Ukraine implements all the reforms prescribed in the ESU 2035, for the 2019-2030 period, power generation companies will be able to invest USD 29.8 billion, which represents 11.5 times more funding than the amount that will be invested without the reforms being introduced. This could help to finance the full introduction of new power units and prevent a deficit of baseload capacity. Moreover, as an outcome of the transition to market tariffs and the end of cross-subsidisation, the distribution and transmission system operators that operate in Ukraine will be able to invest EUR 7.5 billion in the grid, which, compared to the amount without the reform, is nearly twice as much. With the increase in investment volumes, losses in distribution grids are expected to decrease – from 8.6% in 2017 to 7.2% in 2030, in transmission grids – from 2.6% to 2.1%. Finally, the introduction of reforms to synchronise Ukraine's power system with the ENTSO-E could increase the export of electricity by almost 5 times – from 5.6 billion kWh in 2017 to 25 billion kWh in 2030. Consequently, the surplus export earnings in 2019-2030 could reach USD 6.7 billion. However, in case of failure to carry out synchronisation, Ukraine would remain dependent on imports of electricity from the Russian Federation and Belarus (Wilson Center, 2019[51]). It is worth noting that in May 2021, NEURC decided to limit the imports of electric energy to the Integrated Power System of Ukraine from Belarus and the Russian Federation as of 1 October 2021.

The ESU 2035 suffers from a number of structural weaknesses, which affect the quality of implementation, such as the lack of alignment between the ESU 2035 and 2020 Action Plan, the lack of methodological clarity regarding the lower-and-higher-level components of energy sector reform, and the lack of mechanisms for effective risk assessment. In addition, despite the broad consistency of ESU 2035 with the energy commitments outlined in Ukraine's Sustainable Development Goals, the strategy is only partially consistent with the EU-Ukraine Association Agreement because it is lacking a set of legal acts to reform energy markets and align energy efficiency standards according to EU rules. Other policy and information gaps may also affect the achievement of objectives, such as the lack of measures to promote the phase out of coal-fired power stations and shortage of information relative to budgeting and costing processes by the Government. Overall as of 2020, progress towards ESU 2035 objectives has been mixed. Progress towards the Market Development and Modern Management System objectives is at an intermediate stage, while progress towards the Energy Efficiency, and Energy Independence, Sustainability and Reliability, Investment Attractiveness and Network Integration objectives is at an initial stage. At the sub-sectoral level however, implementation progress has varied much more significantly (OECD, 2020[52]).

## Key trends for investors in Ukraine´s energy sector

Ukraine has been a bold reformer in the energy sector and, between 2000 and 2015, the country announced ambitious reforms, delivered substantially on them, and sustained them over time (World Bank, 2020[42]). For example, Ukraine reformed its gas sector and increased the participation of private corporations in the wholesale and retail markets. As a result, over the past five years, Naftogaz ceased to be the near-monopoly supplier of the domestic market. Its share of imports was nearly cut in half, it imported 7 bcm (billion cubic metres) of the total 10.6 bcm imported in 2018, while 7.2 bcm of 14.3 bcm imported in 2019. The remainder was imported by a range of wholesale traders (65 companies in 2018 and 76 in 2019). The share of gas produced in Ukraine by companies other than Naftogaz has also grown to 4.7 bcm, in 2019.

Despite the advances in Ukraine's reform programme, to finance the much-needed modernisation of ageing energy infrastructure while maintaining fiscal discipline the government should increase the availability of mechanisms to leverage public-private financing instruments. Furthermore, Ukraine should bear in mind that investments in mid-stream and downstream infrastructure, which are badly-needed in the country, are contingent on regulatory frameworks that enable companies to recover their fixed investment cost.

### *Direct private participation in Ukraine´s energy sector*

For Ukraine to achieve the objectives and goals set out in the ESU 2035, the country requires long-term investments, the majority of which can come from the private sector. Successful private investments in upstream, mid-stream and downstream projects in all energy sub-sectors rely on having adequate legal schemes that allow the participation of private companies (Fitch Solutions Country Risk and Industry Research, 2021[53]). There are six main forms of direct private participation in the energy sector that have been used in Ukraine (Figure 2.6): concessions, permits and licences, production sharing agreements

(PSA), service contracts, public-private partnerships and joint ventures (see Chapter 5 for an analysis on joint ventures, public-private partnerships and service contracts).

**Figure 2.6. Forms of direct private participation in the energy sector**

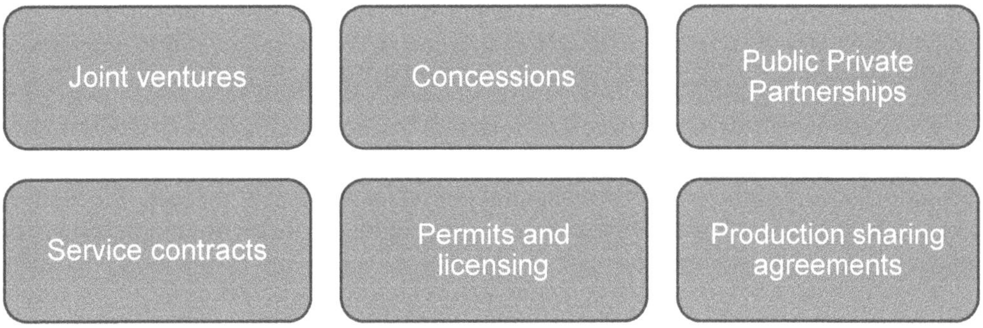


Source: (Fitch Solutions Country Risk and Industry Research, 2021[53])

Concessions are regulated by the Law on Concessions, which was approved in September of 2019. The Law introduces clear and non-controversial procedures for initiating concessions, with both contracting authorities and concessionaires having the right to initiate the transfer of infrastructure objects into the concession, conducting concession tenders and choosing concessionaires. This takes place through a competition or competitive dialogue as envisaged by the UNCITRAL's Model Legislative Provisions on Privately Financed Infrastructure Projects. In addition, the 2019 Concession Law allows investors leasing state property to obtain concession rights for the property by negotiating directly with the contracting authorities. The Law also includes new rules, providing investors with more options when resolving disputes. Parties to concession contracts may, by mutual consent, choose which law will apply. They may also choose to resolve disputes via mediation, non-binding expert assessment, international commercial arbitration or investment arbitration - including arbitration sitting abroad, if the concessionaire is a subsidiary of a multinational enterprise (Government of Ukraine, 2019[54]).

For permits and licensing, the State Service for Geology and Subsoil of Ukraine, in accordance to the Subsoil Code, issues licences to private investors granting the right to explore and produce hydrocarbons. In return, companies are required to pay royalties, taxes and fees to the government (Fitch Solutions Country Risk and Industry Research, 2021[53]). A special permit must be obtained for each stage of development: for the geological survey, up to 5 years onshore and 10 years offshore, for the production permit it is up to 20 years onshore and 30 years offshore and for a special permit associated with a Production Sharing Agreement (PSA) up to 50 years (Government of Ukraine, 1994[55]).

Regarding PSAs, private companies have similar rights, but only containing "cost oil" and a share of any "profit oil" produced, with the state recouping the remainder in lieu of, or sometimes in addition to, collecting royalties (Government of Ukraine, 1994[55]). The investor also pays taxes and fees. Under a service contract, the private corporation explores for and produces hydrocarbons on behalf of the government and is paid a fee for its services, with the possibility to buy a portion of the production. Association or joint venture agreements involve private investors partnering with host governments or state-owned enterprises, as in a PSA, sharing hydrocarbon production. In practice, these forms and labels tend to be much less important than the specific content of a contract.

As part of its efforts to implement a more enabling investment framework in the sector, the Government of Ukraine has modernised its Law on Production Sharing Agreements (PSA) and adopted the 2018 Law on Deregulation of the Oil and Gas Industry (Fitch Solutions Country Risk and Industry Research, 2021[53]). The Law on Deregulating Oil and Gas Industry simplifies regulatory procedures relating to exploration and commercial development of oil and gas fields. Such deregulation involves cancelling procedures for construction approvals from local authorities, state approvals for pilot production of hydrocarbons, state approvals for transfer of the company's geological information to third parties, approval for transfer of the company's geological information to third parties and environmental impact assessments (EIA). These shall be required only for production activities, but special permits for exploration works may be obtained without the EIA. Regarding the simplification of land allocation procedures, a specific type of servitude is introduced for construction of oil and gas extraction facilities and pipeline infrastructure without the need for changing their designated purpose (Government of Ukraine, 2018[10]).

Ukraine eased the granting of subsoil licences and permits through the 2019 Law on Extraction of Amber and other Minerals (Government of Ukraine, 2020[56]). Despite its name and main focus, the Amber Law also contains provisions that will have an impact on the production of other mineral resources in Ukraine, including oil and gas, such as lifting the requirement for a regional council's approval as a necessary step in the process of granting the right for subsoil geological survey and extraction of hydrocarbons. Additionally, the requirement of an Environmental Impact Assessment for PSAs was amended, from prior to signing the agreement to after the contract was signed but before the start of activities (CMS, 2020[27]). In line with the Amber Law, in February 2020, the CMU restated the procedure of issuance of special permits for subsoil use and made it possible to submit applications electronically, in order to obtain and extend special permits. This all became possible through the usage of subsoil users' online accounts on the State Geological Service website (Government of Ukraine, 2020[57]).

### *Public procurement, auctions and privatisation in the energy sector*

Public procurement reform is considered as one the most successful reforms over the last years in Ukraine. It has contributed to fighting corruption and to increasing participation of private companies in the procurement market (World Bank, 2019[58]). In 2016, a new Law on Public Procurement was approved in Ukraine, introducing mandatory eProcurement through the ProZorro platform, an electronic system that ensures open access to public procurement wherein public procurement contracts are disclosed on open data standards so citizens can search them (ProZorro, 2021[59]). Starting from August 2016, all public procurements performed by all government agencies, including local ones, were made through the ProZorro centralised electronic procurement system. Since the amendment of the Law on Public Procurement in 2019, ProZorro has remained Ukraine's electronic procurement system and more functions have been enabled, such as identifying abnormally low prices, correcting errors in tender proposals, establishing the grounds for automatic cancellation of tenders and allowing simplified procurement procedures for goods, works or services of low value.

In 2017, an additional platform, ProZorro.Sales, was launched to serve as an electronic system for auction sales of non-specialised state-owned assets (Ukrenergo, 2017[60]). Through this second platform the government also sells leasing rights to land plots managed by the State of Ukraine for Geodesy, Cartography and Cadastre (State Geocadastre), as well as the sale of special permits for the use of subsoil in Ukraine, managed by the State Service of Geology and Subsoil. More recently, in September 2021, the state enterprise ProZorro.Sale was designated the administrator of land tenders for the sale of land plots (including state and communal property) and the acquisition of rights to use them such as lease, superficies, emphyteusis, as well as being responsible for approving the requirements for the preparation and conduct of land tenders through the electronic system.[4]

In January 2018, the government enacted the new Law on Privatisation to simplify both large-scale and small-scale privatisation transactions at state and municipal levels (Government of Ukraine, 2018[61]). The law aims to enhance transparency, integrity of individual transactions and provides a guarantee for private investors. The IMF, IFC and EBRD considered the approval of the new privatisation law an essential step for facilitating an influx of private capital into Ukraine, especially in the energy sector (International Monetary Fund, 2020[62]). Per the regulation, the State Property Fund (SPFU) is the primary institution leading the privatisation of SOEs that have been pre-identified by the CMU. The privatisation process is split into so-called small-scale assets with a value of up to UAH 250 million, and large-scale assets. Privatisation auctions are held through the Prozorro.Sales online platform, a system that intends to ensure bidding transparency and open access to participation. The SPFU ensures full disclosure of asset information. All documents become available to investors after signing a non-disclosure agreement.

As of December 2020, the SPFU was responsible for 11 entities in the energy sector that were in the process of being privatised as part of the large-scale privatisation efforts. When SOEs are selected to be privatised, their assets are transferred to the SPFU which is responsible for their restructuring, with the purpose of maximising assets' value before putting them on sale. Therefore, the SPFU conducts the appointment of company management and representatives to the board of directors, reviews and approves company financial plans, business strategies and is responsible for evaluating the performance of SOEs. The State Property Fund of Ukraine announced its plans to sell shares of six power distribution companies: 78.3% of the stakes of Centrenergo, the largest electricity generating company in the country, 50.9% of Ternopiloblenergo, 60.3% of Zaporizhiaoblenergo, 65% of Kharkivoblenergo, 70% of Mykolaivoblenergo and 70% of Khmelnytskyioblenergo (BakerMckenzie, 2020[63]). However, in 2020 due to COVID-19, the government required the SPFU to suspend all large-scale privatisation efforts until the markets had been stabilised. To unblock large-scale privatisations, in March 2021, the Ukrainian parliament approved the second reading of Law N. 4543 on Privatisation of State and Communal Property, which was signed by the President in April 2021. The SPFU forecasts that around USD 430 million of budget revenues will come from privatisation. Of this amount, USD 320 million is expected to come via large-scale privatisation and another USD 110 million will include revenues from the sale of smaller privatisation objects. If Ukraine seeks to attract quality investors that take responsible business conduct considerations into account as well as economic profitability, it must focus on creating transparent conditions for the upcoming auctions and expanding the participant list as much as possible.

On 2 October 2019, Ukraine's parliament abolished the Law "On List of State-Owned Property Prohibited for Privatisation" that included a number of state-owned infrastructure objects. The law prohibits the full privatisation of industries such as energy, railway, space, and communications. In the Energy sector, full privatisation is not permitted for Naftogaz, Magistralni Gazoprovody Ukrainy, Ukrtransgaz, Ukrnafta, Ukrgasvydobuvannya, Ukrtransnafta, Centrenergo, Energoatom, Ukrenergo and Ukrhydroenergo.

#### *Increased public-private synergies in oil and gas exploration and production*

In 2019, the Ukrainian hydrocarbons sector advanced private participation and, for the first time in several years, licensing rounds and PSA tenders for new oil and gas blocks were offered. Of the nine PSA tender rounds for onshore blocks offered in May 2019, six were solely awarded to Ukrainian SOEs, one to an American company and two to a venture between the SOE Ukrgasvydobuvannya and Vermilion Energy, a Canadian company. The four concession rounds held in 2019 by the State Service of Geology and Subsoil of Ukraine (SSGS) resulted in awarding 19 blocks with exploration and production (E&P) licences for 20 years, out of the 29 proposed blocks. Fourteen blocks were awarded to Ukrgasvydobuvannya (UGV), and the remaining five were sold to five different private companies (State Service of Geology and Subsoil of Ukraine, 2019[64]). Ukraine offered concessions for 12 new onshore oil and gas fields, which were available for private investors under PSAs. In terms of subsoil auctions, the SSGS held new licensing rounds, offering 20-year exploration and production licences of 34 onshore petroleum blocks. Out of 19 blocks, 14 were awarded to the SOE Ukrgasvydobuvannya. State participation in oil and gas exploration and production activities are carried out by Nadra Ukrayny, which entered into joint-venture agreements with private investors.

In 2019, Naftogaz was awarded four PSAs after open bidding competitions and two of them were given in conjunction with Canadian company, Vermilion Energy. The partnership of Naftogaz and Vermilion Energy did not materialise. In mid-2020, Vermilion Energy decided not to proceed with these projects due to changes in their strategy and significant decline in prices for natural gas and oil compared to 2019. Furthermore, the pandemic and global economic recession affected the Company's plans regarding participation in projects in new regions (Naftogaz, 2020[65]).

On July 2020, at the request of private investors that were awarded PSAs to exploit gas fields with Ukrgazvydobuvannya (UGV), a wholly owned subsidiary of Naftogaz, the CMU extended the term to conclude agreements by six months. The order to prolong the signing of the production-sharing agreements was adopted because the awarded companies applied to the Interdepartmental Commission requesting an extension. The investors referenced the complexity of the negotiation process and the highly technical terms contained in the contracts, which require deep analysis prior to the final signing (Cabinet of Ministers of Ukraine, 2020[66]). On December 2020, UGV signed PSAs with local players DTEK Oil & Gas for the Zinkivska blocks, Geo Alliance for Sofiyivska, and Zakhidnadraservis for Uhnivksa (S&P Global Platts, 2021[67]).

Despite Ukraine's efforts to increase public-private synergies in oil and gas exploration and production as described above, new forms of synergies between SOEs and private investors would be welcome to attract foreign investments in Ukraine's energy sector, particularly for projects that involve depleted hydrocarbon resources. An example of an innovative association is the Production Enhancement Contract (PEC) that Naftogaz and Expert Petroleum signed in March 2020. It is the first ever full-scale PEC in the history of Ukraine's oil and gas industry and will generate an additional 300 million cubic meters of gas within five years, from small fields in Western Ukraine (Naftogaz, 2019[3]).

### *Fragmented land reforms to advance energy projects*

In Ukraine's agenda of reforms to advance private investments in the energy sector, one crucial adjustment has been the approval of regulations that help to ease the acquisition of permits and licences related to subsoil usage, which enables the use of land to install energy infrastructure.

According to the Constitution of Ukraine, mineral resources belong to the Ukrainian people and governmental authorities dispose of the subsoil rights on their behalf. Therefore, an investor in the extractive industry must obtain a land use permit as well as a subsoil licence. The State Service of Geology and Subsoil (SSGS) is responsible for issuing contracts, permits and licences related to extracting hydrocarbons or minerals from the subsoil, which are awarded through auction. The regulation determines that a subsoil user becomes an owner of the mineral resources once the minerals reach the surface (CMS Cameron McKenna LLC, 2019[68]).

The SSGS plays a relevant role with regards to land subsurface management, as it administers the use and transfer of geological information. The subsurface users must notify the SSGS of the creation, acquisition or transfer of ownership. Alongside the rights to use the geological information shall be recorded in the catalogue of data on geological information maintained by the state-owned company GeoInform of Ukraine (GeoInform of Ukraine, 2021[69]). On November 2018, to streamline the procedure for acquisition of state geological information and to enhance transparency in the sector, the CMU adopted a resolution on new procedures for the disposal of geological data, mandating that all the information should be accessible online. In 2019, the SSGS started publishing online licensing agreements and special permits granted to private investors. It also presented an online investment atlas containing basic information about subsoil areas nominated for the upcoming auctions (BakerMckenzie, 2020[63]).

In addition to these reforms, in February 2020, the CMU approved Resolution 124 with the new version of the Procedure for Granting Special Permits for Subsoil Use (Hillmont Partners, 2020[70]). The key point was to eliminate the need to agree with regional councils on a procedural basis, for the provision of subsoil use and the extraction of minerals of national importance. The changes have helped reduce the administrative burden and political influence on investors, minimise corruption risks and stimulate the development of subsoil exploitation.

In 2011, Ukraine introduced the Law on Energy Lands and the legal regime of Special Zones for Energy Facilities, which defines the principles for granting use of land plots for energy facilities. To ease land permits for RES investments, in 2018, the Law was reformed so that solar and wind companies could develop energy projects not only on land designated as "land for energy" but also on land designated within the generic category of "land for industry, transport, telecommunications, defence and other designation" with no need to change the designated use of land (Government of Ukraine, 2021[71]).

## Securing sustainable energy investments in a challenging global reality

### *Investing in the energy sector and the COVID-19 crisis*

COVID-19 has dealt a devastating blow to the global economy, disrupting supply chains while stifling demand. In Ukraine, all parts of the energy value chain were affected - upstream, midstream, downstream and service companies. The challenge from the COVID-19 crisis for oil and gas companies was compounded by the oil price crisis that started before the pandemic. Ukraine's oil and gas industry has remained affected due to the ongoing impact of the COVID-19 pandemic on consumption, in particular of refined fuels, notably due to lingering restrictions on travel. Transport and industrial decrease in demand for refined fuels has led to an estimated 10% contraction in consumption in total (Fitch Solutions Country Risk and Industry Research, 2021[53]).

In addition to implementing COVID-19 safety measures, energy companies need to pull all the traditional downturn levers, such as reductions in capital expenditures and cash conservation. The implications of current hedging positions and future hedging positions need to be carefully evaluated, and procurement and risk mitigation strategies will need to be based on effective scenario and demand curve data analysis (PWC, 2020[72]). High-cost producers, such as oil and gas extraction, may need to go further and consider ways of partnering to reduce their cost base, including Production Enhancement Contracts.

As the crisis evolves, power utility companies need to build strategic forecast tools that examine various possible scenarios under different timeframes, so that the organisation is ready for fast decision-making. Business continuity and preparedness plans will need continual review to ensure that operations and infrastructure are properly supported. More than ever, it will be important to work closely with governments and regulators to consider the implications for energy affordability, sustainability and security of supply.

COVID-19 has further deepened the existing crisis in the energy sector of Ukraine. The full range of consequences for the energy sector are yet to be revealed and are difficult to predict, however it is already clear that demand for energy resources has dropped, prices have plummeted and non-payment of utility bills by end-consumers has had a detrimental effect along the supply chain, from DSOs, TSOs, to suppliers and producers (EnergyWorld Magazine, 2020[73]).

In Ukraine, the fall in electricity demand has also been driven by a decrease in the volume of industrial production, caused mainly by COVID-19, given that the largest consumers of electricity are industrial enterprises. The drop in electricity consumption amounts to approximately 5% in 2020 compared to the same period of the last year (Diahovchenko and Morva, 2020[74]).

Lockdowns pose challenges for the implementation of RES projects as there is a significant risk that companies with concluded pre-PPAs will not be able to complete the construction of RES projects on time. Prohibition of entry to the territory of Ukraine for foreigners came into effect during March of 2020 and many RES projects involve participation of foreign companies, from Engineering to Procurement and Construction (EPC) specialists (IMEPOWER, 2020[75]). Consequently, due to the force-majeure situation and restrictions on entry into Ukraine, many companies could be forced to temporarily suspend their activities in Ukraine.

The sharp drop in power demand in 2020, due to the COVID-19 pandemic and the decline in business activities, contributed to a deep financial crisis in the power sector. But the financial indebtedness of the SOE Guaranteed Buyer was just a reflection of several problems in the market, such as the imbalances of power produced by RES. According to Ukraine's National Action Plan for Renewables, the country set the objective to produce 2 300 MW of solar energy, 2 280 of wind and 950 of biomass by the end of 2020 (Government of Ukraine, 2020[76]). However, as of the end of June 2020, 4 593 MW of solar, 1 064 MW of wind and 171 MW of biomass capacities were installed. This huge injection of power capacities to the grid prevented remedial action needing to be taken, and solar power, the most expensive in terms of the feed-in tariff, has not only exceeded other renewables, but also the planned benchmark for itself.

The abovementioned factors coupled with the simultaneous overregulation of electricity market design and attempts to maintain artificially low prices for households were significant contributors to the debts shadowing the RES market.

### *Renewable energy potential and opportunities in Ukraine*

With a population of around 42 million and $CO_2$ equivalent emissions per capita of 5.02mt, Ukraine is one of the most energy-intensive economies in Europe. The largest greenhouse gas (GHG) emitter in the country is the energy sector, with around 66% of emissions. As part of the country's commitments derived from the Paris Climate Agreement, the government approved the Renewed Nationally Determined Contribution (NDC), which sets a new GHG emission target not to exceed 65% of 1990 GHG emission levels in 2030 (UNFCCC, 2021[77]). The 2030 target will be achieved through aligning climate policy and legislation with the European Green Deal, particularly in the areas of renewables, hydrogen and the transformation of the coal sector. The government aims to phase out coal-fired power generation and increase the share of renewables in the energy mix.

At the national level, Ukraine has set a goal of sourcing 25% of its total energy mix from renewables by 2035. In 2035, bioenergy is expected to have the largest contribution with 11 Mtoe – having a share of 11.5% of total primary energy supply, followed by wind and solar energy with 10 Mtoe together – a combined share of 10.4% (Government of Ukraine, 2017[45]).

Ukraine has huge potential for generating energy from biomass, wind and solar (International Renewable Energy Agency, 2015[78]). The country's wind energy potential is estimated at 30,000GW, with about half of the country suitable for establishing wind farms. Ukraine has most notably been making progress in deploying solar equipment and developing solar power facilities, exhibiting substantial growth in the sub-segment. There are five main regions in southern Ukraine where approximately 66% of all renewable generation is located, namely Odesa, Zaporizhzhia, Mykolaiv, Kherson and Dnipro regions. Those regions have the best wind resources and highest solar radiation (US Department of Commerce, 2021[79]). While Ukraine's hydropower sector makes up only a minor share of the energy mix, it is the most developed renewable source in Ukraine, through the use of large-scale hydro power plants. As such, the sector is attracting some investment, primarily focused on the modernisation of existing large plants (US Department of Commerce, 2021[79]).

The government incentivised private sector investments in RES by granting generous FITs for variable renewable projects with no capacity caps, which resulted in the rapid installation of over 8GW of RES capacity at the end of 2020, with the bulk of these additions occurring in 2019. Ukraine's RES sector boomed over 2019, as a number of developers rushed to capitalise on the country's high green FITs for wind and solar capacity before they were cut in 2020. The renewables expansion in Ukraine was aimed at decreasing GHG emissions and diversifying the market's power mix, in the face of ageing nuclear capacity and the rapid drop in coal production. This follows the separatists taking control of significant swathes of the Donbass region, where much of the country's coal production capacity is located (Fitch Solutions Country Risk and Industry Research, 2021[80]).

As a result of the FITs, Ukraine quickly emerged as one of the fastest expanding renewables markets in Europe. Tariffs, which awarded USD150.2/MWh and USD100.2/ MWh for solar and wind power projects respectively were very attractive relative to other European renewables markets and led activity in the Ukrainian renewables sector to surge over the previous two years. Hence, at the beginning of 2020, the share of renewables in energy reached 11% and by the end of the year reached 12.4% (US Department of Commerce, 2021[79]).

With the surge of renewable generation from solar and wind resources, the grid is increasingly in need of balancing capacities. In this regard, the electricity market has provided opportunities for the evolution of a completely new segment of balancing services and auxiliary services. Hence, there are prospects for private companies to invest in: a) grid-scale energy storage systems b) distribution equipment c) energy infrastructure d) storage technologies and batteries f) smart grid technology and metering and e) technical consultancy (US Department of Commerce, 2021[79]). However, some investment projects like storage technologies and batteries, in order to be implemented in Ukraine at large scale, are dependent on the adoption of new regulations, which define important legal conditions for such projects.

### *Amendments to the regulatory framework for renewable energy*

Although Ukraine has made significant progress in planning out the future of its energy system and developing its renewable energy generation (International Renewale Energy Agency, 2015[81]), the RES market has faced limitations for structural reasons, including budgetary deficits, price interventions and cross-subsidisation, insufficient capacity of the grid, lack of a legal framework that adequately regulates imbalances and flexibility in the grid, as well as non-payment of the Guaranteed Buyer.

The rapid increase of RES project has changed the structure of generation in the power system of Ukraine. In 2020, compared to 2019, the generation from RES was projected to almost double to 10.284 TWh. During 2019, the installed capacity of SPPs and WPPs in Ukraine increased 2.7 times and reached 4.7 GW, which is the largest amount that the state power system can accept without serious operational deviations and imbalances (Diahovchenko and Morva, 2020[74]). As of the end of 2020, the installed capacity of RES had already reached 8GW, thereby posing a major challenge to the grid balance.

The rapid increase in the capacity of renewables has created financial and operational challenges for Ukrenergo, the TSO and the Guaranteed Buyer, the latter of which ultimately has accumulated large debts, approximately USD 1.2 billion by the end of 2020, to renewable energy companies (World Bank, 2020[8]). Moreover, there is a lack of flexibility when balancing this 8GW of renewable energy generation, which is produced by private investors. Often times, wind and solar generation is curtailed, and the compensation comes from the take or pay of PPAs.

When RES electricity is curtailed, part-loaded thermal power plants have to intervene and provide the required reserves. The large SOEs that supply 60% of electricity are not allowed to participate in the WEM and are obliged to provide power at low regulated prices, which increases their financial stress, particularly, as higher priced RES power puts a squeeze on their volumes. These practices result in market distortions and price manipulations in the bulk power prices (World Bank, 2020[8]). Adding to the abovementioned challenges, since the launch of the new wholesale electricity market in mid-2019, tariff-setting mechanisms for electricity transmission and dispatching have been characterised by its constant changes and the contesting of prices by industrial consumers who are reluctant to cross-subsidise electricity (Box 2.3).

**Box 2.4. The incomplete transition to market-base tariff setting of Ukraine's wholesale electricity market and its impact to the Green Feed-In Tariff**

On July 2019, the wholesale electricity market started its operations in a phased manner to enable a smoother transition to the new structure by imposing various restrictions, including constrained bidding in the DAM and bidding caps in the BM and ASM. Additionally, two Public Service Obligation (PSO) mechanisms were introduced: (i) a Household PSO to protect household consumers by keeping electricity tariffs below full cost recovery; and (ii) a Renewable Energy PSO to cover RES obligations under the FIT mechanism, since FITs are significantly above wholesale electricity market prices.

Under the household PSO, nuclear and hydro producers – Energoatom and Ukrhydroenergo – are obliged to sell a bulk of their production at low regulated rates to meet residential consumption needs. On the other hand, the Renewable Energy PSO is funded through Ukrenergo's revenues from its transmission tariff, which must be approved by NEURC. Since NEURC does not consider the Renewable Energy PSO to be part of Ukrenergo's mandate, this PSO is not fully funded in the transmission tariff calculation. This leads to a large and growing unfunded mandate of Ukrenergo towards RES.

Since end-consumer tariffs – both for households and for industrials, that include transmission tariff – are regulated by NEURC, there is a disconnect between the legislated household, renewable PSO requirements and the approved end-user tariffs, leaving a large and growing unfunded gap that is at the heart of the sector's financial stress

Source: (OECD, 2020[24])

As of end of 2020, the accumulated arrears of Ukrenergo to guaranteed buyer and power suppliers exceeded UAH 26 billion or USD 0.9 billion. Per preliminary estimate, nearly UAH 50 billion or USD 1.8 billion will be necessary for RES purchases under FIT in 2021. This is expected to grow to about UAH 55 billion or USD 2 billion in 2029.[5] The current financial stress on Ukrenergo has made it difficult for the TSO to perform its core functions, including attracting investments to modernise the grid resilience capabilities, such as rapid response frequency technology, which is needed for timely UkrES grid synchronisation with the EU. According to Ukrenergo's calculations, the Ukrainian energy system, among others measures, will need around 2GW of manoeuvrable capacities with quick start for the next 10 years, and 2GW energy storage capacities (UkraineInvest, 2020[82]). Thus, as more renewables are connected to the grid, more efficient balancing capacities will be needed to enable proper balancing, to limit curtailment of renewables and to continue attracting private investors of RES projects. The implementation of Law 810-IX and Law 2712-VII will be essential for restoring the trust of RES investors. Law 810-IX changes the terms of the agreement that were signed by investors, in several ways (PV Magazine, 2020[83]) : it reduces green FITs, increases local content bonuses, limits new SPP and WPP capacity addition under green FITs, sets partial payment to RES producers using state budget funds, accelerates the balancing responsibility for RES power plants, introduces a compensation mechanism for curtailment due to TSO instructions, updates the stabilisation clause for PPA of RES producers and extends the list of potential sources of financing for the off-taker's costs, related to payments for the FIT to RES producers. Meanwhile, Law 2712-VII on Promotion of Competitive Conditions for Producing Electric Power from Alternative Energy Sources sets the framework for the implementation of RES auctions.

It is worth mentioning that, in Europe, investments in the renewable energy sector have been largely driven by regulatory policies such as quotas, obligations and pricing instruments. Past experiences in Spain and France show that Feed-In Tariffs and Premiums need to evolve continuously, and regular tariff-level adjustment is one example of measures that are needed to reflect the falling cost of technology. As such, auctions are being increasingly adopted, given their ability for real-price discovery. In addition, corporate PPAs for renewable energy are increasingly relevant for achieving the energy transition. Notably, the success of auction and corporate PPAs relies on the design and deployment of policies that are adequate to the country conditions. Ukraine must develop policies that are adequate to its energy market, technology and economics. Hence, the government should consider implementing a policy agenda that advances transparent auctions and corporate PPA from RES.

### Box 2.5. RES auctions as a mechanism to restore investor's trust in Ukraine's energy market

The Law on RES auctions prescribes the procedure that companies producing variable renewable energy should follow to be part of the electricity market. Originally, auctions were foreseen to take place two times a year, but Law 810-IX abolished these provisions and gave the CMU full discretion regarding the auction schedule and dates. The annual quotas are set for wind, solar and other RES technologies separately. In addition, when setting the annual quotas, the CMU can decide to conduct multi-technology or site-specific auctions, for example, the Chernobyl Exclusion Zone. To have control over the RES introduced to the electricity mix, the quotas are based on proposals of the TSO and the State Agency on Energy Efficiency and Energy Savings of Ukraine.

Bidders are required to submit their sealed bids through the ProZorro system. The bid shall include the technical proposal or power capacity of the power plant (kW) and the price offer (EUR/kWh). The winners are determined by opening the bids simultaneously, with the price offers being the sole selection criteria.

The SOE Guaranteed Buyer is mandated to buy the electricity from the producer at the awarded auction price, under the Power Purchase Agreement, which needs to be signed within 15 working days after the auction results are published in the electronic trade system. Until the end of 2029, RES producers are exempted from balancing costs in hours during which their imbalance rate is below 10% for wind operators, 5% for solar and 5% for all other RES operators.

To avoid imbalances, and as stated in Law 810-IX, from January 2021, RES operators with projects over 1 MW will have to bear 50% of the cost for imbalances created by their RES projects, while starting from 2022, they will have to bear the full cost. Also, to level the participation between large and small RES projects, wind power plants with more than 5 MW (Law 810-IX deleted the exception of projects with up to 3 turbines) and solar plants with more than 1 MW are obliged to take part in the auctions. All other RES types can take part on a voluntary basis regardless of their power capacity in the auctions or use of the FIT-scheme, with support until the end of 2029.

Companies that want to participate in the bidding process have to comply with pre-qualification requirements, including: a) Material pre-qualifications, such as confirmation of a right for land use/ownership, concluded grid connection agreement for the project, and disclosure of beneficial owners and b) Financial pre-qualifications in the form of a bid bond of 5 EUR/Kw. The bond is refunded to an unsuccessful bidder after signing the PPA. Additionally, successful bidders must submit a performance bond of 15 EUR/kW, after signing the PPA with the GB. Winning companies will guarantee the purchase of electricity for 20 years after the project is commissioned.

To foster the participation of investors, the content rule of the FIT schemes stays in place. Projects with more than 30% local equipment get a 5% increase in the awarded bid price. If more than 50% are of local origin the support increases by 10%. Law 810-IX introduced a 20% increase in support if more than 70% of the equipment is from a local origin.

Although the auction scheme itself seems to be suitable to ensure an efficient and effective RES expansion, the greatest challenge will be to win back investor confidence after the recent FIT cuts, as well as the delayed auction implementation.

Source: (AURES, 2020[84])

### *International co-operation to advance energy projects*

#### Support to advance energy reforms and the integration of Ukraine into the EU energy system

Ukraine has established strong cooperation ties with actors of the international community to reform and develop its energy industry. Ukraine-EU co-operation is based on a comprehensive partnership in line with the Energy Charter Treaty, the Ukraine-EU Memorandum of Understanding on Energy Cooperation, the Ukraine-EU Association Agreement and the Energy Community Treaty. Currently, Ukraine is implementing measures to further reform its energy sector in accordance with the EU's Third Energy Package, as well as, provisions of the updated Memorandum of Understanding on the Strategic Energy Partnership between Ukraine and the European Union (Government of Ukraine, 2021[85]).

**Box 2.6. Tripartite co-operation to achieve a new gas transit between Naftogaz and Gazprom**

Ukraine is a key transit country for Russian gas exports to Europe. Nevertheless, there was a dispute from 2014 to 2019 between Gazprom and Naftogaz over the price of gas and its transit through Ukrainian territory. This put in peril the flow of Russian gas and the revenue collected by the Ukrainian government from transit tariffs. In December 2019, Gazprom and Naftogaz reached an agreement to continue the transit of Russian gas through Ukraine for the period 2020-2024.

The European Commission facilitated trilateral talks between the parties. This effort led to a new gas transit agreement with Russia based on EU rules. It outlines that 65 bcm are to be transited in 2010 and 40 bcm per year from 2021 to 2024, for a total of 225 bcm, with provisions for additional volumes to be shipped if required. The agreement expressed the two sides' intention to co-operate further on transit in 2025-2034. It was the first major trading agreement between Russia and Ukraine since the outbreak of military conflict in eastern Ukraine in early 2014. The arbitration clauses in the agreement state that disputes are to be settled at the International Chamber of Commerce in Zurich. This differentiates the agreement from the previous practice, where Gazprom-Naftogaz contracts were subject to arbitration in Stockholm. Gazprom will pay USD 7.2 billion to Naftogaz as part of the transit contract and 2.9 billion USD in compensation under the Stockholm arbitration award.

Source: (Pirani and Sharples, 2020[86])

The European Union and Ukraine entered into the Deep and Comprehensive Free Trade Agreement (DCFTA) on 1 January 2016. Although the Association Agreement and the DCFTA are separate from the Energy Community agreements, the provisions of the DCFTA includes references to the provisions and actions being implemented as part of the Energy Community. The DCFTA is primarily focused on issues concerning trade in energy and raw energy materials, including setting prices, customs duties, infrastructural co-operation, transport of energy resources and the flow of investments (European External Action Service, 2019[87]).

As part of the international co-operation that Ukraine receives from the European Union, the EU4Energy Initiative helps the country to improve the quality of energy data and statistics, shape regional policy-making discussions, strengthen legislative and regulatory frameworks and improve access to information. The initiative's main objective is to support its partners on their way towards a low-carbon economy. The program is implemented by the International Energy Agency, Energy Community Secretariat and Energy Charter Secretariat. The project has five key components: data project, policy project, governance project, web portal and communications project. Among the six partners of the project (International Energy Agency, 2016[88]), Ukraine is the country which is closest to achieving the objectives set by the EU4Energy initiative.

Multilateral Development Banks (MDBs) have afforded substantive support to the Government of Ukraine and SOEs in order to spur indirect positive effects to private sector participants. For instance, Ukrenergo's co-operation with MDBs has enabled an increase in the flow of foreign investments into the country. In July 2019, the European Bank for Reconstruction and Development (EBRD) agreed to provide EUR 149 million to Ukrenergo, to support the upgrading of the country's power transmission network (EBRD, 2019[89]). Ukrenergo committed to using the EBRD funding to upgrade its key transmission and infrastructure, which is necessary in order to enable synchronisation with European electricity networks. The funding is accompanied with technical assistance, which will support the country's efforts to align its legal framework and operational practices with the EU Third Energy Package, a legislative package for gas and electricity markets within Europe. The EBRD financing is also promoting the commercialisation and institutional development of Ukrenergo through the implementation of a comprehensive Corporate Governance Action Plan and robust procurement standards.

The International Bank for Reconstruction and Development (IBRD) leads the second power transmission project (PTP-2), with a total cost of USD 378 million. The main objective of the PTP-2 project is to increase the level of security, reliability and efficiency of electricity transmission. Additionally, the PTP-2 will improve compensation of reactive power in the grids, thus creating technical conditions to advance the integration of the IPS of Ukraine into the European Network of Transmission System Operators (ENTSO-E), ultimately, thereby enabling it to become a competitive member of the European electricity markets. This project includes investments in the smart grid and advancements to the institutional development of the power company (Ukrenergo, 2021[90]).

Not only has the electricity sector received assistance from MDBs. On May 2018, the CMU formalised the Action Plan created by the EBRD and WB for the Implementation of the State Policy in the Area of Heat Supply. This will help to create a transparent, stable and predictable regulatory and business environment, under which District Heat Companies (DHCs) will be able to attract private investments for modernisation (See Figure 2.7).

**Figure 2.7 Ukraine's DHCs Action Plan created by the EBRD, EIB and WB**

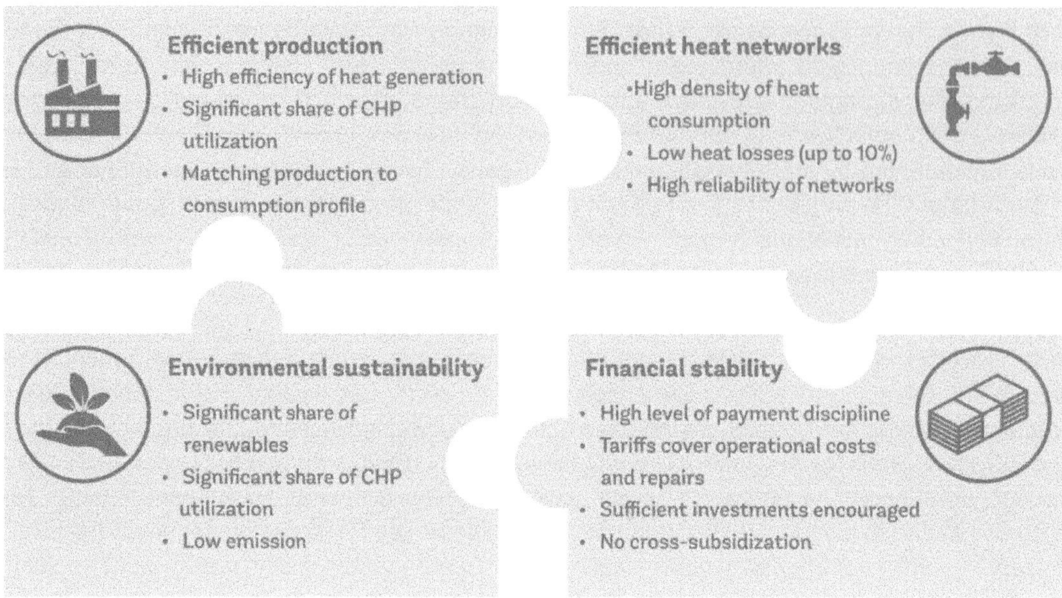


Source: (EBRD, EIB, WB, 2019[91])

In Ukraine, the European Investment Bank (EIB) has invested in large-scale infrastructure projects focused on increasing the utilisation of NPPs, reducing pollution and enhancing stability of the electricity supply to consumers. The EIB supports Ukraine in implementing an ambitious energy efficiency programme. A EUR 300 million loan will allow Ukraine to improve the energy efficiency of some 1,000 public-owned buildings, including schools, cultural centres, kindergartens and hospitals (European Investment Bank, 2021[92]).

In August 2019, Ukraine and Germany signed a 'Memorandum of Understanding on Establishing an Energy Partnership". The energy partnership consolidates the activities of the German government, which has been working on bilateral energy projects with Ukraine for several years. Its main priorities include: increasing energy efficiency in buildings and industry, modernising the electricity sector, expanding and integrating renewable energy and reducing carbon emissions. With financial and technical aid from Germany, the government established a Coordination Centre for the Transformation of Coal Regions of Ukraine (Ministry for Communities and Territories Development of Ukraine, 2018[93]).

*Support to advance private investments in the energy sector*

To reach the next stage of development and close the gap with its more advanced neighbours, such as Poland and Hungary, Ukraine needs to support innovation and consolidate a dynamic, competitive, and robust private sector. This is where international development institutions, such as development aid agencies, multilateral development banks (MDBs), can provide key support (Emerging Europe, 2018[94]). Regarding the energy sector, Ukraine has strengthened its relationship with MDBs in specific areas, including: (i) overcoming persistent investment gaps, which persist despite policy reforms (ii) focusing on infrastructure needed over the long term, including the important dimension of innovation and scaling up of low-carbon technologies (iii) supporting new market-based investment in the energy sector, in particular, for relatively new types of infrastructure, such as auctions, demand response and storage technology and (iv) advancing regulatory and policy reforms.

Ukraine is a partner of the Eastern Europe Energy Efficiency and Environment Partnership (E5P). The E5P fund provides Ukraine with access to financial support for the implementation of 25 energy efficiency projects valued at over EUR 962 million. The projects approved for implementation in Ukraine have shown that the E5P grants can leverage, on average, investment volumes that are five times the size of the committed grants. Moreover, E5P projects in Ukraine have reduced 790,466 tonnes of $CO_2e$ emissions. The grant allocations are flexible and recognise the priorities of each recipient country. The overall aim is to reduce energy use, pollution and greenhouse gas emissions. The fund also supports policy dialogue and regulatory reform (Eastern Europe Energy Efficiency and Environment Partnership (E5P), 2021[95]). The grants from E5P are used as an incentive for clients to take loans provided by those participating as Implementing Agencies:

- Council of Europe Development Bank (CEB)
- European Bank for Reconstruction and Development (EBRD)
- European Investment Bank (EIB)
- International Finance Corporation (IFC)
- KfW Entwicklungsbank
- Nordic Environment Finance Corporation (NEFCO)
- Nordic Investment Bank (NIB)
- World Bank (WB)

Due to the relevance of the co-operation between Ukraine and the E5P, the Ministry of Energy signed an agreement of contribution to continue participation in July 2019. The agreement provides a 10 million EUR contribution to the fund, which will provide access to financial support and technical assistance for energy efficiency. This will result in significant reductions in electricity consumption, carbon dioxide emissions and other greenhouse gases (Ministry of Energy of Ukraine, 2020).

The EBRD has been the most important provider of financing with regards to advancing RES projects in Ukraine. In order to encourage businesses to pursue sustainable energy projects, the EBRD launched Ukraine's Sustainable Energy Lending Facility (USELF), a loan program that goes beyond providing tailor-made financing, and also affords assistance by providing technical consultants for businesses and local authorities. USELF supports the fulfilment of the goals of the Ukrainian government on its path to higher shares of RES and brings more competition into Ukraine's electricity sector, which is currently dominated by state-owned enterprises. Loans within USELF are available to local and international project developers in the renewable energy business. Programs like USELF have led to a total investment of EUR 1 billion by the EBRD in Ukraine's power sector (Ukraine Sustainable Energy Lending Facility (USELF), 2021[96]). Despite the RES crisis in 2020, the EBRD aims to continue its engagement in Ukraine for the duration of the transitional period, from the FIT to the auction scheme. Similar to the FIT scheme, investments from international financing institutions will play a crucial role in de-risking auctions in Ukraine (European Commission, 2020[35]).

The financing for private solar and wind projects in Ukraine have also been made possible due to the participation of development banks and export credit agencies from different countries, including: the Dutch development bank (FMO), the Norwegian Export Credit Guarantee Agency (GEIK), the German development bank (KfW), Proparco as a subsidiary of the French development agency (ADF), the Nordic Environment Finance Corporation (NEFCO), the Nordic Investment Bank (NIB), the US EXIM bank, etc.

## Outlook and policy recommendations

Ukraine has successfully implemented regulatory reforms in the energy industry that have led to the participation of private companies in the power, oil & gas, coal and heating markets. The country has shifted the energy sector from an industry with absolute control by the government to one that encourages free market principles.

In terms of ownership and management, Ukraine has developed policies and regulations that have enabled private sector participation and privatisation of energy assets. Major reforms have been implemented to modernise SOEs and enhance their governance, while opening the sector to private companies.

An important advancement has also been the enactment of laws that have allowed the introduction of renewable energy into the energy mix and the deployment of energy efficiency programmes. However, renewable energy generators have faced severe challenges derived from the imbalances of the power sector and the regulatory changes that Ukraine approved in 2020. The crisis caused major arrears to key actors in Ukraine's power market and affected the trust of private investors in the rule of law.

Despite these challenges, Ukraine has the opportunity to continue encouraging investments in the energy sector, particularly in projects that will help to achieve the country's National Determined Contributions, by offering legal certainty to private investors. Such an approach could lead to positive outcomes, including reducing the country's dependence on energy imports, securing a just energy transition and creating sustainable returns for investors.

- **Progressively move from feed-in tariffs to more competitive support mechanisms. In addition to the feed-in tariffs**, Ukraine's renewable energy market offers the possibility of auctions and the introduction of corporate power purchase agreements that will play an important role in energy transition efforts. Ukraine may wish to consider putting in place awareness campaigns that highlight the benefits of renewable energy.
- **Advance the implementation of regulations on the development of bioenergy potential of Ukraine** related to the development of solid biofuels market, development of liquid biofuels market, development of bio methane market, development of energy crops on marginal lands, reduction of the tax burden on bioenergy facilities running on biofuels by setting a zero rate of C02 emissions tax for them.
- **Move forward with the implementation of regulations that promote competition in the electricity sector,** while placing a special emphasis on the Auctions Law.
- **Assess electricity and gas tariff schemes for consumer households, abolish cross-subsidies and provide targeted subsidies to benefit the poorest households**. In this regard, ensure that tariff and pricing policies reflect the costs of production, transmission, and distribution and allow for a profit for investors. In addition, gradually reduce public service obligations and ensure that those applicable in the country are in line with the EU acquis.
- **Develop a regulatory framework and action programmes that expedite the economic switch from hydrocarbons to renewable energy sources at a faster rate** by strengthening national and regional efforts to phase out coal power plants and eradicating policy support mechanisms for the consumption of fossil fuels.
- **Continue implementing policies and programmes that pursue the integration of Ukraine's power and gas system with the EU through synchronisation with the ENTSO-E and the ENTSO-G,** including integration measures such as reinforcements of the transmission network, realisation of frequency regulation reserves, establishment of a telecommunication network, and studies on future grid stability.
- **Establish a mandatory condition for power quotas for entities generating electricity from renewable energy investors, according to which they must simultaneously provide highly manoeuvrable generation, efficient balancing capacities, or Energy Storage-type systems**. Incite policy investments that allow RES producers to use the grid to store surplus generated power for a long time and to consume it later.

- **Adopt a progressive regulatory framework to attract players with new technologies, such as battery energy storage systems, demand response technologies, and green hydrogen to energy markets.** This step will encourage the implementation of many more investment projects with these technologies.
- **Ensure that public procurement and privatisation processes in the whole energy sector are transparent, open to quality private investors, free of corruption and continue using public procurement e-platforms such ProZorro and ProZorro.Sales**, Continue providing training for public officials, both at the central and local levels of governments, on the use of ProZorro and ProZorro.Sales.
- **Take additional actions to ensure that state-owned enterprises active in the energy sector observe high standards of transparency and are subject to the same high quality accounting, disclosure, compliance and auditing standards** as listed companies, as was recommended in the OECD 2021 *Review of the Corporate Governance of State-Owned Enterprises: Ukraine*

## Notes

[1] See https://data.worldbank.org/indicator/BX.KLT.DINV.CD.WD?locations=UA, https://data.worldbank.org/indicator/BX.KLT.DINV.WD.GD.ZS?locations=UA.

[2] See https://www.flandersinvestmentandtrade.com/export/sites/trade/files/market_studies/Ukrainian%20Energy%20Market.pdf.

[3] In accordance with the amendments (made by the Resolutions of the Cabinet of Ministers of Ukraine of 24 April 2020 No 303 and of 30 April 2021 No 444) to the Resolution of the Cabinet of Ministers of Ukraine dated 19 October 2018 No 867 "On Approval of the Regulations on the imposition of special duties on the subjects of the natural gas market to ensure public interests in the functioning of the natural gas market" the Resolution ceased to be in force as of 20 May 2021, and the Public Service Obligations were withdrawn from Naftogaz.

[4] See https://land.gov.ua/proekt-postanovy-kabinetu-ministriv-ukrainy-deiaki-pytannia-pidhotovky-ta-provedennia-zemelnykh-torhiv-dlia-prodazhu-zemelnykh-dilianok-ta-nabuttia-prav-korystuvannia-nymy-orendy-superfitsiiu-emfit/, https://www.kyivpost.com/business/cabinet-authorizes-prozorro-sale-to-conduct-electronic-land-auctions.html?fr=operanews.

[5] According to the Law of Ukraine “On Amendments to Certain Laws of Ukraine on Improving Conditions for Supporting Electricity Production from Alternative Energy Sources” of 21 June 2020 № 810-IX, new generating capacities on biogas / biomass put into operation after 2023 will not receive FIT. New solar power facilities will receive 40% of the FIT, which is almost equal to the current electricity prices at day-ahead market. According to the latest estimates, it is expected that in 2029 the volume of payments under FIT (including industrial stations and solar power plants installed on the roof of the property) will not exceed UAH 55 billion excluding VAT (in prices and at the rate of EUR / UAH 2021).

## References


Atlantic Council (2020), *Ukraine quietly launches a gas market revolution*, https://www.atlanticcouncil.org/blogs/ukrainealert/ukraine-quietly-launches-a-gas-market-revolution/. [29]

Atlantic Council (2020), *Ukraine's gas market reform: A success story that needs to be acknowledged*, https://www.atlanticcouncil.org/blogs/energysource/ukraines-gas-market-reform-a-success-story-that-needs-to-be-acknowledged/. [19]

AURES (2020), *Auctions for the support of renewable energy in Ukraine : Auction design for the planned 2020 RES auctions*, http://aures2project.eu/wp-content/uploads/2020/11/AURES_II_case_study_Ukraine_final.pdf. [84]

BakerMckenzie (2020), *Conducting Business in Ukraine 2020*, https://www.bakermckenzie.com/-/media/files/insight/guides/2020/conducting-business-in-ukraine-2020_090420.pdf?la=en. [63]

Cabinet of Ministers of Ukraine (2020), *Decree of 22 July 2020 n°642 "On extension of the term of concluding agreements on distribution of hydrocarbons"*, https://zakon.rada.gov.ua/laws/show/642-2020-%D0%BF#Text. [66]

CMS (2020), *Progress in the Ukrainian oil and gas sector in 2019 and the outlook for 2020*, https://www.cms-lawnow.com/ealerts/2020/01/progress-in-the-ukrainian-oil-and-gas-sector-in-2019-and-the-outlook-for-2020. [7]

CMS (2020), *Ukraine: important changes to subsoil use legislation*, https://www.cms-lawnow.com/ealerts/2020/01/ukraine-important-changes-to-subsoil-use-legislation. [27]

CMS Cameron McKenna LLC (2019), *Mining in Ukraine: overview*, https://uk.practicallaw.thomsonreuters.com/w-019-9318?transitionType=Default&contextData=(sc.Default)&firstPage=true&bhcp=1. [68]

Diahovchenko, I. and G. Morva (2020), *Effects of COVID-19 on the electricity sectors of Ukraine and Hungary: challenges of energy demand and renewables integration*, https://ieeexplore.ieee.org/stamp/stamp.jsp?arnumber=9337785. [74]

Eastern Europe Energy Efficiency and Environment Partnership (E5P) (2021), *E5P Projects in Ukraine*, http://e5p.eu/ukraine. [95]

EBRD (2019), *EBRD €149 million loan to support upgrade of Ukraine's transmission network*, https://www.ebrd.com/news/2019/ebrd-149-million-loan-to-support-upgrade-of-ukraines-transmission-network.html. [89]

EBRD, EIB, WB (2019), *Setting the agenda for further district heating reform in Ukraine*. [91]

Emerging Europe (2018), *What Ukraine needs to do to achieve its vast potential*, https://emerging-europe.com/voices/what-ukraine-needs-to-do-to-achieve-its-vast-potential/. [94]

Energy Charter Secretariat (2021), *Statistics of ECT Cases*, https://www.energychartertreaty.org/fileadmin/DocumentsMedia/Statistics/All_statistics_-_20_March_2021.pdf. [39]

Energy Community (2020), *Annnual Implementation Report*, http://dx.doi.org/EnC_IR2020_Ukraine.pdf. [25]

Energy Community (2020), *Renewable energy investments in Ukraine at a critical junction*, https://www.energy-community.org/news/Energy-Community-News/2020/07/17.html. [40]

Energy Community (2020), *Two billion euros burnt in coal subsidies by Energy Community Contracting Parties in 2015-2019*, https://energy-community.org/news/Energy-Community-News/2020/12/02.html. [21]

Energy Community Secretariat (2019), *Annual Implementation Report*. [16]

Energy Community Secretariat (2018), *Public Service Obligations: a blackbox case*. [32]

EnergyWorld Magazine (2020), *The impact of Covid-19 crisis on global energy sector*, https://www.energyworldmag.com/the-impact-of-covid-19-crisis-on-global-energy-sector/. [73]

EU Neighbours (2018), *Energy reforms: the challenge for Ukraine's gas market*, https://www.euneighbours.eu/en/east/eu-in-action/stories/energy-reforms-challenge-ukraines-gas-market. [12]

European Business Association (2020), *Gas market of Ukraine: general overview*, https://eba.com.ua/en/gas-market-of-ukraine-general-overview/. [6]

European Commission (2020), *Auctions for the support of renewable energy in Ukraine: Auction design for the planned 2020 RES auctions*, http://aures2project.eu/wp-content/uploads/2020/11/AURES_II_case_study_Ukraine_final.pdf. [35]

European Commission (2019), *Association Implementation Report on Ukraine*, https://eeas.europa.eu/sites/default/files/swd_2019_433_f1_joint_staff_working_paper_en_v4_p1_1056243.pdf. [28]

European External Action Service (2019), *The EU-Ukraine Association Agreement and Deep and Comprehensive Free Trade Area*, https://eeas.europa.eu/archives/delegations/ukraine/documents/virtual_library/vademecum_en.pdf. [87]

European Investment Bank (2021), *EIB records high investments in Ukraine in 2020: over €1 billion for infrastructure, environment, innovation and post-COVID-19 recovery*, https://www.eib.org/en/press/all/2021-042-eib-records-high-investments-in-ukraine-in-2020-over-eur1-billion-for-infrastructure-environment-innovation-and-post-covid-19-recovery#. [92]

European Union (2016), *EU–Ukraine Association Agreement "Quick Guide to the Association Agreement"*, http://eeas.europa.eu/archives/docs/images/top_stories/140912_eu-ukraine-associatin-agreement-quick_guide.pdf. [43]

Financial Times (2021), *Germany and US reach truce over Nord Stream 2 pipeline*, https://www.ft.com/content/49210a4e-17ed-4a2e-a986-4efcadc7f342. [5]

Fitch Solutions Country Risk and Industry Research (2021), *Ukraine Energy Market Overview*, https://www.ogel.org/article.asp?key=1730. [53]

Fitch Solutions Country Risk and Industry Research (2021), *Ukraine Power Repoer*. [80]

GeoInform of Ukraine (2021), *SSE GeoInform of Ukraine*, https://geoinf.kiev.ua/pro-pidpriemstvo/. [69]

Government of Ukraine (2021), *On amendments to some resolutions of the Cabinet of Ministers of Ukraine*, https://www.kmu.gov.ua/npas/pro-vnesennya-zmin-do-deyakih-postanov-kabinetu-ministriv-t180121. [33]

Government of Ukraine (2021), *On energy lands and the legal regime of special zones of energy facilities*, https://zakon.rada.gov.ua/laws/show/2480-17#Text. [71]

Government of Ukraine (2021), *Sectorial dialogue: Energy*, https://ukraine-eu.mfa.gov.ua/en/2633-relations/galuzeve-spivrobitnictvo/energetika. [85]

Government of Ukraine (2020), *Law on Extraction of Amber and other Minerals*, https://zakon.rada.gov.ua/laws/show/402-IX#Text. [56]

Government of Ukraine (2020), *National Action Plan for Renewable Energy for the period until 2020*, https://saee.gov.ua/sites/default/files/documents/Presentation_NAPRES_Norw_OCT_3_Eng%20.pdf. [76]

Government of Ukraine (2020), *Report on the state of implementation of the Energy strategy of Ukraine until 2035*, http://mpe.kmu.gov.ua/minugol/control/uk/publish/officialcategory?cat_id=245001827. [49]

Government of Ukraine (2020), *Resolution on Modification of the Procedure for GRanting Special Permits for Subsoil Use*, https://zakon.rada.gov.ua/laws/show/124-2020-%D0%BF#Text. [57]

Government of Ukraine (2019), *Law On Concession № 155-IX*. [54]

Government of Ukraine (2018), "Energy Sector Reform", https://www.kmu.gov.ua/en/reformi/ekonomichne-zrostannya/reforma-energetichnogo-sektoru. [47]

Government of Ukraine (2018), *Law of Ukraine on Deregulating the Oil and Gas Industry*, https://zakon.rada.gov.ua/laws/show/2314-19#Text. [10]

Government of Ukraine (2018), *Law on Privatization of State and Municipal Property*, https://zakon.rada.gov.ua/laws/show/2269-19#Text. [61]

Government of Ukraine (2017), *Energy Strategy of Ukraine for the period up to 2035 "Security, Energy Efficiency, Competitiveness"*, https://razumkov.org.ua/uploads/article/2018_Energy_Strategy_2035.pdf. [45]

Government of Ukraine (2017), *Law on the Electricity Market*, https://zakon.rada.gov.ua/laws/show/2019-19#Text. [23]

Government of Ukraine (2015), *Gas Storage Code*, https://zakon.rada.gov.ua/laws/show/z1380-15#Text. [15]

Government of Ukraine (2015), *Gas Transmission System Code*, https://zakon.rada.gov.ua/laws/show/z1378-15#Text. [14]

Government of Ukraine (2015), *Law On Natural Gas Market*, https://zakon.rada.gov.ua/laws/show/329-19#Text. [13]

Government of Ukraine (2004), *Law on Oil and Gas*, https://zakon.rada.gov.ua/laws/show/2665-14?lang=en#Text. [9]

Government of Ukraine (1999), *Law on Mining*, https://zakon.rada.gov.ua/laws/show/1127-14#top. [20]

Government of Ukraine (1994), *Subsoil Code of Ukraine*, https://zakon.rada.gov.ua/laws/show/132/94-%D0%B2%D1%80#Text. [55]

Hillmont Partners (2020), *New Rounds of Subsoil Use E-Auctions in 2020*, https://hillmont.com/wp-content/uploads/Hillmont-Partners_New-Rounds-of-Subsoil-Use-E-Auctions_Legal-Alert_15062020.pdf. [70]

ICIS (2020), *Ukraine gas market faces major changes as foreign companies seek its short-haul, storage services*, Independent Commodity Intelligence Services, https://www.icis.com/explore/resources/news/2020/05/13/10506796/ukraine-gas-market-faces-major-changes-as-foreign-companies-seek-its-short-haul-storage-services. [30]

IEA (2019), *Data and statistics*, https://www.iea.org/data-and-statistics?country=UKRAINE&fuel=Energy%20supply&indicator=TPESbySource. [2]

IMEPOWER (2020), *Law of Ukraine Introducing Amendments to the Renewable Energy Support System*, https://www.imepower.com/wp-content/uploads/2020/08/Law-810-Draft-Law-3658-Summary-Eng-v2.pdf. [75]

International Energy Agency (2020), *Ukraine Energy Profile*, https://www.iea.org/reports/ukraine-energy-profile/energy-security#energy-infrastructure-and-investment. [1]

International Energy Agency (2019), *World Energy Investment*, https://www.iea.org/reports/world-energy-investment-2019. [44]

International Energy Agency (2016), *About EU4Energy Programme*, https://www.eu4energy.iea.org/about. [88]

International Monetary Fund (2020), *Ukraine : Request for Stand-by Arrangement-Press Release; Staff Report; and Statement by the Executive Director for Ukraine*, https://www.imf.org/en/Publications/CR/Issues/2020/06/10/Ukraine-Request-for-Stand-by-Arrangement-Press-Release-Staff-Report-and-Statement-by-the-49501. [62]

International Renewable Energy Agency (2015), *REmap 2030 Renewable Energy Prospects for Ukraine*, https://www.irena.org/-/media/Files/IRENA/Agency/Publication/2015/Apr/IRENA_REmap_Ukraine_paper_2015.pdf. [78]

International Renewale Energy Agency (2015), *REMAP 2030: Renewable Energy Prospects for Ukraine*, https://www.irena.org/publications/2015/Apr/Renewable-Energy-Prospects-for-Ukraine. [81]

Ministry for Communities and Territories Development of Ukraine (2018), *Coordination Center for the Transformation of Coal Regions holds the first meeting – Minregion*, https://www.minregion.gov.ua/en/eng-press/eng-news/coordination-center-for-the-transformation-of-coal-regions-holds-the-first-meeting/ (accessed on 25 October 2021). [93]

Ministry of Energy of Ukraine (2020), *Resolution of the Cabinet of Ministers of Ukraine of July 1, 2020 № 542 "On Amendments to the Regulations on Imposition of Special Obligations on Natural Gas Market Entities to Ensure Public Interests in the Process of Natural Gas Market Functioning"*, http://mpe.kmu.gov.ua/minugol/control/uk/publish/article?art_id=245451008&cat_id=35109. [31]

Ministry of Energy of Ukraine (2020), "The memorandum with the participants of the "green" energy market takes into account the interests of investors, the state and consumers", http://mpe.kmu.gov.ua/minugol/control/uk/publish/article?art_id=245447139&cat_id=35109. [41]

Naftogaz (2020), *Anual Report of Naftogaz*, https://www.naftogaz.com/files/Zvity/Annual_report_Naftogaz_2020_EN_28_04_2021_3.pdf. [65]

Naftogaz (2019), *Annual report 2019*, https://www.naftogaz.com/files/Zvity/Naftogaz_2019_EN.pdf (accessed on 20 July 2021). [4]

Naftogaz (2019), *Annual Report 2019*, https://www.naftogaz.com/files/Zvity/Naftogaz_2019_EN.pdf. [3]

NEURC (2020), *Basic tasks and functions*, https://www.nerc.gov.ua/?id=11804. [26]

NEURC (2019), *Annual Report of the National Energy and Utilities Regulatory Commission*, https://www.nerc.gov.ua/data/filearch/Catalog3/Report_NEURC_2019-ENG.pdf. [17]

OECD (2020), *Investment Perspectives in Eastern Partner Countries*, https://www.oecd.org/investment/Investment-perspectives-in-Eastern-Partner-countries.pdf. [37]

OECD (2020), *Monitoring the Energy Strategy of Ukraine 2035*, https://www.oecd.org/eurasia/competitiveness-programme/eastern-partners/Monitoring-the-energy-strategy-Ukraine-2035-EN-.pdf. [52]

OECD (2020), *State-Owned Enterprise Reform in the Electricity Sector in Ukraine*, OECD, https://www.oecd.org/corporate/SOE-Reform-Electricity-Sector-Ukraine-ENG.pdf. [24]

OECD (2020), *State-Owned Enterprise Reform in the Electricity Sector in Ukraine*, https://www.oecd.org/corporate/SOE-Reform-Electricity-Sector-Ukraine-ENG.pdf. [36]

OECD (2019), *Snapshot of Ukraine's Energy Sector*, https://www.oecd.org/eurasia/competitiveness-programme/eastern-partners/Snapshot-of-Ukraines-Energy-Sector-EN.pdf. [22]

OECD (2018), *Monitoring the Energy Strategy of Ukraine 2035*, https://www.oecd.org/eurasia/competitiveness-programme/eastern-partners/Monitoring-the-energy-strategy-Ukraine-2035-EN-.pdf. [48]

Pirani, S. and J. Sharples (2020), "The Russia-Ukraine gas transit deal: opening a new chapter", *The Oxford Institute for Energy Studies*, https://www.neweurope.eu/article/ceasefire-russias-gazprom-ukraines-naftogaz-eus-gas-link-team/ (accessed on 19 July 2021). [86]

ProZorro (2021), *ProZorro Platform*, https://prozorro.gov.ua/en. [59]

PV Magazine (2020), *Impact of Covid-19 on the Ukrainian energy sector*, https://www.pv-magazine.com/2020/04/28/impact-of-covid-19-on-the-ukranian-energy-sector/. [83]

PWC (2020), *Energy industry and COVID-19 (coronavirus): strategising for the 'new normal'*, https://www.pwc.com/gx/en/issues/crisis-solutions/covid-19/energy-utilities-resources-coronavirus.html. [72]

Razumkov Centre (2019), *Assessment of the implementation of the Energy Strategy of Ukraine*, https://razumkov.energy/meny/news/analysis-energy-strategy.html. [50]

S&P Global Platts (2021), *Commodities 2021: Ukraine makes new upstream push as gas output falters*, https://www.spglobal.com/platts/en/market-insights/latest-news/natural-gas/010821-commodities-2021-ukraine-makes-new-upstream-push-as-natural-gas-output-falters. [67]

Sayenko Kharenko (2019), "Ukraine has adopted Law about auctions to support renewable energy projects", https://sk.ua/news/ukraine-adopted-law-auctions-support-renewable-energy-projects/. [38]

State Service of Geology and Subsoil of Ukraine (2019), *Results of Oil & Gas Licensing Rounds 2019 in Ukraine*, https://www.geo.gov.ua/en/licensing-round-2019/. [64]

The Government of Ukraine (2017), *ESU 2035*, https://razumkov.org.ua/uploads/article/2018_Energy_Strategy_2035.pdf. [46]

Ukraine Sustainable Energy Lending Facility (USELF) (2021), *Investment in renewable energy - a step for the future!*, http://www.uself.com.ua/. [96]

UkraineInvest (2020), *Invest in Ukraine NOW*, https://ukraineinvest.gov.ua/wp-content/uploads/2020/04/UkraineNOW_b.pdf. [82]

Ukrenergo (2021), *Cooperation with the World Bank (IBRD)*, https://ua.energy/european-integration/cooperation-with-imf/cooperation-world-bank/. [90]

Ukrenergo (2017), "Ukrenergo in ProZorro", https://ua.energy/procurement/ukrenergo-in-prozorro/. [60]

UNFCCC (2021), *Updated Nationally Determined Contribution of Ukraine to the Paris*, https://www4.unfccc.int/sites/ndcstaging/PublishedDocuments/Ukraine%20First/Ukraine%20NDC_July%2031.pdf. [77]

US Department of Commerce (2021), *Market Intelligence: Ukraine Renewable Energy Market*, https://www.trade.gov/market-intelligence/ukraine-renewable-energy-market. [79]

US Energy Information Administration (2013), *Feed-in tariff: A policy tool encouraging deployment of renewable electricity technologies - Today in Energy*, https://www.eia.gov/todayinenergy/detail.php?id=11471. [34]

US Energy Information Administration (n.d.), *Analysis on Ukraine*, https://www.eia.gov/international/analysis/country/UKR. [11]

US-Ukraine Business Council (2020), "Progress in the Ukrainian oil and gas sector in 2019 and the outlook for 2020", https://www.usubc.org/site/recent-news/progress-in-the-ukrainian-oil-and-gas-sector-in-2019-and-the-outlook-for-2020. [18]

Wilson Center (2019), *Liberalising Ukraine's Electricity Market: Benefits and Risks*, https://www.wilsoncenter.org/blog-post/liberalizing-ukraines-electricity-market-benefits-and-risks. [51]

World Bank (2020), *Improving Power System Resilience for European Power Grid Integration*, https://pubdocs.worldbank.org/en/596881617115808469/14576-GESP-WB-Ukraine-Improving-Power-System-Resilience-for-European-Power-Grid-Integration-PUBLIC.pdf. [8]

World Bank (2020), *Rethinking Power Sector Reform in the Developing World*, https://www.esmap.org/sites/default/files/RPSR_English%20_Overview_Final.pdf. [42]

World Bank (2019), *Public Expenditure and Financial Accountability (PEFA) Performance Assessment Report Ukraine*, http://documents1.worldbank.org/curated/en/739681586466657490/pdf/Ukraine-2019-Public-Expenditure-and-Financial-Accountability-PEFA-Performance-Assessment-Report.pdf. [58]

# 3 The Policy Framework for Investment

This chapter provides an overview of Ukraine's framework for investment relevant to investment in the energy sector. It assesses Ukraine's restrictions on the entry of foreign investors in the energy sector and the extent to which the country provides national treatment once they are established. The chapter notably looks into the rules for property protection and access to land, as these issues are important for investors interested in operating in the energy sector.

## Introduction

Ukraine has a regulatory framework that guarantees national treatment to foreign economic operators. The Constitution, the Foreign Regime Law and the Economic Code of Ukraine are essential primary legal instruments that allow the participation of foreign investors with local ones. In addition, the country has implemented specialised laws that protect the interests of private investors in the Electricity, Oil & Gas, and Energy Efficiency markets.

Attracting investment and further improving the country's institutional framework are key government priorities, as is evidenced by Ukraine's strategic documents, such as "The Energy Strategy of Ukraine 2035", which was adopted in 2017.[1] The key standards of investor treatment and protection are guaranteed under the Constitution[2] – the highest legal authority – and in dedicated laws. Ukraine's FDI legal regime includes enforceable principles for foreign investors' protection, investment promotion, and transparency requirements.

### Box 3.1. The OECD National Treatment instrument for foreign-controlled enterprises

National treatment is the commitment by an Adherent to the *Declaration on International Investment and Multinational Enterprises* to treat enterprises that operate on its territory, but which are controlled by the nationals of another country, either directly or indirectly, no less favourably than domestic enterprises in like circumstances.

The term "operating in its territory" in the instrument conveys the idea of doing business from a place of business in the host country, as distinct from conducting business in the country from abroad. This recognises that adhering countries' practices differ regarding recognised forms of business but that the main forms of doing business are through locally incorporated subsidiaries and branches. The principle of national treatment applies regardless of the home country's treatment of enterprises from the host country (OECD, 2005[1]).

The National Treatment instrument consists of two elements: a declaration of principle, which forms part of the Declaration, and a procedural OECD Council Decision which obliges Adherents to notify their exceptions to national treatment and establishes follow-up procedures to deal with such exceptions The Decision comprises an Annex that lists exceptions to national treatment, as notified by each Adherent and accepted by the OECD Council. The Investment Committee periodically examines these exceptions.

Only measures concerning legal entities are reported for the purpose of the National Treatment instrument, and thus any measure that may apply to natural persons is not reflected in the list contained in the Annex to the Council's decision.

To ensure transparency, Adherents to the Declaration also undertake to report any measures that, while not representing exceptions to national treatment, have an impact on it. The lists of exceptions to National Treatment and measures reported for transparency by country are published and regularly updated (see www.oecd.org/daf/inv/investment-policy/nationaltreatmentinstrument.htm)

## Ukraine has a legal regime conducive to the attraction of investment in its energy sector

For the past few years, Ukraine has made important efforts to raise the quality, efficiency, and fairness of the legal and regulatory framework for investment in the energy sector by adopting laws to improve the business climate and the business environment, without distinction between foreign and domestic companies.

In the aftermath of the Euromaidan revolution of 2014, the Ukrainian government has been seeking to improve the country's business environment by implementing a series of structural and institutional reforms. Key reforms have included deregulation and improvements within the justice and the tax areas, promotion of anti-corruption policies, and the establishment of a Business Ombudsman Council. Some of these reforms have been introduced to comply with Ukraine's obligations under the EU-Ukraine Association Agreement and the Deep and Comprehensive Free Trade Area (DCFTA) between the EU and Ukraine.

## *Protection of foreign investors*

Both the 1996 Constitution of Ukraine[3] and the 1996 Foreign Investment Regime Law[4] guarantee the national treatment of foreign economic operators and this applies to foreign investors operating in the energy sector. The Constitution of Ukraine provides that the State protects the rights of all property rights holders and economic operators which are equal before the law (Article 13, para. 4, the Constitution of Ukraine). Through the Foreign Investment Regime Law, Ukraine guarantees the principle of equal treatment between national and foreign citizens or entities with the exceptions provided for by its national legislation and international agreements (Article 7, the Foreign Investment Regime Law). According to the Foreign Investment Regime Law, investors are entitled to certain privileges and guarantees such as protection against legislative changes, protection against nationalisation, compensation, and reimbursement of losses and repatriation of profits.

In addition, the 2003 Economic Code of Ukraine[5] covers definitions of enterprises with foreign investments (Article 116), foreign enterprises (Article 117), and foreign investors (Article 390); types (Article. 391) and forms (Article 392) of foreign investments; the activity of business entities with foreign investment (Article 396); and the guarantees to foreign investors in case of termination of investment activities (Article 399). Since 2016, as seen in the previous chapter of this *Review*, the UkraineInvest agency assists foreign and local investors by providing information, contacts, and project management support at different stages of the investment.

Furthermore, local and foreign investors are protected against unlawful expropriation, in a non-discriminatory manner. According to the Ukrainian Constitution, expropriation of immovable property may be carried out only as an exception for reasons of social necessity, on the grounds of and by the procedure established by law, and on the condition of advance and complete compensation of their value (Article 41, the Constitution of Ukraine). The legal framework for investment protection (both domestic and foreign) is analysed in detail in chapter 4 of this *Review*.

## *Non-discrimination in domestic regulations applying to investors in the energy sector*

Reforming the energy sector to achieve energy independence and attract FDI is one of Ukraine's main priorities for the country's future economic development. The government has made important efforts to comply with the principles of the EU's Third Energy Package by adopting new laws in the natural gas and electricity markets, simplifying the legal and regulatory requirements for these sectors.

### *Non-discrimination in the natural gas market*

In April 2015, Ukraine adopted a new Natural Gas Market Law[6] (effective since October 1st 2015) as part of the EU's Third Energy Package commitments to create a fully functional natural gas market. In particular, the Natural Gas Market Law transposes the unbundling requirements of Directive 2009/73/EC, allowing for the ownership unbundling as well as the independent system operator model.

According to the Natural Gas Market Law, the authorities and subjects of the natural gas market are required to comply with the principles of proportionality[7], transparency[8] and non- discrimination[9] when taking decisions (Article 2, Legal basis of the natural gas market).[10] According to the same law, the Regulator in the natural gas market is required to ensure non-discriminatory access to the market for all customers, both domestic and international (Article 4, para.4, Natural Gas Market Law). Besides, the Gas Market Law sets forth the legal basis for a new market model based on good faith and fair competition, free trade and equal treatment of domestic and foreign investors, free choice of supplier for consumers, equal rights for exporting and importing natural gas and non-intrusion of the state into the functioning of the market (Article 3, Natural Gas Market Law).

*Non-discrimination in the electricity market*

As part of Ukraine's legal commitment to the Third Energy Package on the European electricity markets, the country started reforms to liberalise its electricity sector. In 2017, the Ukrainian Verkhovna Rada) adopted the Law on Electricity Market[11], effective since July 2019.

While establishing the economic and structural electricity market framework, the new Electricity Market Law also promotes energy efficiency, fair competition and equal rights to sell and buy electricity, non-discriminatory and transparent access to the transmission system and distribution systems, non-discriminatory participation in the electricity market, development of alternative and renewable energy, non-discriminatory tariff setting, and free supplier choice (Article 3, Law on the Electricity Market). Also, restrictions in the electricity market shall be managed through non-discriminatory market mechanisms (Article 38, para. 4, Law on the Electricity Market).

### ***Investment promotion***

Ukraine's investment framework contains several investment incentives, applicable to both national and foreign investors in line with the principles outlined in the OECD *Declaration on International Investment*. According to Ukraine's Investment Regime Law, investment incentives may be granted to businesses operating in priority sectors of the economy (Article 7, the Foreign Investment Regime Law).[12] More recently, in December 2020, Ukraine adopted a new law on the State Support of Investment projects (also known as Law on "Investment Nannies"), which is Ukraine's new flagship law to attract investment. The Investment Nanny Law, which entered into force on February 13, 2021, offers support and additional guarantees to both foreign and domestic investment projects satisfying certain criteria[13], in particular regarding the industry of the project's implementation. The total amount of state support would not exceed 30% of the amount of investments in the project.[14]

According to article 3 of the Law on "Investment Nannies", state support provided for investment projects may be in the form of:

- Exemption from certain taxes.
- Exemption from import duty of new equipment and components to it, which are imported for the implementation of the investment project.
- Land-related privileges such as a land plot of state or communal property for use (lease) for the implementation of an investment and the possibility to be the first to acquire the land once the special investment agreement expires.
- Development of infrastructure to facilitate the creation of investment projects at the expense of local budgets or other sources.

Such state assistance will be provided starting from 1 January 2022.

According to Article 5 of the Law on "Investment Nannies", key criteria (not exclusive) of an investment project to be eligible for state support include:

- Being implemented on the territory of Ukraine in the sectors of processing industry (except for the production and circulation of tobacco products, ethyl alcohol, cognac and fruit, alcoholic beverages), extraction for further processing and/or enrichment of minerals and lignite, crude oil and natural gas), waste management, transport, warehousing, postal and courier activities, logistics, education, scientific and technical activities, health, arts, culture, sports, tourism and resort, and recreational sphere.
- Providing for the construction, modernisation, technical, and/or technological re-equipment of investment objects in the sectors specified above.
- Creating at least 80 new workplaces annually, with the average remuneration of employees with remuneration exceeding the average remuneration of employees working at the same location/area in the region by at least 15%.
- Bringing at least EUR 20 mln of new investments.
- Being implemented within five years.

Also, to attract and retain FDI, Ukraine has established investment promotion agencies and dedicated bodies to help and assist foreign investment projects. In 2014, the National Investment Council, a consultative and advisory body under the President of Ukraine, was established. In 2015, Ukraine established a Business Ombudsman, which provides a platform for domestic or foreign businesses to file complaints about unjust treatment by public authorities, state-owned or controlled companies, or their officials (OECD, 2016[2]). In 2016, the Ukrainian government established UkraineInvest, an independent advisory agency aimed at promoting investment in the country. UkraineInvest disposes of a user-friendly and regularly updated online portal that helps investors to access information and to follow recent legal and regulatory changes as well as upcoming investment opportunities in different sectors such as energy. Chapter 6 of this report provides a detailed analysis of Ukraine's framework for investment promotion and facilitation.

Following the adoption of the Energy Strategy of Ukraine 2035 (ESU) in 2017, Ukraine has adopted additional laws, regulations, targets and incentive schemes to encourage investment in renewable power and to improve energy efficiency, security, competitiveness, and integrations with the EU energy market, which are further discussed in chapter 4 of this *Review.*

### *Transparency requirements*

Ukrainian and foreign investors have the right to access public information, in line with the 2011 Law on access to public information.[15] In general, laws, regulations, and administrative procedures in Ukraine are published in one of the State official gazettes such as the Official Bulletin of Ukraine[16] and the Governmental Courier or Bulletin of Verkhovna Rada.[17] Some of Ukraine's institutions also make available laws, guidelines in English on their official webpages, thus facilitating foreign investors' access to public information.

## Ukraine is open to foreign investors

As can be seen from above, Ukraine has a relatively open regime for international investment according to the OECD *FDI Regulatory Restrictiveness Index* (FDI index).[18] Exceptions under the OECD *National Treatment instrument* are limited to foreign ownership restrictions in a few sectors that are detailed below. Ukraine maintains a relatively open investment environment in nearly all business activities related to energy. When compared to the OECD average, regulatory restrictions on FDI are lower in the mining and quarrying sector and higher in the other sectors such as oil, electricity, electricity generation, and electricity distribution (Figure 3.1). Nonetheless, the regulatory environment for FDI in the energy sector must not be seen in isolation from the overall business environment, given that Ukraine's FDI index is considerably higher (1.21) than the OECD average FDI Index (0.064)

When foreign investors incorporate in Ukraine they are generally treated as domestic legal entities, benefiting from the rights and obligations as national investors (OECD, 2016). There are no generalised screening or approval mechanisms for new investments or to establish companies in Ukraine and there are only few horizontal exceptions to national treatment, such as the foreign acquisition of agricultural land. Ukraine does not impose limits on access to local finance and incentives (e.g., tax, public procurement, concessions) or government purchasing markets for foreign-controlled enterprises incorporated on the territory (OECD, 2016[2]).

## Figure 3.1. OECD FDI Regulatory Restrictiveness Index, by sectors 2020

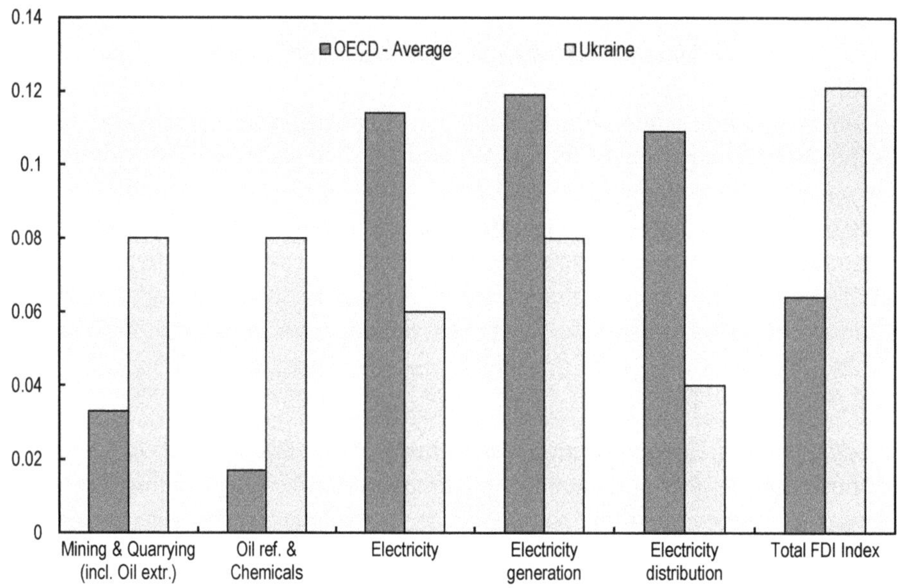


Source: OECD FDI Regulatory Restrictiveness Index, (OECD, n.d.[3])

### *Measures affecting foreign investment in the energy sector in Ukraine*

Foreign investors in Ukraine have the same basic rights and obligations as Ukrainian investors and, in general, when industry-specific restrictions exist, they apply equally to foreign and Ukrainian operators. There are a few general restrictions on foreign investment in the energy sector, such as the acquisition of land, participation in privatisation processes as well as some restrictions related to national security concerns.

#### *Purchase of state-owned land remains restricted for foreign investors*

According to Ukraine's Land code, the purchase of state and municipal land by foreign legal entities is subject to a specific screening procedure. Foreign legal entities must have a representative office in Ukraine. The purchase requires the approval of the Cabinet of Ministers. In the case of state-owned land, the approval of the Ukrainian Parliament (Verkhovna Rada) is also required (Article 129, the Land Code of Ukraine as amended in April 2021). Moreover, some state-owned lands cannot be transferred to private ownership, including lands of nuclear energy and space system (Article 84, para.4a). These restrictions apply to both foreign and domestic investors.

The law on acquisition of energy lands applies equally to foreign and domestic investors but there are some restrictions. According to Article 116 of the Land Code, legal and natural persons (both foreign and domestic) may acquire property rights of state and municipal land plots on the basis of auctions, as set by the Land Code. Still, there are some restrictions as to the transfer of ownership of lands of the energy system.[19]

### *Restrictions with respect to ownership of agricultural land*

Ukraine, possibly more than other transition economies, has experienced complexities when seeking to establish a formal ownership registration for agricultural land. In 2020, Ukraine adopted the Law on Amendments to Certain Legislative Acts of Ukraine on the Conditions of Circulation of Agricultural Land[20], abolishing the moratorium on agricultural land that lasted for more than 20 years. As a result of these amendments, since July 2021, individual Ukrainian citizens can acquire up to 100 hectares of agricultural land, while legal entities with 100% local capital will be able to acquire agricultural land starting from January 2024.

At the time of publication, however, foreign nationals and companies with foreign participation are still prohibited from purchasing agricultural land, something that could change with a national referendum as foreseen in Article 130, para. d of the Law on Amendments to Certain Legislative Acts of Ukraine on the Conditions of Circulation of Agricultural Land. In addition, agricultural lands inherited by foreign legal entities are subject to alienation within one year (Article 82, para.4, the Land Code of Ukraine). The law also introduced some limitations and prohibitions for foreign legal entities with Russian participants, terrorism-related organisations, foreign states, unknown beneficiaries, and entities under sanctions. Ukraine should consider further opening its agricultural land for foreign investors to attract more investors and develop not only agricultural but also energy-related industries.

### *Privatisation*

In March 2018, Ukraine adopted the Law On Privatisation of State-Owned and Municipal Property. The privatisation programme is open to domestic and foreign investors, except the following cases:

- Investors that are registered in offshore zones as well as investors coming from countries defined as aggressor of the state.
- Legal entities, beneficial owners of more than 10% of shares of a company residing in a country recognised by the Verkhovna Rada as aggressor of the state.
- Natural persons - citizens and / or residents of the state recognised by the Verkhovna Rada of Ukraine as the aggressor of the state.
- Legal entities registered in a state included in the FATF list of states that do not cooperate in combating money laundering (Article 8, the Law On Privatisation of State-Owned and Municipal Property).[21]

### *Natural monopolies restricting foreign investment in the energy sector*

In Ukraine, as in many other countries and including other Adherents to the OECD *Declaration on International Investment*, certain types of business activities may be pursued only by natural monopolies which are regulated by the Law on Natural Monopolies. The Ukrainian legislation defines a natural monopoly as an activity for which the absence of competition is beneficial to the market due to specific features of production, and products cannot be replaced by equivalent substitutes.

Article 5 of the Law on Natural Monopolies lists a number of energy related activities and markets as natural monopolies, notably:

- Transport of oil and oil products by oil pipelines;

- Transport of natural and oil gas by pipelines;
- Distribution of natural gas by pipelines;
- Storage of natural gas beyond certain volumes defined by the Ukrainian legislation;
- Transport of other products by pipelines;
- Transmission and distribution of electricity;
- Centralised heating supply.

### *Concessions*

Concessions play a central role in the provision of public services in Ukraine.[22] In October 2019, a new Law on concession, developed in accordance with the EU laws, came into force (Law of Ukraine on Concession, 2019).[23] The Law introduces a number of important changes to the Law of Ukraine On Private Public Partnership dated 1 July 2019 (the "PPP Law") as well as several positive novelties aimed at simplifying the involvement of private capital of both domestic and foreign investors in public-private partnerships. Concessions can be used for project implementation in all fields of economic activities, except for the objects falling under the restrictions for concession according to the Ukrainian legislation, which means, for instance, that concessions in the extraction industry shall be governed by the Law of Ukraine On Production Sharing Agreements. While any legal entity (both domestic and non-resident) can take part in the selection procedure under concession, only a Ukrainian legal entity can become a concessionaire. This means that if the concession tender is won by a non-resident legal entity, such a legal entity shall register a legal entity under Ukrainian law in order to enter the concession agreement.

### *Public-Private Partnerships*

Public-Private Partnerships (PPPs) are viable tools to attract investment in the energy sector. As is further discussed in the chapter of this *Review* on addressing investment in infrastructure, Ukraine PPP legislation is extensive, although it includes some burdens for investors: as determined in article 7 of the Law of Ukraine "on Public-Private Partnerships" (Article 7, para 5. PPP Law)[24], PPPs are not possible if a public partner is subject to a privatisation procedure. This limitation has affected in practice the potential opportunities for private companies to direct their investments in energy infrastructure, as it has been the case with the six SOE oblenergos that have been in the process of privatisation for the last ten years.

### *National security concerns*

The OECD Investment Instruments recognise that policies for safeguarding national security are an important part of investment policies in many countries. In Ukraine, foreign investor's activity may be restricted in some sectors or territories for national security reasons (Article 116, para. 5, Economic Code of Ukraine). Circumstances under which a national security exception can be invoked are set out in the Law on Fundamentals of National Security of Ukraine.[25] The latter law gives the list of "potential and real economic threats to the national security of Ukraine". For instance, some strategic energy sectors (such as fuel and energy resources) are restricted to investment in case of "*ineffective use, insufficient diversification for their supply and the absence of an effective energy-saving strategy*" (Article 7, Law on Fundamentals of National Security of Ukraine). Such prohibitions apply equally to domestic and foreign investors.

## Efforts to reduce administrative burden are producing results and should be pursued

Despite Ukraine's openness to foreign investment, the country suffers from various shortcomings that investors experience when establishing a business which are further described in this *Review*. The Ukrainian energy sector remains vulnerable wide-ranging risks such as controlled pricing, corruption, and favouritism (Bayramov and Marusyk, 2019[4]). As is further discussed in chapters 5, 7 and 8 of this *Review*, corruption and favouritism in energy infrastructure projects continue to be of high concern for investors.

For the past five years, Ukraine has improved its performance in the World Bank's *Doing Business* indicators. For instance, in 2020 Ukraine ranked 64th out of 190 countries in the World Bank's 2020 edition, ranking 19 positions higher than in 2016 (World Bank, 2020[5]). Ukraine has notably improved its performance in issuing construction permits. Despite this progress, when compared with non-OECD countries that are, like Ukraine, Adherents to the *OECD Declaration*, Ukraine is behind countries such as Croatia at 51 and Morocco at 53 (Table 3.1).

### Table 3.1. Ukraine's international rankings

| Indicator | Rank | Past Ranking |
|---|---|---|
| Doing Business 2020 edition (World Bank) | **64/190** | **In Doing Business 2019 edition 71/190** |
| Starting a business | 61/190 | 56/190 |
| Dealing with construction permits | 20/190 | 30/190 |
| Getting electricity | 128/190 | 135/190 |
| Registering property | 61/190 | 63/190 |
| Getting credit | 37/190 | 32/190 |
| Protecting minority investors | 45/190 | 72/190 |
| Paying taxes | 65/190 | 54/190 |
| Trading across borders | 74/190 | 78/190 |
| Enforcing contracts | 63/190 | 57/190 |
| Resolving insolvency | 146/190 | 145/190 |
| Global Competitiveness Index Report 2019 (WEF) | **85/141** | **83/140 in 2018** |
| First pillar: institutions | 104/141 | 110/140 |
| Second pillar: infrastructure | 57/141 | 57/140 |
| Third pillar: ICT adoption | 78/141 | 77/140 |
| Fourth pillar: macroeconomic stability | 133/141 | 232/240 |
| 2019 Corruption Perceptions Index (Transparency International) | **117/180** | **126/180 in 2019** |
| Rule of Law Index of the World Justice Project | **72/128** | **77/126** |

Source: Doing Business 2020 (World Bank, 2020[5]), Global Competiveness Index Report 2019 (WEF, 2019[6]), Corruption Perception Index 2020 (Transparency International, 2020[7]), (World Justice Project, 2020[8]).

The 2019 *Global Competitiveness Index of the World Economic Forum* ranked Ukraine 85 out of 141 countries, placing it below countries such as the Russian Federation at 43, Kazakhstan at 55, and Azerbaijan at 58. The *Index* provides additional perspectives on Ukraine's policies and practices when doing business. Despite its good ranking in areas such as digital skills and innovation, the main obstacles for doing business in Ukraine, as perceived by entrepreneurs, remained those signalled above such as inefficient government bureaucracy and corruption. This situation can be observed in other international rankings such as the *Transparency International Corruption Index*. Perceived corruption in Ukraine remains relatively high, not only by regional standards (Ukraine was ranked 117th among 180 countries in the *Transparency International's Corruption Perception Index* in 2020). When compared with other non-OECD countries that are Adherents to the OECD *Declaration on International Investment*, Ukraine is ranked alongside countries such as Egypt (117th) and below Kazakhstan (94th). As it will be discussed later in this *Review*, the establishment of Ukraine's High Anti-Corruption Court and the restart of the National Agency for the Prevention of Corruption (NAPC) resulted in a 3-point increase of Ukraine's score compared to 2019. Nevertheless, in 2020, the Rule of Law Index of the World Justice Project ranked Ukraine 72nd out of 128 countries, scoring the lowest in the component measuring absence of corruption.

## Outlook and policy recommendations

Ukraine has made important efforts to create an open and transparent environment for foreign investment in the energy sector by adopting new laws reinforcing and simplifying the protection of businesses operating in the energy sector. Under Ukraine's investment regime, foreign and domestic investors are in most cases treated equally.

The country applies rules on ownership that prohibit foreigners from owning a company or operating in specific sectors; it also has rules on acquisitions, which regulate the extent to which a foreigner can acquire stakes in a company operating in given sectors. The number of such sectors is nevertheless limited and is expected to decrease even further, except for those sectors that are seen by the Ukrainian authorities as national security-sensitive due to on-going tensions with the Russian Federation. Public monopolies still apply in some significant sectors such as energy transport, the transmission of electricity, supply and distribution of water, centralised heating supply, and railways (OECD, 2016[2]), all relevant to investment in the energy sector.

Despite important progress in the natural gas and electricity market, Ukraine still needs to ensure the coherence and the implementation of its energy sector reform agenda. Laws are not always properly implemented, in particular due to corruption and the presence of oligarchs in the energy sector. Ukraine's high number of natural monopolies in the energy sector, along with the regulatory barriers of some state-owned enterprises in this sector, are also constraints for both domestic and foreign private investment. As of August 2020, Ukraine had 87 natural monopolies conducting economic activity in the energy sector.[26]

- **Consider further liberalisation in sectors that remain relatively closed to foreign investment** as already highlighted in the 2016 *Investment Policy Review of Ukraine*.
- **Finalise the pending reform on land and evaluate the restriction on foreign companies to acquire agricultural land**, especially if Ukraine would like to activate the biofuel industry.
- Given that the energy sector is still characterised by the prevalence of monopolies, **keep strengthening the competition law regime**, notably in the areas highlighted in the 2016 OECD *Review of Competition Law and Policy in Ukraine* such as improving the impartial and transparent functioning of the Anti-Monopoly Committee of Ukraine, and **ensuring that privatisation encourages more competition** in previously monopolistic sectors instead of merely replacing public with private monopolies.

## Note

[1] See https://zakon.rada.gov.ua/laws/show/605-2017-%D1%80#Text.

[2] Available in English at: https://rm.coe.int/constitution-of-ukraine/168071f58b.

[3] English version of Ukraine's Constitution (1996), http://extwprlegs1.fao.org/docs/pdf/ukr127467E.pdf.

[4] English version available at: https://investmentpolicy.unctad.org/investment-laws/laws/253/ukraine-law-on-the-regime-of-foreign-investments.

[5] Economic code of Ukraine, (Vidomosti Verkhovnoi Rady Ukrainy (VVR), 2003, № 18, № 19-20, № 21-22, p.144), https://zakon.rada.gov.ua/laws/show/436-15#Text.

[6] Law of Ukraine on Gas Market (Vedomosti Verkhovnoi Rady (VVR), 2015, № 27, p.234), https://zakon.rada.gov.ua/laws/show/329-19#Text.

[7] According to the proportionality principle, decisions (measures) of authorities shall be necessary and minimally sufficient for the achievement of an objective of general public interest (the Natural Gas Market Law).

[8] According to the transparency principle, decisions (measures) of authorities shall be duly substantiated and notified to the subjects to which they shall apply within a reasonable time before their entry force or effect (the Natural Gas Market Law).

[9] According to the non-discrimination principle, decisions, actions, inactions of authorities shall not lead to: legal or actual scope of rights and obligations of a person which is different than the scope of rights and obligations of other persons in similar circumstances unless such difference is necessary and minimally sufficient for the achievement of an objective of general public interest; Legal or actual scope of rights and obligations of a person which is the same as the scope of rights and obligations of other persons in different circumstances unless such similarity is necessary and minimally sufficient for the achievement of an objective of general public interest (The Natural Gas Market Law).

[10] Available in English at www.naftogaz.com/files/Information/Ukraine%60s%20Natural%20Gas%20Market%20Law_engl.pdf.

[11] Law of Ukraine on the Electricity market (Vedomosti Verkhovnoi Rady (VVR), 2017, № 27-28, p.312) https://zakon.rada.gov.ua/laws/show/2019-19#Text.

[12] The Law of Ukraine On the Regime of Foreign Investments (the Foreign Investment Regime Law), Article 9, available in English at https://investmentpolicy.unctad.org/investment-laws/laws/253/ukraine-law-on-the-regime-of-foreign-investments .

[13] Law of Ukraine on state support of investment projects with significant investments in Ukraine, Article 5: Requirements for an investment project with significant investments for the implementation of which state support may be provided, https://ips.ligazakon.net/document/T201116?an=37. The law does not apply to investment projects with significant investments in the fields of processing industry such as crude oil and natural gas.

[14] Law of Ukraine on state support of investment projects with significant investments in Ukraine, Article 3. Forms of providing state support for investment projects with significant investments, https://ips.ligazakon.net/document/T201116?an=37.

[15] Law of Ukraine on access to public information, (Vidomosti Verkhovnoi Rady Ukrainy (VVR), 2011, № 32, p. 314), https://zakon.rada.gov.ua/laws/show/2939-17#Text.

[16] Verkhovna rada of Ukraine, Official Gazette of Ukraine, https://zakon.rada.gov.ua/laws/main/b19.

[17] Available at: https://ukurier.gov.ua/uk/.

[18] The OECD FDI Regulatory Restrictiveness Index covers 22 sectors, almost all sectors of the economy except health and education. The economy-wide index is obtained by averaging the scores for all 22 sectors. Scores range from 0 (open) to 1 (closed), https://www.oecd.org/investment/fdiindex.htm.

[19] Lands of the energy system are lands provided for electric generating objects (nuclear, thermal, hydroelectric power plants, power plants using wind and solar energy and other sources), for objects of electricity transportation to the user, except for cases of placement of such objects. Projects on lands of other purpose (Article 76, Land Code of Ukraine).

[20] See https://zakon.rada.gov.ua/laws/show/552-20#Text.

[21] Law On Privatisation of State-Owned and Municipal Property (Vedomosti Verkhovnoi Rady (VVR), 2018, № 12, p.68, https://zakon.rada.gov.ua/laws/show/2269-19#Text.

[22] According to the Ukrainian authorities, as of April 2020, 166 concession agreements had been concluded 34 agreements were being implemented in the areas of water supply, electricity, and transport.

[23] Available at: https://zakon.rada.gov.ua/laws/show/155-20#Text.

[24] Law (in Ukrainian), https://zakon.rada.gov.ua/laws/show/2404-17#Text.

[25] Law No. 964-IV "On Fundamentals of National Security of Ukraine" (19 June 2003), https://zakon.rada.gov.ua/laws/show/964-15#Text.

[26] Ukraine's Anti-monopoly authority keeps a public register. A list of natural monopolies in the country is available at www.nerc.gov.ua/data/filearch/litsenziini_reestry/reestr_monopol_energo.pdf.

## References

Bayramov, A. and Y. Marusyk (2019), "Ukraine's unfinished natural gas and electricity reforms: one step forward, two steps back", Vol. 60/1, pp. 73-96, http://dx.doi.org/10.1080/15387216.2019.1593210. [4]

OECD (2016), *OECD Investment Policy Reviews: Ukraine 2016*, OECD Investment Policy Reviews, OECD Publishing, Paris, https://dx.doi.org/10.1787/9789264257368-en. [2]

OECD (2005), *National Treatment for Foreign-Controlled Enterprises: 2005 Edition*, OECD Publishing, Paris, https://dx.doi.org/10.1787/9789264012912-en. [1]

OECD (n.d.), *FDI Regulatory Restrictiveness Index*, https://www.oecd.org/investment/fdiindex.htm (accessed on 20 July 2021). [3]

Transparency International (2020), *Corruption Perception Index 2020*, https://www.transparency.org/en/cpi/2020/index/nzl. [7]

WEF (2019), *The Globalal Competitiveness Report*, https://www3.weforum.org/docs/WEF_TheGlobalCompetitivenessReport2019.pdf. [6]

World Bank (2020), *Doing Business 2020*, http://dx.doi.org/10.1596/978-1-4648-1440-2. [5]

World Justice Project (2020), *The World Justice Project Rule of Law Index*, https://worldjusticeproject.org/sites/default/files/documents/WJP-ROLI-2020-Online_0.pdf. [8]

# 4 The Protection of Investment in Ukraine

This chapter provides an overview of the legal protections that Ukraine offers to investors in domestic legislation and international investment agreements. It focuses on several core investment policy issues – protections for investors' property rights and mechanisms for resolving investment disputes – under Ukrainian law and Ukraine's investment treaties. In terms of investment treaty policy, this chapter addresses Ukraine's investment treaties, analyses the main substantive protections and investor-state dispute settlement provisions in these treaties and identifies considerations for possible policy reforms.

## Introduction

Ukraine has a domestic legal framework that adequately protects investors and provides strong guarantees against expropriation for energy companies. The guarantees to protect foreign investments in the country include protection against changes in legislation, nationalisation, and termination of investment activities, profit repatriation and compensation.

Intellectual Property Rights are essential to advance technology upgrades in the energy sector. As such, Ukraine has a robust regulatory framework to protect intellectual property rights. On July 2020, the newly-adopted law completing institutional IP reform in Ukraine was published, setting out the basis for the new National Intellectual Property Authority (NIPA). This new law on IP aims to harmonise the national legislation with the provisions of the EU acquis.

Deep reforms in the judiciary have been implemented in Ukraine as part of the Justice Sector Reform Strategy and Action Plan 2015-2020. In the absence of a holistic approach, various pieces of legislation were adopted to transform the judiciary. The positive effects of the judicial reform in Ukraine have been captured by the World Bank Doing Business report, with Ukraine's distance to frontier score improving from 57.1 points in 2015 to 63.6 points in 2020. However, there are still challenges that investors face when accessing the court system, including vested interests affecting civil and commercial procedures and a limited respect for due process.

As of September 2021, Ukraine is party to 67 investment protection treaties and has had several experiences with investment treaties as a basis for legal claims by investors. Based on publicly-available information, foreign investors have filed at least 31 treaty-based claims against Ukraine. Many of the ISDS cases involving Ukraine concern investments in long-term energy projects (e.g. electricity, gas, steam and air conditioning supply projects) and natural resource projects in the country.

## The domestic legal framework for the protection of investors

The most recent Global Investment Competitiveness report found that the three top factors affecting decisions multinational investors face are political stability and security, a fair and predictable legal and regulatory environment, and market size. Ukraine has a large domestic market, and is close to other attractive export markets, but, as discussed throughout this Review, further efforts are required to improve the country's investment climate. Ukraine can no longer delay more decisive actions to reduce corruption, improve transparency in the public and private sectors, and protect property rights. Without those actions, private sector growth will remain stunted, preventing Ukraine from achieving its vast potential.

### *Strong guarantees against expropriation*

As identified in the 2016 *Investment Policy Review of Ukraine* (IPR), the regulatory framework of the country establishes the undisputed and sovereign right of the government to expropriate property. Article 41 of the Constitution provides that the right of ownership is guaranteed and can only be affected as an exception, for reasons of public necessity. Expropriation can only be carried out under due process of law on the condition of advance and complete compensation of the property's value (Verkhovna Rada of Ukraine, 1996[1]). The protection of property rights for both domestic and international investors has not been reformed and, as mentioned in the IPR of 2016, diverse domestic laws, including the Law on Investment Activity, the Commercial Code and the Tax Code, recognise property rights.

The laws of Ukraine that specifically set guarantees against expropriation of foreign investors are the Law on the Regime of Foreign Investing and the Law on Protection of Foreign Investments. The set of legislation implemented by Ukraine defines a range of guarantees for foreign investments, including national treatment, protection from expropriation, free transfer of funds and a ten year protection clause in case of changes to the foreign investment legislation (See Box 4.1).

### Box 4.1. Guarantees to protect foreign investment in Ukraine

**Protection against changes in legislation:**

- Foreign investors are guaranteed protection against changes in foreign investment legislation for a period of ten years, but this protection does not prevent changes in other areas of Ukrainian legislation, which limits the applicability of this guarantee.

**Protection against nationalisation**

- Foreign investments may not be nationalised. State bodies may not expropriate foreign investments, except in cases of emergency, such as national disasters, accidents or epidemics. The CMU is the authority that will decide which governmental body will oversee the exceptional procedures.

**Guarantee for compensation and reimbursement of losses**

- Foreign investors have the right to compensation for losses, including lost profits and non-pecuniary damage caused as a result of actions, omissions or improper performance by state bodies of Ukraine. Compensation paid to a foreign investor must be prompt, adequate and effective. It must reflect the fair market value.

**Guarantee in case of termination of investment activity**

- In case of termination of an investment activity, foreign investors are guaranteed the right to remit their revenue and withdraw their investments from Ukraine free from export duties within six months of the termination.

**Guarantee of profit repatriation**

- After the payment of taxes, duties and other mandatory payments, foreign investors are guaranteed the right to the unimpeded and immediate transfer abroad in a foreign currency of all profits and other proceeds legally earned as a result of their investment activity.

Source: Law of Ukraine On the Regime of Foreign Investments

Whilst the 2016 IPR noted the obligation of foreign investors to register with the government in order to qualify for the guarantees provided by the domestic legislation, the government positively advanced its laws by adopting, in 2016, the "Amendments to some legislative acts regarding the cancellation of mandatory state registration of foreign investments". This law abolished article 395 of the Commercial Code and amended the Law on the Regime of Foreign Investments by cancelling the requirement for foreign investors to be registered to enjoy the benefits and guarantees provided by the Ukrainian applicable laws and regulations. The implementation of the amendments has positively affected foreign investments in Ukraine by removing discrimination measures against foreign investors and preventing corruption when registering foreign investment projects (CMS Law Tax, 2016[2]).

Particularly relevant to investments in the energy sector, article 22 of the Law "On the Regime of Foreign Investments" determines that any disputes arising out of a concession agreement shall be settled through the dispute settlement mechanism agreed by the parties and business activities of foreign companies related to the use of state or municipal-owned objects shall be granted through concession agreements.

Article 2 indicates that foreign corporations can sign contracts for Production Sharing Agreements and any other type of joint investment activities. The inclusion of PSA and joint production agreements as contracts feasible for signing with foreign corporations allows for protection guarantees and protections against expropriation for major projects in the upstream and midstream sectors.

### *Intellectual Property rights*

The energy sector is characterised by developing technologies in all different areas – oil and gas, petroleum, electricity and green technology. With these technological advancements determining the future of energy usage, the protection of intellectual property (IP) rights is essential for attracting investments in the sector.

#### Box 4.2.WIPO GREEN platform and its potential for private enterprises

The World Intellectual Property Organisation is actively and directly encouraging the use of green technologies through its WIPO GREEN initiative, launched in 2013, to catalyse and accelerate green technology innovation and its transfer to expand the uptake and use of environmentally friendly technologies in support of the global transition to a low-carbon future. WIPO GREEN includes three main players:

- Technology providers: Green technology inventors, entrepreneurs, and companies can list their products on the WIPO GREEN database to give them global visibility, helping to attract partners and finance.
- Technology seekers: Organisations seeking eco-friendly technology solutions can use the WIPO GREEN database to publicise their needs and try to find a match. The database is also a useful tool for investors looking to make green tech deals as it provides access to technologies and entrepreneurs from around the world.
- Partners: The WIPO GREEN network provides exciting opportunities for collaboration and partnership by bringing together a range of key stakeholders, such as multinational companies, academic and research institutions, intergovernmental organisations, and small and medium-sized enterprises.

Source: (WIPO, 2021[3])

IP rights are protected by Ukraine's Constitution and in diverse domestic and international laws and regulations. Ukraine's main national legal instruments on IP rights include Copyright Law, Trademarks and Service Marks Law, Inventions and Utility Models Law, Industrial Designs Law, State Regulation of Activities in the Sphere of Transfer of Technology Law, and the Protection against Unfair Competition Law. Ukraine is a member of the World Intellectual Property Organisation (WIPO) and is a signatory of all the most relevant international treaties in the field, including agreements under the World Trade Organisation (WTO) such as the Agreement on Trade-Related Aspects of Intellectual Property Rights (TRIPS).

In June 2020, the Parliament of Ukraine adopted the Law of Ukraine No. 703 "On Amendments to Certain Legislative Acts of Ukraine Concerning the Establishment of a National Intellectual Property Authority" in force as of 14 October 2020, which introduces a two-tier structure of the state system of legal protection of intellectual property. The body responsible for granting rights and coordinating the national IP rights system is the Ukrainian Intellectual Property Institute (Ukrpatent), which performs the functions of the National Intellectual Property Authority, while the Ministry of Economy is responsible for ensuring the formation and implementation of state policy in the field of intellectual property.

One month later, in July 2020, the Rada approved legislative amendments to strengthen the protection of trademarks and industrial designs and patent law, which are now in force. The availability of opposition procedures provides an alternative to lengthy and costly litigation required to invalidate a patent. The new dispositions provide two opportunities for an opposition: a pre-grant opposition, which can be filed within six months after the patent application is published, and an post-grant opposition, which can be filed within nine months after publication of the grant of the patent. Examination guidelines with exact provisions on added proceedings were due by February 2021, however, at the time of writing of this Review, this had not yet been completed.

In 2017, the President of Ukraine signed a Decree establishing the High Court of Intellectual Property in Kyiv. The creation of a specialised court aimed to: (1) resolve a range of issues in the area of intellectual property that have hindered the development of intellectual property relations and, (2) raise the standards of protection of the intellectual property rights in Ukraine. However, as of now, the selection of the judges has not been completed and the court is not operational.

Under Ukrainian legislation, IP protection remedies are available through administrative procedures, civil litigation and criminal proceedings. Civil litigation is the most frequently used means of enforcing IP rights in Ukraine. The vast majority of IP civil litigation cases in the country are filed for termination of IP infringement, compensation for damages resulting from infringement, cancellation of a patent, extension of a patent term, invalidation of an IP-related contract, and termination of unfair competition in the IP domain (European Union Intellectual Property Office, 2015[4]).

### *Ukraine should continue reinforcing its levels of IP protection and enforcement*

The EU-Ukraine Association Agreement requires Ukraine to reinforce its level of IP protection and enforcement in order to comply with EU standards. The Agreement represents a regulatory opportunity to push Ukrainian IP law closer to the EU acquis in the area of copyright, trademarks, designs, topographies of semiconductors, patents, and civil and border enforcement. The government has an opportunity to reinforce its levels of IP protection and enforcement. On this matter, in a 2021 report "on the protection and enforcement of intellectual property rights in third countries", the European Commission acknowledged that Ukraine has made progress in reforming its IP protection regime. A number of new laws were adopted in 2019 and 2020: on trademarks and designs (815/2020)83, on patents (816/2020)84, on Gis (123/2019)85 and on IPR border measures (202/2019)86. Ukraine is also in the process of reforming its copyright regime. The adoption of these laws, the ongoing copyright reform and the new co-operation activities with the EPO and the EUIPO have brought Ukraine's IP regime closer to international standards and thus also to EU law and practice [European Commission, SWD(2021) 97 final]. Nevertheless, in 2020, the EC highlighted that some of the laws and regulations proposed by the Rada are not in line with international standards set by the WIPO, WTO and the European Patent Convention (European Commission, 2020[5]).

Although the government has made consistent progress in the protection and enforcement of intellectual property, the US Trade Representative's 2021 report concluded that Ukraine's IP regime remains not fully satisfactory in certain areas, notably including administration of the system for collective management organisations (CMOs), – which are responsible for collecting and distributing royalties to rights holders – continued use of unlicensed software by Ukrainian government agencies and the ongoing failure to implement an effective means to combat online copyright infringement.

### *Legal and institutional framework for judicial contract enforcement*

When justice institutions operate effectively and regulations are adequately implemented, trust in the government is enhanced, and businesses can invest with the confidence that their property rights will be protected. Strong justice institutions can address breaches of law, provide redress for violations of rights and entitlements, and facilitate peaceful resolution of disputes that may affect national and foreign investors. The UN, World Bank, IMF, OECD and European Union have supported, at both national and oblast level, judicial reform in Ukraine.

Coordination of the justice sector reform is necessary to successfully implement changes in the investment arena. With this in mind, the Judicial Reform Council (JRC) of Ukraine was established in 2014, and since then has been the reform champion and the ultimate filter for all reform initiatives. The Justice Sector Reform Strategy and Action Plan 2015-2020 (JSRSAP) serves as blueprint of the reforms that Ukraine has implemented in the last five years. To achieve the implementation of the reforms, Ukraine has produced annual implementation plans for each JSRSAP Chapter since 2016.

Empirical evidence shows that efficient, fair, and accessible justice systems promote security, encourage investment and growth, and provide fundamental protections to foreigners and national citizens. As a result, the government has devoted substantial efforts to reforming its justice system, aiming to lower barriers access, reducing delays, tackling corruption, and improving the quality of judicial system as further discussed in chapter 7 of this Review. One major step was taken on June 2016 when the Parliament adopted the Law №1401-VIII "On Changes to Constitution of Ukraine (regarding justice)", settling the terms of reforming the justice system. Subsequently, the adoption of the Law № 2136-VIII "On the Constitutional Court" in 2017 allowed for individual complaints to be brought before the Constitutional Court. This meant a significant step forward in the workings of the judiciary, with any citizen of Ukraine now able to challenge the constitutionality of Ukraine's laws applied to them in a final court decision before the Constitutional Court. To operationalise the new functioning of the judiciary, Law №1402-VIII "On the judiciary and the status of judges" and Law №1798-VIII "On High Council of Justice" were adopted in 2016.

The 2016 reforms transferred the authority to appoint judges from parliament to the High Council of Justice (HCJ), a key body conceived to be self-governing and autonomous from the rest of the judiciary, and the other two branches of power. Together with the High Qualification Commission of Judges (HQCJ), it was given the responsibility of coordinating the evaluation of the fitness of judges. By the end of 2019, after the qualification assessment of 2 038 judges, the HCJ dismissed 15 judges from the system. As discussed further in chapter 7 of this *Review*, there have been numerous issues with these two bodies, including integrity and corruption concerns. To face this challenge, in July 2021, the President of Ukraine adopted a new reform supported by international partners, notably the EU, aiming at rebooting the two judicial bodies in Ukraine dealing with the selection, disciplinary liability, and dismissal of judges, notably the HCJ and the HQCJ. The two laws adopted in July 2021, notably Law No 1629-IX and Law No1635-IX, envisage the creation of two bodies, notably the Selection Commission that will conduct the competition for HQCJ membership and the Ethics Council, which could conduct a one-time vetting of current HCJ members and advise on candidates for four vacant positions by assessing their compatibility with integrity and ethics requirements. In addition, the two laws foresee the engagement of international organisation professionals in both the HQCJ and the HJC in the selection of their members

The 2016 judicial reform advanced with the creation of a new Supreme Court and the reduction of the number and levels of courts from four to three. In addition, a new electronic asset declaration system was introduced, which obliged officials to declare all the assets they possess inside and outside Ukraine, as well as all assets officially registered in the name of their relatives. The need to comply with this policy made more than 2 000 judges voluntarily leave their positions, and thus brought fresh cadres to the system. The recruitment process for the new Supreme Court, which ended in late 2017, was nevertheless only partially transparent according to some observers (Gherasimov and Solonenko, 2020[6]).

The judicial reform process has addressed many of the key issues raised by the Council of Europe. Nevertheless, a number of shortcomings remain, including in relation to the enforcement of judgments as illustrated by the case Ostchem Holding Ltd. and the State Property Fund of Ukraine v. PJSC Odesa Portside Plant (see Box 4.3) as well as with respect to disciplinary proceedings against judges, the risks of undue interference with judicial independence and issues related to the enforcement of Law 193-IX "On

Amendments to Certain Laws of Ukraine Regarding Activities of the Bodies of Judicial Governance" (see Box 4.4) (Council of Europe, 2020[7]). Other shortcomings have related to the understaffing of the Constitutional Court as well as of local and appellate courts, raising concerns about the extent to which Ukraine can effectively provide judicial protection. Well-functioning commercial courts are essential for investors and businesses, as was highlighted in a September 2021 climate survey conducted by the American Chamber of Commerce of Ukraine (American Chamber of Commerce of Ukraine, 2021[8]).

### Box 4.3. Ostchem Holding Ltd. v. PJSC "Odesa Portside Plant"

**Economic sector: electricity, gas, steam, and air conditioning supply**

By its decision of July 25, 2016, the Arbitration Institute of the Stockholm Chamber of Commerce issued a partial consent award recording an agreement reached in a dispute between Ostchem Holding Limited and the state-owned Odessa Portside Plant. The parties agreed that Odessa Portside Plant (OPP) would pay approximately USD 251 million to Ostchem Holding Limited to settle a contractual debt and penalties owed to OPP under a gas supply contract of 2013.

Odesa Portside Plant and its majority shareholder, State Property Fund of Ukraine, resisted enforcement of the arbitration award. The decision of the Kyiv Court of Appeal of April 24, 2019, satisfied the application of Ostchem Holding Limited and granted permission to execute the said arbitration award. The decision was made despite allegations of non-compliance with a contractually agreed cooling-off period for negotiations and public policy violations. However, on June 8, 2021, the Civil Court of Cassation of the Supreme Court of Ukraine revoked the decision of the Kyiv Court of Appeal of April 24, 2019, and denied Ostchem Holding Ltd. in the execution of the decision of the Stockholm Arbitration Court. It is worth noting that the Supreme Court's decision was made in the context of the planned privatisation of the Odesa Portside Plant.

Source: (Jus Mundi, 2021[9]), (Supreme Court of Ukraine, 2021[10])

**Box 4.4. Law №193-IX On Amendments to the Law of Ukraine "On Judiciary and Status of Judges" and Some Laws of Ukraine on the Activity of Judicial Governments**

On November 2019, Law №193-IX came into force. One of the major changes introduced by the law concerned the bodies of judicial self-government in Ukraine. The law proposed to thoroughly examine the High Qualification Commission of Judges. It gave the High Council of Justice (HCJ) a prerogative to appoint the members of the HQCJ. The HQCJ is in charge of selecting judges and conducting their assessment as well as recommending judges to the HCJ for their subsequent appointment or transfer. The law also established a separate Commission on Integrity and Ethics endowed with the power to put forward disciplinary charges against the justices of the Supreme Court, members of the HQCI and the HCJ. It also reduced the number of Supreme Court judges from 200 to 100.

The law's stipulation to halve the number of Supreme Court judges was controversial from the outset. Furthermore, the Venice Commission also criticised the law's provisions for failing to specify procedures for selecting a new Supreme Court. According to its issued opinion, the lack of such procedures might lead to the politicisation of the selection process, for example, through the dismissal of judges who are disloyal to the government or by retaining those who have integrity issues.

On March 2020, in response to a submission by the Supreme Court, the Constitutional Court of Ukraine ruled that most provisions of Law №193-IX were unconstitutional. This was not the first act of the Constitutional Court to halt the judiciary reform. In February 2020, the Constitutional Court had already annulled parts of the judicial reform of 2016, when it declared the liquidation of the former Supreme Court to be unconstitutional and restored the rights of the 'old guard' judges.

Regarding the issue of the number of Supreme Court justices, the Court pointed out that such reorganisation made without substantive revisions of the Supreme Court's functions in the Constitution was inadmissible. The Court noted that, in any case, the change in the number of justices may be possible after prior consultations of the Presidency and the HCJ, which was not adhered to in case of Law №193-IX. Additionally, the Court pointed out that intervening in the incumbency terms of Supreme Court justices constitutes a violation of their judicial independence.

On the account of the ethics and integrity commission, the Court argued that creating a body that would oversee the bodies of judicial self-government and the Supreme Court and endowing it with the prerogative to charge the incumbents of those bodies constitutes a violation of judicial independence. In view of the Court, the law created a prerequisite to 'control' the judiciary by creating a new commission without any constitutional foundation behind such body. The Court called on the parliament to amend the legislation in light of its decision.

Source: Opinion of the Venice Commission, "Ukraine. Law No. 193 of Ukraine 'On Amending Certain Laws of Ukraine Regarding Activity of Judicial Governance Bodies' and Explanatory Note," Opinion No. 969/2019, November 20, 2019

## *Transparency through publication of court judgments*

Pursuant to part one of Article 11 of the Law № 1402-VIII, court decisions, court hearings and information on cases considered by the court are open, except in cases established by law. No one may be restricted in the right to receive in court oral or written information on the results of his court proceedings. Any person has the right to free access to a court decision in the manner prescribed by law. To access court decisions of courts of general jurisdiction, the State Judicial Administration of Ukraine ensures the maintenance of the Unified State Register of Court Decisions. Judicial decisions are open for free with round-the-clock access to the official web portal of the judiciary of Ukraine, although it has been reported that representatives of courts such as clerks may sometimes purposefully delay the uploading of court decisions on the portal.

**Box 4.5.COVID-19 and its implications for Ukrainian court proceedings**

Due to COVID-19, in April 2020, the changes to the Procedural Codes went into effect, introducing rules that will apply to all court cases pending in the commercial, civil and administrative courts in Ukraine:

- During the officially declared quarantine, the parties may attend the court hearings online by using personal video-conference equipment. The changes to the procedural codes instruct court employees on the technical aspects of handling videoconferencing tools necessary for hearings and detail the requirements that must be adhered to by participants in order to participate remotely. To take part in a court hearing via videoconferencing, a participant must file a respective motion with the court no later than five days before the hearing and send a copy of this motion to other participants in the case.
- The decision to allow such a participant to take part in a court hearing remotely is made by the judge based on the availability of the relevant technical equipment in a given court. The regulations state that participation in a court hearing via videoconferencing can only take place using special software called EasyCon.
- Most of the procedural terms, established by the law, are extended for the duration of the officially declared quarantine (e.g., terms for challenging the court decisions, amending claims, consideration of cases).
- Where the procedural term is established by the court, it will not be shorter than the term of the officially declared quarantine (for commercial and administrative courts only).

Source: Recommendations of the Council of Judges of Ukraine establishing specific work regime of the courts of Ukraine to protect the population of Ukraine from the spread of acute respiratory diseases and COVID-19 coronavirus classified as extremely dangerous infectious disease, https://rm.coe.int/09000016809e3f74.

### *Reform efforts to strengthen the judiciary*

As noted earlier in this *Review*, the reforming efforts of Ukraine in the judiciary are reflected in the increase of the country's score related to the *Enforcing Contracts* indicator of the World Bank. In the 2015 *Doing Business Report*, Ukraine scored 57.1 points, whereas in 2020, it scored 63.6 points out of one hundred. The increment in the score of 6.5 points is likely a consequence of the reforms implemented by Ukraine in 2017, when the judiciary made enforcing contracts easier by introducing a system that allows the parties to pay court fees electronically and, in 2019, when the commercial courts introduced a simplified procedure for small claims and pre-trial conferences as part of their case managements techniques (World Bank Group, 2020[11]). Despite these advancements, the time involved in solving a commercial dispute for a breach of contract has not significantly decreased. According to businesses consulted in the framework of this *Review*, it would take over one year to obtain an adjudication from a judge of a first instance court. Another challenge relates to the high costs associated with litigating commercial matters, given that in Ukraine, the total disbursement that a company should assume to bring a case to a first instance court represents 46.3% of the claim value, whereas the average cost in Europe and Central Asian countries is 26.6% and in OECD high income countries the cost is 21.5%.

Despite the positive momentum from Ukraine's justice sector reforms, as discussed later in this *Review*, there has been a lack of court judgments in top corruption cases, underscoring the need for greater institutional efficiency, transparency and independence in the process of prosecution (IDLO, 2018[12]).

Ukraine's experience suggests that high levels of corruption and entrenched vested interests impede governance and judicial reforms (International Monetary Fund, 2017[13]).

As corruption cases often involve complex financial schemes with elements of money-laundering, the need to delegate them to a specialised court has been strong. In 2017, the OECD recommended addressing this issue through the establishment of specialised anti-corruption courts insulated from corrupt and political influences, which can fairly and effectively hear and resolve high level corruption charges and select the judges through transparent, independent and highly trusted selection process, which in turn should guarantee integrity and professionalism (OECD, 2017[14]). In response to these needs and in order to implement numerous international recommendations, in June 2018 Ukraine adopted Law № 1402-VIII, which envisioned that the judicial system should include higher specialised courts to consider certain categories of cases, and particularly the High Anti-Corruption Court (HACC). The adoption of Law № 1402-VIII was a major break-through, in response to pressure from IMF. The jurisdiction of the court coincided with NABU and SAPO jurisdiction. However, the Law № 1402-VIII contains a provision that significantly narrows its jurisdiction: it provides that cases that have already been investigated by NABU and transferred to ordinary courts can be appealed in ordinary courts as well but not in the HACC (OECD, 2019[15]). The HACC was formally established on 11 April 2019 and it will be able to discharge the courts of general jurisdiction and, in turn, be limited to a specific type of court case.

The short-term positive impact of the HACC is that it should significantly speed up the timeframe for dealing with corruption cases. The number of judges in a court (except for the Supreme Court) is determined by the High Council of Justice (HCJ) taking into account the advisory opinion of the State Judicial Administration of Ukraine, court workload, and expenditures for the maintenance of courts and remuneration of judges (Part 6 of Article 19, the Law № 1402-VIII). In July 2018, the HCJ approved the number of judges in the Supreme Anti-Corruption Court - 39 full-time staff units, of which 12 - the number of full-time judges of the Appellate Chamber of the High Anti-Corruption Court.

Ukraine's justice sector shares governance challenges with many transition countries, suggesting that historical legacies could play an important role, such as the emergence of oligarchs who have often exercised strong influence over government institutions. The significance of the challenge is illustrated by the high cost of enforcing contracts (46% of the total cost of the claim (compared to the ECA average of 26.2% according to DB2018) and the impact of non-enforcement of civil claims (Ukraine's recovery rate is estimated to be 9 cents on the dollar compared to, for example, 27 cents for the United States).

Since contracts are weakly enforced by Ukraine's courts, property rights are reliant on connections with top officials or international guarantees such as bilateral investment treaties. While such arrangements might work for large enterprises and large transactions, they are too costly for small firms, thereby undermining the country's economic growth potential. In fact, given the perceived deficiencies of the court system, vertical integration has remained a primary means of ensuring contract enforcement, protecting business interests relative to competitors, and helping to ensure good relations with various state organs (World Bank Group, 2019[16]).

The 2019 amendment to the Law on Concessions allows investors to request the state to waive its immunity against disputes, which means that foreign investors will be able to bring disputes involving the protection of their rights in any chosen forum around the world. The law also includes new rules providing investors with more options in resolving disputes (article 43). Parties to a concession agreement may freely choose the mechanism of dispute resolution, including mediation, non-binding expert appraisal, national or international commercial arbitration and investment arbitration.

### *Alternative Dispute Resolution*

In 2017, the Law №2147-VIII implemented some changes to the Civil Procedure Code and in Commercial Procedure Code to support the functioning of international commercial arbitration in Ukraine. According to the law, any dispute that meets the requirements of the legislation of Ukraine on international commercial arbitration may be referred to international commercial arbitration by agreement of the parties, except in cases specified by law (part 5 of Article 4 of Commercial Procedure Code).

On October 2017, the Rada adopted Law № 6232 On Amendment of the Commercial Procedure Code of Ukraine, Civil Procedure Code of Ukraine, Code of Administrative Procedure of Ukraine and Other Legislative Acts restating in full three procedural codes (commercial, civil and administrative) and placing substantive advancements in the field of arbitration (US - Ukraine Business Council, 2017[17]).

Ukrainian legislation provides two separate sets of regulations applicable for domestic arbitration proceedings and international commercial arbitrations in Ukraine.

The domestic arbitration regime applicable to disputes between Ukrainian parties is primarily governed by the 2004 Law of Ukraine on Arbitral Courts (Treteyski Sudi). The rules governing domestic arbitration differ significantly from the provisions of the UNCITRAL Model Law.

Disputes involving a foreign party do not fall within the jurisdiction of Ukrainian domestic arbitration courts. They may be referred to either national courts or international arbitration. The main national legislation rules applicable to international arbitrations with the seat in Ukraine are set forth by the 1994 Law of Ukraine On International Commercial Arbitration (the ICA Law), as well as by the Civil Procedural Code of Ukraine (the CPCU) providing for procedural rules for challenging and enforcing arbitral awards by Ukrainian courts.

Law № 6232 ensures that arbitration clauses will be enforced by Ukrainian courts by introducing presumption in favour of the validity and enforceability of arbitration agreements (i.e., it provides that any inaccuracies in the text of the arbitration agreement or doubts regarding its operability, validity and possibility of performance will be interpreted in its favour) (Art. 22 of the Commercial Procedure Code). It broadens the meaning of the arbitration agreement and brings it into compliance with the amended 2006 Model Law by stipulating that the "writing requirement" is met by an electronic communication if the information contained therein is accessible so as to be useable for subsequent reference (i.e., is capable of being reproduced and read). It also identifies the list of non-arbitral disputes and to some extent resolves the problem with non-arbitrability of corporate and public procurement disputes. In particular, Article 22(1)(2) of the Commercial Procedure Code provides that disputes arising from corporate relations, including disputes between business entity participants (founders, shareholders, members) or between a business entity and its participant (founder, shareholder, member), including a former participant, regarding the business entity's establishment, activity, management and liquidation, cannot be referred to arbitration. However, if such a dispute arises from a contract, it can be arbitrated if there is an arbitration agreement between the business entity and all of its participants. Similarly, the civil law aspects of the disputes arising from execution, modification, termination and performance of the public procurement agreements can be arbitrated. The Law transfers competence on setting aside and enforcement proceedings from the first instance courts to Kyiv Appellate Court.

Law № 6232 introduces judicial support to international arbitration undertaken by the Ukrainian courts. The courts may order the provision of evidence (Art. 84 of the Civil Procedure Code), inspect evidence (Art. 85 of the Civil Procedure Code), examine a witness (Art. 94 of the Civil Procedure Code), preserve evidence (Art. 116 of the Civil Procedure Code), and order other interim measures (Art. 149 of the Civil Procedure Code). The Law also provides for a cross-undertaking in damages if the arbitration tribunal rejects the claim in full or in part (Art. 159 of the Civil Procedure Code).

## *The need for mediation in Ukraine*

The implementation of mediation has been proposed in Ukraine by scholars and practitioners, but the legal framework for mediation is currently non-existent – while between 2015 and 2019, several draft laws on mediation were registered in Verkhovna Rada, none of them were approved (Fursa, 2015[18]).

In May 2020, the Cabinet of Ministers submitted to the Parliament the draft Law № 3504 "On Mediation" that the Ukrainian Parliament passed on 15 July 2020 on its first reading. The draft sets the legal basis for mediation as an out-of-court mechanism. According to the draft law, mediation could be applied in any matter, including civil, family, labour, commercial, and administrative or in cases of criminal or minor offences. Mediation could take place before or during the court proceedings. Most importantly, mediation would be conducted with the mutual consent of the parties based on the principles of voluntary participation, self-determination and the equal rights of the parties.

## Investment treaties

Ukraine is party to 67 investment protection treaties that remain in force today. These include 66 bilateral investment treaties (BITs) and one multilateral treaty – the Energy Charter Treaty (ECT) (see summary table in Annex 4.A.). Ukraine is also a member country of two important multilateral treaties related to the enforcement of arbitral awards issued in investor-state arbitration cases under investment treaties – the New York Convention (in force for Ukraine since January 1961)[1] and the Washington Convention (in force for Ukraine since July 2000).

Ukraine signed many of its bilateral investment treaties in the 1990s and early 2000s just after it gained independence. A timeline of the signature and entry into force of its treaties appears in Figure 4.1. Six of these treaties are not in force today – with the Democratic Republic of Congo (signed in 2000), Equatorial Guinea (2005), Gambia (2001), Kyrgyzstan (1993), Romania (1995) and Yemen (2001) (see summary table in Annex 4.A).

### Figure 4.1. Evolution of Ukraine's investment treaty relationships

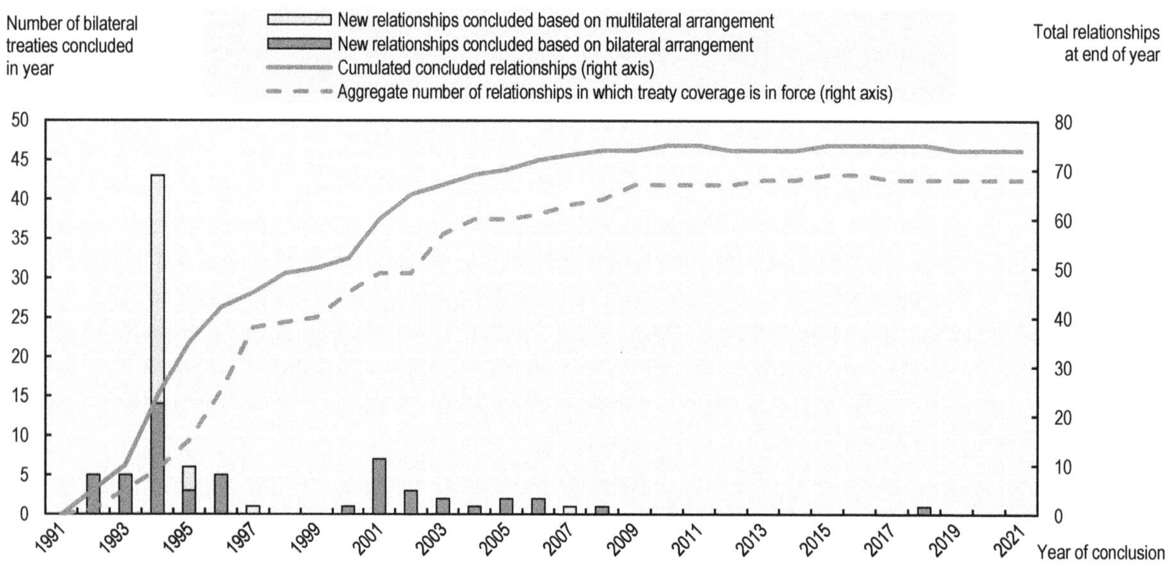


Source: OECD calculations based on OECD investment treaty database (not public) and consultations with the Ukrainian government during the preparation of this Review.

Ukraine has concluded several other investment-related agreements. The Ukraine-EFTA Free Trade Agreement, which has been in force since 2012, contains provisions on investment protection subject to state-to-state dispute settlement in Ukraine's investment relations with Iceland, Liechtenstein, Norway and Switzerland. Likewise, Ukraine's Association Agreement with the EU (2014) contains some investment protections and other commitments on investment co-operation and facilitation, notably on energy efficient investments. The parties have also agreed to consider "including investment protection provisions and investor-to-state dispute settlement procedures" as part of future reviews of the Agreement. A similar agreement was concluded with the United Kingdom in October 2020. Ukraine has also concluded several association and co-operation agreements related to international investment.[2]

Ukraine's treaty making activity and choice of treaty partners has led to significant coverage of its inward (approx. 46%) and outward (approx. 83%) FDI stock (see Figure 4.2 below). It is notable that treaty relationships with the Netherlands and the Russian Federation cover significant portions of Ukraine's inward FDI stock (16% for the Netherlands) and outward FDI stock (58% for the Russian Federation). Treaty relationships with four countries (Germany, Russian Federation, Switzerland, and Syrian Arab Republic) also cover a sizable portion of inward FDI stock (approx. 19% in total) and relationships with another three countries (Estonia, Hungary, Latvia) cover sizable portions of outward FDI stock (approx. 16% in total). Many Ukrainian investment treaties in force today cover none of Ukraine's FDI stock (inward or outward) or only negligible portions of it. This is a common phenomenon in many countries' treaty samples (Pohl, 2018[19]).

## Figure 4.2. Approximate evolution of Ukraine's inward and outward FDI stock coverage from investment treaties in force

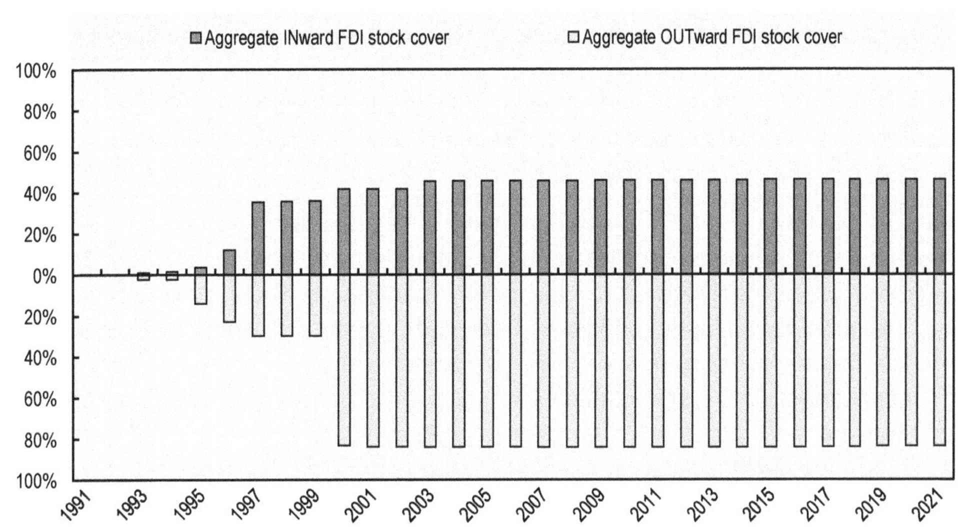


Note: This graph shows the approximate share of overall inward and outward FDI stock by matching investment treaty relationships in force as of May 2021 with aggregate immediate bilateral FDI data. FDI data shown here does not cover relationships or stock in country pairs where only the ECT is in force due to the lack of bilateral sector-specific FDI stock data.
Source: OECD calculations based on OECD investment treaty database. FDI data was taken from OECD FDI database and IMF Direct Investment Positions and reflects FDI stock as of 2018 rather than historical values corresponding to a given year.

### *Treaty use: ISDS claims under Ukraine's investment treaties*

Ukraine has had several experiences with investment treaties as a basis for legal claims by investors. Based on publicly available information, foreign investors have filed at least 31 treaty-based claims against Ukraine: 17 administered under the auspices of the ICSID Convention[3], 7 with arbitral tribunals constituted under the UNCITRAL Arbitration Rules[4], 4 under the SCC Rules[5] and three others under rules that are not publicly known.[6] News reports at the time of writing in the second quarter of 2021 indicate that formal notices of dispute have been provided to Ukraine for several additional disputes.[7]

Many of the ISDS cases involving Ukraine concern investments in long-term energy projects (e.g. electricity, gas, steam and air conditioning supply projects) and natural resources projects in Ukraine. As of May 2021, at least nine cases are still pending. Some of these cases are described in further detail in the 2016 OECD Investment Policy Review of Ukraine (OECD, 2016[20]).

Aside from ISDS cases filed by treaty-covered investors operating in Ukraine, another fourteen treaty-based ISDS claims have been brought, as of May 2021, by Ukrainian investors operating abroad against one of Ukraine's treaty partners.[8]

### *Reconsidering Ukraine's investment treaty policy*

Ukraine's investment treaty policy deserves continued attention as part of the country's approach to attracting and retaining investment in the energy sector for several reasons.

The role of investment treaties to achieve policy objectives. Many countries have concluded investment protection treaties in the hope of attracting long-term investments in their economies, including in their energy sectors. This is a goal for many countries, including Ukraine. Ukraine's ESU 2035 and the European Commission's 2020 Association Implementation Report on Ukraine attest to the government's eagerness to attract energy-efficient investments in Ukraine. The fundamental assumption that international investment can contribute to prosperity, help overcome challenges such as the climate crisis and the need to transform economies, create employment, and address crises remains valid. Most immediately, international investment has a central role to play in a sustainable recovery from the COVID-19 pandemic.

Attempts to document that protection components of treaties help to attract investment have not been conclusive (Pohl, 2018[19]). Some studies suggest that reducing barriers and restrictions to foreign investments are positively correlated with greater FDI flows (Mistura and Roulet, 2019[21]). These assumptions continue to be investigated by a growing strand of empirical literature on the purposes of investment treaties and how well they are being achieved.

Investment treaties can play a role in fostering predictable rules for investment and providing more enforceable remedies than domestic courts in some countries. Investors need assurance that any dispute with the government will be dealt with fairly and swiftly, particularly in countries where investors have concerns about the reliability and independence of domestic courts and where they are uncertain about overall governance. Many also recognise that foreign investors may be exposed to specific risks, at least under certain circumstances, and that mitigating such risks may contribute to enabling foreign investment. These concerns may be more pronounced for energy-related investments, which often require long-term commitments to host countries and large upfront capital expenditure. Government acceptance of legitimate constraints on policies can provide investors with greater certainty and predictability, lowering unwarranted risk and the cost of capital.

Notwithstanding any potential benefits of being a party to international investment agreements, these should not be confused with or perceived as a substitute for long-term improvements in the domestic business environment. Any active approach to international treaty making should be accompanied by measures to improve the capacity, efficiency and independence of the domestic court system, the quality of a country's legal framework, and the strength of national institutions responsible for implementing and enforcing such legislation.

Design features of older investment treaties. Many governments are increasingly attentive to whether experience with treaty use and interpretation warrants an update of their older investment treaties. Many Ukrainian BITs in force today contain features often associated with older investment treaties concluded in great numbers in the 1990s and early 2000s. Such treaties are generally characterised by a lack of specificity of the meaning of key provisions and extensive protections for covered investors. Some of Ukraine's most recent BITs contain more precise approaches in some areas. Ukraine's older BITs nonetheless remain in force alongside these newer agreements and form an integral part of the country's legal framework for investment.

This scenario may expose Ukraine to a range of unintended consequences, especially given the potential scope for ISDS claims under these treaties. Government exposure to international investment arbitration has been receiving increasing attention. The number of claims remains modest in comparison with the amounts of international investment that is covered by such provisions but arbitration claims can create significant cost and resource burdens for governments, even if such claims remain ultimately unsuccessful. Energy investors are among the most frequent users of ISDS under Ukraine's older investment treaties. This is not an unfamiliar experience across the global sample of known ISDS cases: around 30% of all known ISDS cases stem from investments in or related to upstream, downstream or transport activities for energy materials or products.[9]

Many governments now recognise that it would be better if their older investment treaties had more specific design approaches used in newer investment treaties. While many countries have revised their approaches to negotiating new investment treaties in response to these and other concerns, retrospectively addressing older BITs has proven to be more challenging. Some governments have negotiated treaty amendments or joint interpretations with existing treaty partners to address individual treaties but these efforts can require significant time and resources and may remain unsuccessful if they do not enter into effect.

The Ukrainian government is well aware of these and other debates through its participation in several inter-governmental discussions regarding possible reforms of investment treaties, including UNCITRAL's Working Group III on ISDS Reform and multilateral negotiations for possible updates to "modernise" the ECT. The ECT modernisation process may have particularly important implications for the energy sector in Ukraine given that the ECT is the most frequently-invoked investment treaty in ISDS cases globally and in Ukraine: investors have filed more than 130 known ISDS cases under the ECT (including at least four involving Ukraine) since the first claim was filed under this treaty in 2001 (Energy Charter Secretariat, 2021[22]). The ECT negotiations will enter their 8th round in 2021. Overall, however, these multilateral initiatives remain relatively limited in scope. The ECT negotiations concern only ECT members and focus on specific sectors (i.e. energy and energy-related sectors), while initiatives at UNCITRAL and ICSID focus on ISDS provisions and ICSID's arbitration rules, respectively. Over 100 governments at the WTO are also negotiating an agreement on ways to facilitate investment by easing administrative burdens and fostering a more transparent, efficient, and predictable environment for FDI.

In response to the need for a broader, forward-looking and global reflection on the future of treaties and treaty reform options, governments at the OECD – including Ukraine – launched in March 2021 a two-track work programme to complement other discussions about investment treaty policy at the multilateral level. One of these work tracks focuses on what governments can do with older treaties in light of collective experiences with treaties and ISDS over recent decades, as well as evidence of convergence on the purpose and language of newer designs that clarify and calibrate treaty obligations. The other work track will seek to identify possible new policy directions for future treaties addressing investment.

Possible priorities and directions for future investment treaties. The government may also wish to reflect on the content that treaties addressing investment could usefully have in the future, including as part of exchanges with other governments at the OECD. A few Ukrainian investment treaties contain examples of this content, but broader inclusion may be possible and desirable. All of these issues potentially affect investment in Ukraine's energy sector. Examples include the potential role of such treaties to: (i) contribute to sustainable development and responsible business conduct, (ii) preserve and improve investment market access and liberalisation of investment, and to facilitate FDI; (iii) promote fair competition for subsidies for investment and with subsidised SOEs; (iv) promote better rules for intellectual property rights protection, data governance and investments in the digital economy; and (v) offer more flexible and varied remedies and implementation mechanisms (Gaukrodger, 2021[23]).

The urgency of addressing the climate crisis has also markedly changed since Ukraine concluded its many older investment treaties. Decisions to integrate climate action across foreign and trade policy – and the necessity to do so – mean there is a pressing need to consider how treaties addressing investment can contribute to and reinforce climate policies. Conversely, it is vital to identify aspects of existing treaties and interpretations that may unduly interfere with such policies, and to promptly address them in effective reforms. Energy investors have used ISDS in recent years as a means to challenge government action related to climate policy in the Czech Republic, Germany, Italy, Netherlands, and Spain, among other countries, including phase-outs or moratoria on fossil fuel activities and regulatory changes affecting incentives for renewable energy. Initial reports of a notice of dispute filed by a Dutch investor against Ukraine under the ECT in March 2021 indicate that similar disputes may arise in relation to the government's recent decision to reduce feed-in tariffs for renewable energy producers.[10] Approaches to investment treaties will be of key importance for creating the necessary incentives for the transition to renewable energy sources.

The balance of this section examines four key aspects of possible reform for Ukraine's older investment treaties – the scope of three frequently-invoked protections (FET, MFN and indirect expropriation) as well as dispute settlement mechanisms and ISDS. It then briefly outlines some other possible aspects of investment treaty reform.

### *Vague provisions referring generally to "fair and equitable treatment" generate risks and costs, and should be addressed where possible*

Most of Ukraine's investment treaties in force today contain provisions that require Ukraine to provide covered investors and/or their investments with FET.[11] Since the early 2000s, the FET standard has become the most frequent basis for claims in ISDS. Most FET provisions were agreed before the rise of ISDS claims related to this treatment standard. Starting around 2000, broad theories for the interpretation of FET provisions by arbitral tribunals emerged as the number of ISDS cases increased markedly. Based on public information, investors in at least twelve of the known ISDS cases against Ukraine have relied on FET provisions for their claims.[12]

Most FET provisions in investment treaties do not provide specific guidance on what treatment should be considered fair and equitable. Arbitral tribunals in ISDS cases under investment treaties have taken different approaches to interpreting such "bare" FET provisions. This creates considerable uncertainty and high litigation costs for governments and investors alike. It has also resulted in some broad interpretations of bare FET provisions that go beyond the standards of investor protection in the domestic legal systems of some advanced economies. Governments have reacted to these developments in various ways, including by adopting more precise or restrictive approaches to FET or excluding FET in recent treaties (Box 4.6). These recent approaches in broader treaty practice can serve as a useful point of comparison for varying approaches to FET in Ukraine's investment treaties.

**Box 4.6. Recent approaches to the FET provision and ISDS for FET claims**

States are becoming more active in the ways in which they specify, address or exclude FET-type obligations in their treaties and submissions in ISDS. Dissatisfaction with and uncertainties about FET and its scope have also led some governments to exclude it from their treaties or from the scope of ISDS. Some important recent approaches are outlined below.

***The MST-FET approach: express limitation of FET to the minimum standard of treatment under customary international law (MST).*** This approach has been used in a growing number of recent treaties, especially in treaties involving states from the Americas and Asia (Gaukrodger, 2017[24]). In addition to using MST-FET, the CPTPP clarifies that the claimant must establish any asserted rule of MST-FET by demonstrating widespread state practice and *opinio juris* (Article 9.6 (3)-(5), Annex 9A). Evidence of these two components has rarely been provided by claimants or arbitrators in ISDS cases. This approach has since been replicated by other states (e.g., Australia-Indonesia CEPA (2019), Article 14.7). The NAFTA governments have further reformed their approach to MST-FET claims in the USMCA (see below).

***Exclusion of FET from ISDS, investment arbitration or from treaties.*** The recently-concluded USMCA (which replaced the North American Free Trade Agreement (1992) on 1 July 2020) includes MST-FET but generally excludes it from the scope of ISDS (except for a narrow class of cases involving certain government contracts) (Article 14.D.3). ISDS under the USMCA generally applies only to claims of direct expropriation and post-establishment discrimination (and only to Mexico-United States relations); only state-to-state dispute settlement (SSDS) is available for MST-FET claims. India's Model BIT does not refer to FET and instead identifies specific elements; Brazil's model treaty and recent treaties also exclude FET.

***The definition approach: stating what FET means or listing its elements.*** Recent treaties negotiated by the European Union, China, France and Slovakia contain defined lists for the elements of FET. This approach can vary greatly depending on the nature of the list. Some lists include elements such as a denial of justice, manifest arbitrariness, fundamental breach of due process, targeted discrimination on manifestly wrongful grounds, and/or abusive treatment of investors. This approach likely results in a broader concept of FET than MST-FET, especially if state practice and *opinio juris* must be demonstrated to establish rules under MST-FET.

***Clarifications of treatment excluded from FET.*** Some recent treaties have also clarified that FET does not protect investors from certain types of treatment. Starting with the Australia-Singapore FTA as revised in 2016, and followed by the CPTPP signed in March 2018 and the Korea-United States FTA as revised in 2018, several treaties now exclude government measures that may be inconsistent with an investor's expectations concerning its investment from giving rise to a breach of the FET provision.[1] Several recent treaties concluded by Australia clarify that the modification of government subsidies or grants is not protected under the FET provision.[2]

Notes:

1. See also Argentina-Japan BIT (2018); Australia-Peru FTA (2018); USMCA (2018); Australia-Hong Kong Investment Agreement (2019); Australia-Indonesia CEPA (2019). Recent EU treaties such as the EU-Singapore Investment Protection Agreement and the EU-Viet Nam Investment Protection Agreement also contain clarifications relating to investor expectations. However, they clarify certain exclusions of liability generally rather than referring specifically to the FET provision.
2. Australia-Singapore FTA (2003), as amended in 2016, Article 6(5); Australia-Peru FTA (2018), Article 8.6(5); Australia-Uruguay BIT (2019), Article 4(5); Australia-Indonesia Comprehensive Economic Partnership Agreement (2019), Article 14.2(3).

Some Ukrainian BITs adopt some of these more precise approaches to FET. Ukraine's BITs with Finland (1992), France (1994), Canada (1994), Kuwait (2002), Oman (2002), Japan (2015), Jordan (2005), and

Turkey (2017) define FET in accordance with international law, albeit using different designs and formulations. The France-Ukraine BIT (1994) also provides an indicative list of what could constitute a breach of the FET provision, including "any restriction on the purchase and transport of raw and auxiliary materials, energy and fuels".[13]

Other formulations of FET in Ukraine's investment treaties may leave scope for broad interpretations by arbitral tribunals. Most of Ukrainian treaties contain an unqualified or "bare" reference to FET without any further specific guidance on its meaning. Some contain several different references to "bare" FET in the same treaty, which may generate additional uncertainty as to how these provisions should be interpreted.[14] The prevalence of "bare" FET provisions and of varying approaches more generally creates uncertainty as to the scope of these FET obligations and exposure to unpredictable interpretations by arbitral tribunals in ISDS cases. More specific approaches to FET provisions could improve predictability for the government, investors and arbitrators alike. They could also potentially contribute to preserving the government's right to regulate in the context of investment treaties (Gaukrodger, 2017[24]). In some cases, governments may be able to achieve greater clarity on the scope of FET by agreeing on joint government interpretations of provisions in existing investment treaties with treaty partners.[15] In other cases, agreement on new treaty language may be required to reflect government intent and preclude undesirable interpretations.

Members of the ECT including Ukraine are considering the scope of FET as part of the ECT modernisation process (Energy Charter Secretariat, 2019[25]). Most ECT Members agree on the need to update the existing provision on FET in the ECT to clarify further its scope. Issues for discussion include whether FET should be linked to the MST under customary international law, whether FET should be linked to other substantive protections or a stand-alone provision, and whether FET should refer to the concept of legitimate expectations. Some ECT Members, such as Switzerland, Turkey and the EU, propose a list-based definition of FET (European Commission, 2020[26]). Other Members propose MST-FET but are open to considering list-based formulations that are consistent with prevailing understandings of the content of MST-FET.

### *Most-favoured nation (MFN) treatment provisions in Ukraine's investment treaties may have a range of unintended consequences*

All of Ukraine's investment treaties that contain investment protection provisions provide for MFN treatment. Like national treatment (NT) provisions, MFN clauses establish a relative standard: they require Ukraine to treat covered investments at least as favourably as it treats comparable investments by investors from third countries. As with FET provisions, most of the MFN treatment provisions in Ukraine's investment treaties and the global sample of investment treaties are vague with little guidance on how to interpret or apply them. More specific approaches to MFN treatment provisions could improve predictability for the government, investors and arbitrators alike (Box 4.7).

#### Box 4.7. Recent approaches to MFN treatment provisions and ISDS for MFN treatment claims

Recent investment treaty policies and debates over MFN have centred on three key issues outlined below.

***MFN clauses and treaty shopping***. ISDS arbitral tribunals have frequently interpreted MFN provisions to allow claimants in ISDS cases to engage in "treaty shopping".[16] These interpretations allow claimants to use MFN provisions to "import" provisions from other investment treaties that they consider more favourable than the provision in the treaty under which their case is filed.[17] This can create uncertainty and also dilute the effect of investment treaty reforms. While MFN claims in trade law have centred on domestic law treatment of traders from different countries, most claimant attempts to use MFN in ISDS have sought to use the clause to access other treaty provisions.

Some governments have clarified in recent treaties that MFN provisions cannot be used to engage in treaty shopping at all. Others have limited treaty shopping to the importation of substantive provisions or limited the application of MFN clauses to cases where government measures have been adopted or maintained under the third country treaty. Article 8.7(4) of the CETA between Canada, the EU and EU Member States, for example, clarifies that "substantive obligations in other international investment treaties do not in themselves constitute 'treatment', and thus cannot give rise to a breach of [the MFN provision], absent measures adopted or maintained by a Party pursuant to those obligations". The CETA also prohibits "treaty shopping" for procedural provisions. The USMCA similarly clarifies that treaty shopping is excluded under its MFN clause for both substantive and procedural matters (Article 14.D.3 (1) (a) (i)(A), footnote 22): "For the purposes of this paragraph [...] the "treatment" referred to in Article 14.5 (Most Favoured Nation Treatment) excludes provisions in other international trade or investment agreements that establish international dispute resolution procedures or impose substantive obligations".

***Comparison criteria in MFN treatment provisions***. A second area of interest and government action with regard to MFN treatment provisions involves the determination of what investments or investors are comparable. Many older-style treaties do not provide any specificity on this issue, leaving it to arbitral interpretations in ISDS. Some recent treaties provide that comparability requires "like circumstances". Further clarifications have also been added. For example, some recent clarifications have stated that deciding on whether there are "like circumstances" requires, among other things, consideration of whether the relevant treatment distinguishes between investors or investments on the basis of legitimate public welfare objectives.[18]

***Negative lists, carve-outs or conditions***. A third area of interest and government action with regard to MFN treatment provisions involves exclusions or limitations. Some recent treaties include negative lists of exclusions from MFN clauses in their investment chapters. Thus, a schedule may specify exceptions to MFN treatment for existing benefits granted under customs unions, other international treaties or specific domestic law schemes.

Ukraine has had first-hand experience of these interpretations in at least two ISDS cases (OAO Tatneft v. Ukraine, PCA Case No. 2008-8; and Krederi Ltd. v. Ukraine, ICSID Case No. ARB/14/17) where the claimants sought to rely on an MFN provision to benefit from more favourable provisions in other Ukrainian investment treaties.

Some of Ukraine's investment treaties include specifications or restrictions on MFN provisions that reflect recent treaty practices and debates. Almost all Ukrainian BITs that contain such provisions exclude benefits granted under existing customs, economic or monetary unions, double taxation agreements and/or multilateral investment agreements from MFN treatment.[19] At least nine of these treaties also require an assessment of MFN treatment with respect to comparable investments,[20] albeit using different formulations.[21] Ukraine's BITs with Turkey, Japan and the United Arab Emirates explicitly exclude the application of the MFN provisions to ISDS provisions in other treaties.[22] A protocol to the Ukraine-United Arab Emirates BIT (2003) provides an energy-specific example of conduct that would breach the MFN provisions, specifying that "[r]estricting [activities involving the purchase, sale, and transport of raw and secondary materials, energy, fuels and means of production and operation of all types] shall be deemed "treatment less favourable" if directed in a discriminatory way against investors of the other Contracting State".[23] While the current text of the ECT does not contain any such specifications, the EU and several other ECT Members propose to update it to include them (Energy Charter Secretariat, 2019[25]).

### *Vague provisions referring to protection for indirect expropriation should be clarified where possible*

All of Ukraine's investment treaties contain provisions that protect covered investments from expropriation without compensation. Many of these provisions refer to direct takings of investor property by the government (direct expropriation) as well as other government measures that have effects equivalent to a direct taking without a formal transfer or outright seizure (commonly referred to as indirect expropriation). Provisions on indirect expropriation have become the second most frequently invoked basis for claims in ISDS cases after provisions on FET. Most of these provisions in Ukraine's treaties and the global sample of investment treaties are vague with little guidance on how to interpret or apply them.

Since 2003, some countries have included a range of clarifications on the scope of indirect expropriation in newly-concluded investment treaties. Clarifications fall into four broad categories: (i) positive definitions of the concept of indirect expropriation, (ii) guidance on how to determine whether an indirect expropriation has occurred, (iii) clarifications that certain regulatory measures do not constitute indirect expropriation, and (iv) restrictions on the types of assets covered by this protection. Only one of Ukraine's BITs – the Ukraine-Turkey BIT (2017) – contains language to circumscribe the notion of indirect expropriation, albeit limited to a clarification that certain regulatory measures do not constitute such expropriation. Some ECT Members have made proposals to update the existing ECT provisions on expropriation with these and other elements (Energy Charter Secretariat, 2019[25]).

Clarifications such as these are likely to improve predictability as to the scope of indirect expropriation and reduce the possibility for unintended interpretations in ISDS cases. They are also likely to continue to feature in debates regarding the balance between investment protections and governments' rights to regulate in investment treaties, including as part of ongoing discussions at the OECD. The impact of these clarifications may depend, however, on the scope of other provisions in the same treaty such as FET that have often been invoked in ISDS cases as a substitute basis for indirect expropriation claims. It also remains to be seen how arbitrators interpret such provisions as very few investor-state arbitrations have been brought under treaties that contain these features. At least one government (Brazil) has responded to this residual uncertainty by excluding indirect expropriation altogether from its investment treaties concluded since 2015 through clear language to that effect.

### *Ukraine's investment treaties contain relatively few specifications or clarifications in dispute settlement provisions*

Aside from Ukraine's treaty with the EFTA countries, all of Ukraine's investment protection treaties in force today contain ISDS provisions. These treaties allow covered foreign investors to bring claims against host states in investor-state arbitration, in addition or as an alternative to domestic remedies. Investor-state arbitration generally involves *ad hoc* arbitration tribunals that adjudicate disputes in an approach derived from international commercial arbitration.

Recent treaty practice has seen both greater specification of ISDS and, in some cases, replacement of investor-state arbitration with more court-like systems. Treaties like the CPTPP and the EU-Canada CETA are among some recent treaties that have included investor-state arbitration reforms to reduce possible exposure to unintended consequences of ISDS. Common features in these treaties include time limits for claims, possibilities for summary dismissal of unmeritorious claims, mandatory transparency requirements, provisions for non-disputing party participation and possibilities for joint interpretations of the treaty by the state parties that are binding on the arbitral tribunal. The United States–Mexico–Canada Agreement (USMCA) contains many similar investor-state arbitration reforms but has reduced the scope for ISDS claims to direct expropriation and post-establishment discrimination (and only to Mexico-United States relations); only state-to-state dispute settlement (SSDS) is available for claims under other provisions, such as MST-FET claims. The EU, which supports the concept of a multilateral investment court, has included court-like dispute settlement in all its recent investment protection treaties. Brazil's treaties omit ISDS and designate domestic entities ("National Focal Points") to act as an ombudsperson by evaluating investor grievances and proposing solutions to a Joint Committee comprised of government representatives from both states. Under this model, state-state dispute settlement is also available if necessary. South Africa has terminated its BITs with European countries. South African domestic legislation governs the claims of foreign investors against the government in domestic courts and provides for the possibility of case-by-case agreement to arbitration.

ISDS provisions in some Ukrainian investment treaties contain reform elements that reflect recent treaty practice. Some of Ukraine's BITs restrict the scope of ISDS to alleged breaches of specific provisions, i.e. only disputes relating to the amount of compensation owing due to an alleged expropriation.[24] Others require investors to obtain prior written consent from the contracting parties before they can initiate ISDS claims.[25] Ukraine's BITs with Canada (1994), Japan (2015), and Qatar (2018) prescribe limitation periods for investor claims starting from when investors knew or should have known about the events giving rise to their claims. The Canada-Ukraine BIT (1994) also provides guidance on the types of remedy that an arbitral tribunal can grant. At least 15 Ukrainian BITs specify the governing law for ISDS cases,[26] albeit using different formulations.[27]

The majority of Ukraine's investment treaties, however, do not contain specifications or clarifications regarding investor-state arbitration procedures. These treaties thus give claimants and their counsel substantial power over key procedural issues in addition to allowing them to choose when to claim. For example, in ISDS, the appointing authority in a case plays a key role notably because it chooses or influences the choice of the important chair of the typical three-person tribunal (Gaukrodger, 2018[27]). Some recent treaties provide for a single appointing authority for all cases. Some Ukrainian treaties – including BITs with Armenia (1994), Italy (1995), Indonesia (1996), Iran (1996), and Oman (2002)[28] – remove this choice by providing for a single forum for investor-state arbitration. However, most Ukrainian treaties give claimants and their counsel a choice between at least two and as many as four different arbitration institutions at the time they file a claim.[29] This allows them to choose or influence the choice of appointing authority and exacerbates the competition for cases between arbitration institutions (Gaukrodger, 2018[27]).

Multilateral reform efforts for ISDS are underway in several fora, including at UNCITRAL and ICSID. The Ukrainian government participates actively in these discussions. Possible ISDS reforms under consideration at UNCITRAL and in the ECT modernisation process (no decisions have yet been reached in either setting) include both structural-type reforms (a permanent multilateral investment court with government-selected judges or a permanent appellate tribunal) as well as more incremental reforms such as a code of conduct for arbitrators or adjudicators.

### *Other possible aspects of investment treaty reform*

*Clearer specification of investment protection provisions would help to reflect government intent and ensure policy space for government regulation*

Specifications on key provisions in investment treaties play an important role calibrating the balance between investor protection and governments' right to regulate. Specifications seeking to achieve this balance should reflect policy choices informed by Ukraine's priorities. Policy-makers should consider the costs and benefits of these choices and their potential impact on foreign and domestic investors, together with the government's legitimate regulatory interests and potential exposure to ISDS claims and damages.

There are a range of techniques that governments can use to affect the balance between the right to regulate and investor protections in investment treaties (Gaukrodger, 2017[28]). The most obvious technique involves decisions about whether to include or exclude particular provisions, whether to draft them narrowly or broadly, precisely or in broader terms. The most important provisions in this regard are likely to be those that are most often the focus of an alleged breach in investor claims such as the FET provision.

Depending on whether the parties wish to clarify original intent or revise a provision in an existing treaty, it may be possible to clarify language through joint interpretations agreed with treaty partners or treaty amendments. These types of government action have been relatively rare in recent years, however, and can require significant time and resources to engage with individual treaty partners. Replacement of older investment treaties by consent in the context of new treaty negotiations may also be appropriate in some cases.

The government's experiences with the COVID-19 pandemic may cause it to recalibrate the appropriate balance between investor protections and the right to regulate. Measures taken by governments to protect their societies and economies during the pandemic affect companies and investors. Investment treaties should be drafted with sufficient precision to provide flexibility for governments to respond effectively to the crisis and to take vital measures such as securing quick access to essential goods and services. While it may be too early to assess the consequences of the pandemic for this area of investment policy, it is likely that experiences with the crisis may refocus government attention on the balance between investor protection and governments' right to regulate, especially in times of crisis (OECD, 2020[29]). Governments have been addressing the balance between investment protection and the right to regulate in investment treaties through analysis and discussion at the OECD (Gaukrodger, 2017[28]).

### *Investment treaties can be used as tools to liberalise domestic investment regimes*

While liberalisation provisions are common features of international trade agreements, they have been much less common in BITs. Investment treaties can be used to liberalise investment policy by facilitating the making or establishment of new investments (Pohl, 2018[19]). This can be achieved by extending the national treatment (NT) and MFN treatment standards to investors seeking to make investments (i.e. the pre-establishment phase of an investment) or by expressly prohibiting measures that block or impede market access.

Overall, provisions that seek to foster liberalisation remain the exception in Ukrainian investment treaties. The Canada-Ukraine BIT (1994), for example, grants so-called pre-establishment NT and MFN treatment to Canadian investors in Ukraine, and vice versa. The government thereby agrees to allow Canadian investors to establish a new business enterprise on the same basis as domestic investors or investors from third countries. Provisions of this type are typically accompanied by lists of exclusions, known as negative lists. Ukraine's on-going efforts to facilitate and attract new FDI could be an opportunity for policy-makers to consider a more widespread inclusion of such liberalisation provisions into new or existing treaties.

### *Opportunities for investment treaties to address investor responsibilities*

Governments at the OECD are considering how trade and investment treaties can affect business responsibilities including through their impact on policy space for governments, provisions that buttress domestic law or its enforcement, or provisions that directly address business by, for example, encouraging observance of RBC standards (Gaukrodger, 2021[30]).

Some Ukrainian BITs contain provisions on RBC-related objectives and investor responsibilities. These provisions vary in terms of scope and level of generality; some are binding on arbitral tribunals in ISDS or SSDS but others may not be. Examples include provisions reiterating the importance of RBC-related objectives,[30] seeking to preserve space for government policy-making in RBC-related areas, or reinforcing domestic law by clarifying the parties' understanding that it is inappropriate to encourage investment by relaxing environmental or health measures.[31]

Almost all of Ukraine's BITs contain provisions that address investors directly on RBC-related issues. Most Ukrainian BITs contain legality requirements that restrict the scope of treaty protections to investments made in accordance with Ukrainian law. These requirements appear most frequently in provisions defining covered investments but also appear in provisions on the scope of application of the treaty.

Investment treaties concluded by other governments address investor responsibilities in various other ways. For example, some treaties reaffirm government duties to regulate in key RBC-related areas, exclude non-discriminatory government measures in these areas from the scope of ISDS claims; exclude investments procured by corruption from the scope of ISDS, impose obligations on investors to uphold human rights and maintain an environmental management system, refer to the parties' commitments to implement international standards related to RBC, or recognise that investments should contribute to the economic development of the host state (Gaukrodger, 2021[30]) (Gordon, Pohl and Bouchard, 2014[31]).

The government may wish to consider whether and how investor responsibilities could be included in its existing and future investment treaties. This may align with the goals of Ukraine's National Contact Point for RBC under the OECD *Guidelines on Multinational Enterprises* and the government's 10-year plan to achieve certain RBC-related targets by 2030 (Order of the Cabinet of Ministers of Ukraine, 24 January 2020, No. 66-r). The government should also engage with intergovernmental discussions on this topic, including as part of the ECT negotiations and at the OECD. Some ECT Members including the EU propose to update the ECT by including new provisions addressing sustainable development and RBC-related objectives (Energy Charter Secretariat, 2019[25]) (European Commission, 2020[26]).

### *Addressing the unique approach to claims for reflective loss in ISDS*

Ukraine should continue to engage in multilateral fora such as at the OECD and UNCITRAL to develop proposals to address the unique approach to claims for shareholders' reflective loss in ISDS. Shareholders incur reflective loss if a company in which they hold shares suffers a loss that results, in turn, in the shareholders suffering a commensurate loss, typically a loss in value of the shares. In contrast to the approach of domestic laws in many countries, many investment treaties have been interpreted to allow ISDS claims by covered shareholders for losses incurred by companies in which they own shares.

Governments have been considering these issues at the OECD since 2013 (Gaukrodger, 2014[32]) (OECD, 2016[33]).[32] Ongoing discussions at UNCITRAL's Working Group III on ISDS Reform are considering possible reforms to address these issues, which were underlined in a recent UNCITRAL Secretariat note (UNCITRAL Commission, 2019[34]). At the request of the Working Group, these discussions are being conducted jointly with the OECD. Given that the current approach towards reflective loss in ISDS provides claimants with exceptional benefits and greatly expands the number of actual and potential ISDS cases, however, only government-led reform is likely to address the issues.

### *Evaluating overlaps between investment treaties*

Ukraine has two investment treaties in force simultaneously with 40 countries and three investment treaties in force simultaneously with one of its treaty partners as of May 2021 (Figure 4.3).

**Figure 4.3. Overview of Ukraine's overlapping investment treaty relationships**

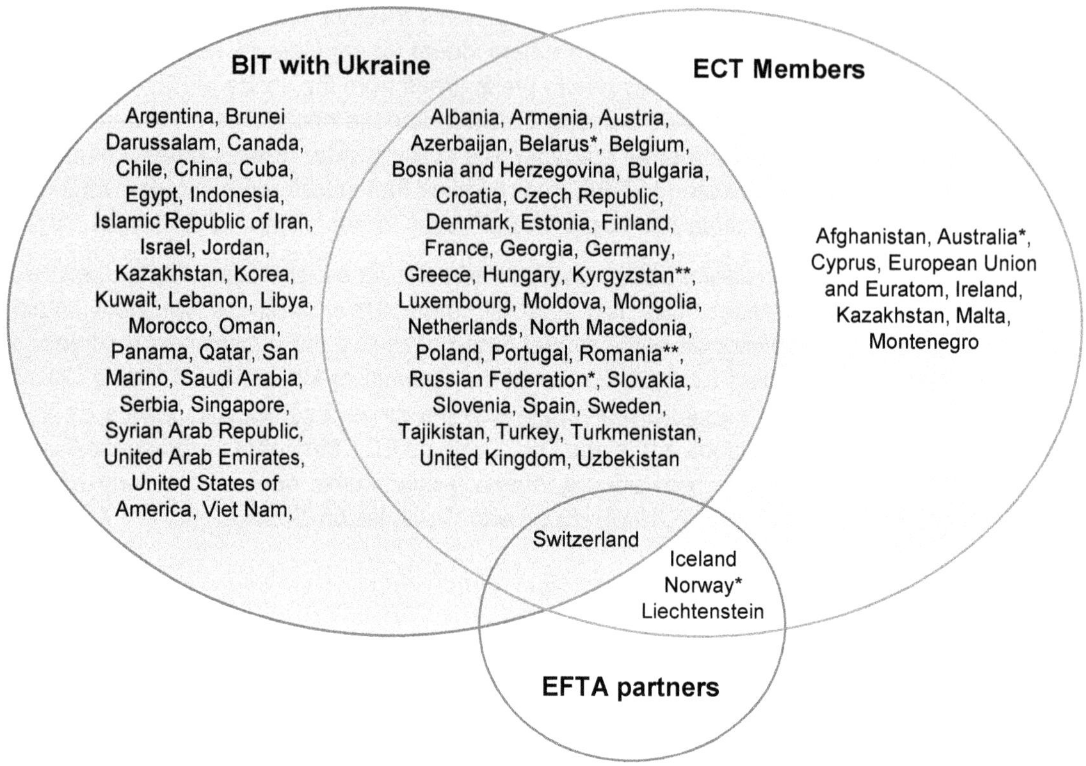


Note: *Belarus, Norway and the Russian Federation have signed but not ratified the ECT; Belarus applies the treaty provisionally. **Ukraine has signed BITs with Kyrgyzstan and Romania but they are not in force.

Note by Turkey. The information in this figure with reference to "Cyprus" relates to the southern part of the Island. There is no single authority representing both Turkish and Greek Cypriot people on the Island. Turkey recognises the Turkish Republic of Northern Cyprus (TRNC). Until a lasting and equitable solution is found within the context of the United Nations, Turkey shall preserve its position concerning the "Cyprus issue".

Note by all the European Union Member States of the OECD and the European Union: The Republic of Cyprus is recognised by all members of the United Nations with the exception of Turkey. The information in this document relates to the area under the effective control of the Government of the Republic of Cyprus.

Source: OECD investment treaty database (not public).

Overlapping investment treaties that apply to investments by investors from the same country may raise some policy concerns. As a general matter, Ukraine should strive to minimise inconsistencies between international obligations entered into with different countries. In the case of the ECT, any potential overlap with protections offered under BITs with the same partners applies to investments in energy or energy-related sectors – while the ECT applies only to these sectors, Ukraine's BITs apply to investments in all sectors. In practice, this means that covered foreign investors in Ukraine's energy or energy-related sectors may be able to rely on more favourably-worded provisions in Ukraine's older BITs in their dealings with the government or in ISDS disputes. This approach could potentially undermine the impact of the ongoing ECT modernisation process if investors in the energy sector can circumvent reforms to ECT provisions by relying on older BITs that are still in force.

Ukraine may wish to evaluate the likely impact of these overlaps in treaty protection for investments in energy or energy-related sectors. It may also wish to consider engaging with relevant treaty partners to consider these overlaps and how they could be addressed as part of the ongoing ECT modernisation process.

Despite the concerns that may arise with overlapping treaties, some governments may consider that they need to provide certain extra incentives or guarantees to some treaty partners over others in order to attract FDI. This may be because they expect that investors from those countries are less likely to invest their capital in the absence of such treatment or assess that the broader benefits associated with attracting FDI from those countries are particularly lucrative. Some governments may also consider that similar provisions in different treaties, while framed differently, are likely to be interpreted in a consistent way. The balance between these interests and assessments is a delicate one and may evolve over time.

#### *Developing approaches to prevention of ISDS claims and ISDS case management*

Ukraine may wish to prioritise the development of strategies to prevent and achieve early settlement of investment-related disputes, as well as its approach to case management of ISDS cases. Aside from participating in inter-governmental discussions on these topics, the government may wish to consider taking certain steps at a domestic level.

As discussed in further detail in the 2016 *Investment Policy Review of Ukraine* (OECD, 2016[20]) and already addressed in previous chapters of this report, Ukraine has established the Business Ombudsman Council (BOC), which is the first point of contact for companies seeking redress against unfair treatment (Wehrle, 2015[35]). Such forms of dispute prevention mechanisms are important tools to manage the exposure of governments to investors' claims because they can reduce the likelihood of formal investment treaty claims arising. Case studies published by the BOC in its annual reports indicate that investors have successfully sought redress through the Ombudsman without having to resort to arbitration. In the Ministry of Justice of Ukraine, there is a special department on international disputes which is responsible for representative of the state during the disputes settlements, including investments disputes settlement at different stages. Investors within the relevant bilateral investment treaties are able to send to the Ministry of Justice the notice of intent to claim against Ukraine in the specific investment dispute, and the Ministry of Justice from its side is authorised to do pre-claiming consultations with the investor, for example, by organising meetings or creation of working group on pre-claiming dispute settlement. The International Disputes department within the Ministry of Justice, which is responsible for representing the government in legal disputes with foreign investors, also conducts pre-litigation consultations aimed at the early resolution of disputes with aggrieved investors through informal meetings and the creation of inter-ministerial working groups in some cases.

The government may wish to consider drawing on examples of other institutional frameworks in other countries for the prevention of investment disputes and policy-setting activities. At a domestic level, some countries, such as Colombia and Peru, have adopted comprehensive legislative and regulatory frameworks to encourage the early detection and resolution of investment disputes (OECD, 2018[36]; Joubin-Bret, 2015[37]). Other countries, such as Chile, have opted for an informal prevention system where sectoral agencies directly manage disputes with investors. Some countries including Croatia and Thailand have reported successful outcomes with inter-ministerial committees established to advise line agencies on investor grievances and formulate proposals to update and revise the government's policies regarding investment treaties and domestic legal frameworks for investment protection. As noted above, Brazil does not include ISDS in its investment treaties but instead establishes with each treaty partner a Focal Point or ombudsman within each government to address investor grievances, with a Joint Committee of government representatives to oversee the administration of the agreement. Korea has also had a successful track-record of early dispute resolution with its Foreign Investment Ombudsman since it was established in 1999 (Nicolas, Thomsen and Bang, 2013[38]). It may also be worth exploring options to build awareness within government ministries, agencies and local or sub-national government entities regarding Ukraine's obligations under investment treaties and the potential impact that government decisions may have on investor rights under these treaties. Internal written guidelines or a handbook could be a useful way to disseminate this information and encourage continuity of institutional knowledge as personnel changes occur over time.

The government may also wish to explore ways to share and learn from its experiences with ISDS and those of other governments. Several states that have been frequent respondents in ISDS cases – including Argentina, Canada, Mexico, Spain and the United States – have developed dedicated teams of government lawyers to advise the government on investment disputes and investment treaty policy. Nurturing internal expertise to evaluate investor claims candidly before a legal dispute arises can be an important step in preventing time and cost protracted and costly legal disputes.

#### *Procedural considerations: exit and renegotiation*

A growing number of countries are considering ways to replace, update or exit older investment treaties that no longer reflect governments' current priorities. Review and renegotiation of investment treaties takes time and significant governmental resources and the option to terminate a treaty is not necessarily available at any moment, as the relevant provisions on temporal validity in the treaty may place limits on exit options (Box 4.8).

### Box 4.8. Designs of temporal validity provisions in investment treaties

Unlike most international treaties, which can be denounced at relatively short notice, investment treaties typically contain clauses that extend their temporal validity for significant periods of time. Three designs can be found, often cumulatively in the same agreement (Pohl, 2013[39]). First, most investment treaties set an initial validity period of often 10 years or more, counting from the treaty's entry into force. After that period, many treaties only allow states parties to denounce the treaty at the end of specific intervals of often 10 years or more. Finally, treaty obligations almost universally continue to apply for a sunset period after the termination of the treaty, again for periods of typically 10 years or more. Many treaties thus bind the treaty parties for at least two decades, and in some extreme cases for up to 50 years.

Treaty designs that automatically extend the validity of the treaty for fixed terms are included in around 30% of the global treaty stock, but this design has been used less frequently in recent years. This design tends to prolong the period for which states parties are bound without granting additional benefits in terms of predictability for investors: on the contrary, the oscillating residual treaty validity is hard to predict without detailed study (see illustrative comparison in Figure 4.4).

**Figure 4.4. Residual validity of treaties depending on the design of their validity clause**

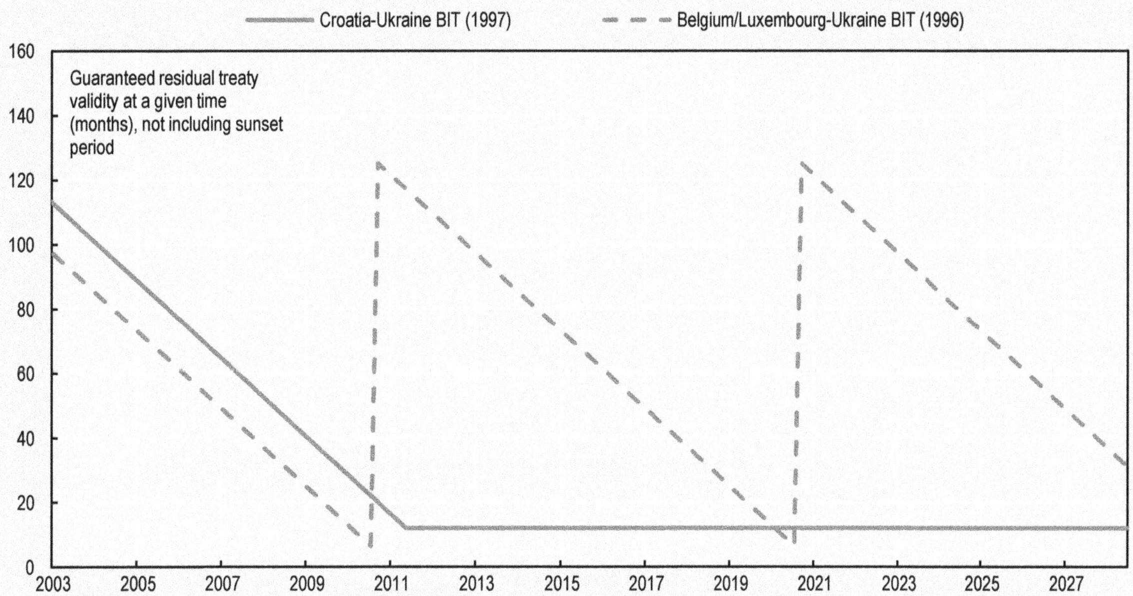


Note: Adapted from OECD work on temporal validity of investment treaties (Pohl, 2013[39]).
Source: OECD calculations based on OECD investment treaty database (not public).

Many Ukrainian investment treaties in force today contain temporal validity provisions that will operate to delay possibilities for unilateral exit from the treaty. Most of Ukraine's investment treaties contain an initial validity period of 10 or 15 years. Ukraine's BIT with Kuwait has a longer initial validity period of 30 years. At least 27 of Ukraine's BITs in force today provide for automatic renewal of the treaty for a fixed time after the period of initial validity and allow either treaty party to denounce the treaty within six or 12 months (depending on the treaty) of the expiry of the renewed period. Treaties that renew for fixed terms require more monitoring as they limit the possibilities to update or unilaterally end the agreement. If no termination occurs in the defined notice period, the treaty automatically renews for the agreed period, thereby committing Ukraine to these treaties for a further five or ten years in most cases – and 30 years in the case of the BIT with Kuwait – before the next opportunity to terminate the treaty will arise.

Even if Ukraine were to terminate unilaterally some or all of its treaties, most of them would continue to apply for a survival period of at least 10 years (often referred to as "sunset" clauses). These provisions are often intended to provide a measure of legal certainty for investors who frequently make long-term capital commitments in the host country. This situation may leave the government potentially exposed to ISDS claims far beyond the termination date. An extreme case is Ukraine's BIT with Belarus, which appears to envisage survival effects for an unlimited duration following termination. Treaty partners may be able to agree mutually to replace or exit an older treaty in such a way that the survival provisions no longer apply.

As a hypothetical example to illustrate the possible effects of these clauses, as of September 2021, the earliest occasion that the government could unilaterally withdraw from all of its investment treaties is 2033 (taking into account the automatic renewal periods in some treaties) and the effects of post-termination "sunset" periods could last until 2053 even if appropriate actions were started today (leaving aside the treaty with Belarus mentioned in the previous paragraph) (Figure 4.5).

**Figure 4.5. Projection of the temporal validity of Ukraine's investment treaties**

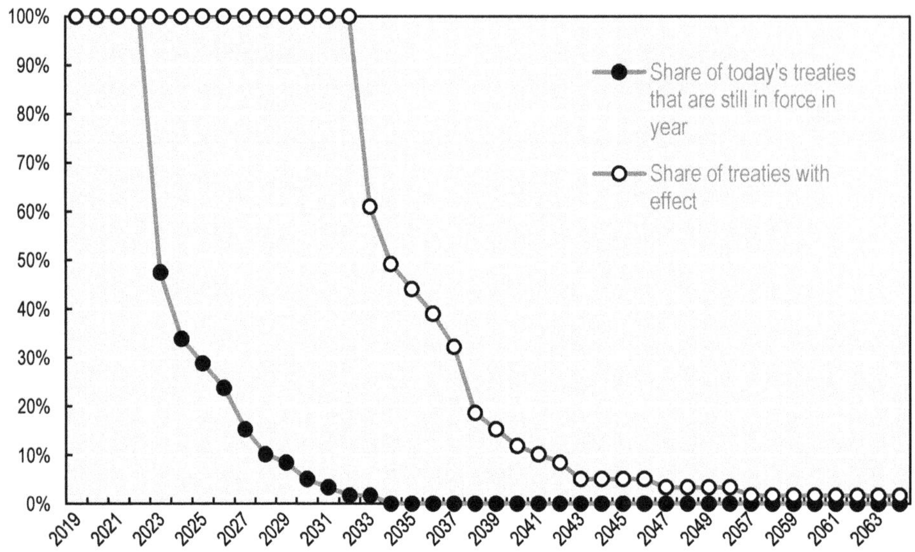


Note: Projections based on a hypothetical scenario of unilateral denunciation of all treaties in the available sample at the earliest possible occasion. Line with black dots shows the share of Ukraine's existing treaties that would remain in force in a given year. Line with white dots shows the share of those treaties that would remain in effect in a given year based on applicable sunset periods.
Source: Calculations based on OECD investment treaty database.

Unilateral action is not the only option to update or address older investment treaties but the impact of temporal validity provisions may influence how treaty amendments or agreed exits can be negotiated with treaty partners, especially if the renewal period is imminent. Ukraine may therefore wish to consider whether the current design of its temporal validity provisions can serve its interests in future discussions with treaty partners.

## Outlook and policy recommendations

Ukraine has a comprehensive regulatory framework to protect intellectual property rights through local and international instruments, including the establishment of a High Intellectual Property Court and the Ukrainian Intellectual Property Institute (UkrPatent).

Judicial reforms have advanced substantially, particularly with the establishment of the High Council of Justice as an independent body that monitors the integrity of judges, nominates judicial appointments and dismiss judges. More recently, in August 2021, new legislation aiming at rebooting the High Council of Justice and the High Qualification Commission of Judges of Ukraine and ensuring the engagement of foreign professionals in the selection of members of the two bodies entered into force. However, there are still actions to be taken that could further enhance the business climate, particularly, by enhancing the transparency of court adjudications, increasing the use of ADR mechanisms and eradicating corruption in the judiciary.

Ukraine's investment treaty policy also deserves continued attention. The government should be proactive in evaluating whether its existing BITs – many of which were concluded decades ago – align with current priorities. These treaties may play a role in attracting and retaining FDI in Ukraine, and they may be important for protecting Ukrainian investors abroad, but evidence of this impact would help to assess whether these and other objectives are being fulfilled. Some aspects of Ukraine's older BITs discussed in this Chapter may render them out of step with the government's assessments of the appropriate balance between investor protection and the right to regulate. Seeking to update these treaties in line with recent treaty practices is a challenge for many governments that involves time, cost and resource allocation constraints. The government is keenly aware of these issues through its participation in reform processes at UNCITRAL and for the ECT, as well as regular discussions about investment treaty policy at the OECD. Continued engagement in government and other action on investment treaty reforms should be a central part of the government's strategy to address these issues in the coming years.

- **Increase the number of IP rights trained judges.** The increase in the number of judges is likely to improve the quality and efficiency of IP dispute consideration. It will contribute to the Ukrainian court system and the state in general as the solution to the jurisdiction problem by boosting the effectiveness of decisions, creating an opportunity to set special court procedures and practice generalisations to enhance efficiency and accuracy, serving as a basis for the consistency and predictability of case outcomes and the source of progressive development and dynamism in IP cases.
- **Expedite the examination for green technology IP applications**. As part of the strategy to enhance the protection of IP rights of green technologies, various national IP offices offer expedited examination for green technology patent applications. In the United Kingdom, the Green Channel platform is open to all patent applications that can make a reasonable assertion of having an environmental benefit.
- **Strengthen international co-operation to nurture innovation**. To stimulate the breakthroughs necessary to advance renewable energy investments, existing platforms designed to foster international collaboration should be prioritised at a national level. This allows countries to share ideas, pool resources and capital, and co-develop programmes that support common interests.
- **Ensure independent, integral and rigorous work of the HACC towards adjudication of corruption without political interference and other undue influence**. As mandated by the Law, the HACC must keep its independence and respect the separation of powers but it must solve the cases brought by NABU and SAPO against designated high-level officials (including ministers, deputies, members of parliament, agency leaders, judges, prosecutors, and heads of state-owned enterprises) for a specified set of corruption-related crimes that entail damage in excess of a monetary threshold (at the time of writing of this *Review*, and as indicated earlier in this report, NABU was conducting a pre-trial investigation into corruption offenses which incurred damages excessing UAH 1 189 500, roughly equivalent to USD 44 500). It is of utmost importance that this final element in the specialised anti-corruption criminal justice system functions effectively and with integrity. The backlog of cases from NABU and SAPO should be eliminated to ensure fair and transparent judgements in corruption cases. This should help strengthen trust in the judiciary, including on the behalf of investors.
- **Adopt a comprehensive legislative package that sets out a complete systemic enforcement framework.** Ukraine should incorporate a comprehensive problem-solving mechanism for genuine enforcement reform. The proposed framework should involve an open discussion with representatives of the legal community, businesses and other service users, professional associations, and scholars, as well as international experts. The final enforcement framework must ensure institutional independence of the enforcement service from state intervention and deliver significant results of judgment enforcements.
- **Implement mediation and ADR mechanism legislation.** It is recommended to further develop mediation and other ADRs in all types of process, which would have a positive impact on the court's workload (the workload of the courts of first instance would be affected directly, also, agreements reached through ADR mechanism could prevent appeals; thus, reducing the workload of appeal courts) Compulsory attempt of pre-litigation settlement in certain categories of cases (mandatory pre-requisite for taking legal action) should also be considered.

- **Continue to reassess and update the government's priorities with respect to investment treaty policy**. An important issue in this regard is an evaluation of the appropriate balance between investor protections and the government's right to regulate, and how to achieve that balance in practice. Many of Ukraine's older investment treaties do not contain the clarifications and more specific design approaches to key clauses used in many newer investment treaties. Clearer specification of these provisions would likely help to reflect government intent and ensure policy space for government regulation, as well as providing greater predictability for covered investors, including in the energy sector. The interface between investment treaties and broader priorities for Ukraine and many other governments – such as tackling climate change, promoting responsible business conduct and fostering sustainable development – may also be important considerations. It has proven difficult for governments to update older treaties to reflect updated priorities but some multilateral reform initiatives are underway. Aside from multilateral action, it may be possible to clarify language through joint interpretations agreed with treaty partners or treaty amendments, depending on whether the parties wish to clarify original intent or revise a provision. Replacement of older investment treaties by consent may also be an appropriate option in some cases (as Ukraine appears to have done with Israel, Finland, Turkey and Slovakia).
- **Continue to participate actively in and follow closely government and other actions on investment treaty reforms at the OECD, UNCITRAL and for the ECT**. Consideration of reforms and policy discussions on frequently-invoked provisions in ISDS cases and whether investment treaties are achieving their intended purposes are of particular importance in current investment treaty policy. The government should prioritise its engagement in these various inter-governmental initiatives.
- **Continue to improve ISDS dispute prevention and case management tools**. The government may wish to consider drawing on examples of institutional frameworks in other countries for the prevention of investment disputes and policy-setting activities. It may also wish to consider ways to promote awareness-raising and inter-ministerial co-operation regarding the government's investment treaty policy and the significance of investment treaty obligations for the day-to-day functions of line agencies. Whatever approach the government adopts towards international investment agreements, complementary measures can help to ensure that treaties are consistent with domestic priorities and reduce the risk of disputes leading to international arbitration.

## Notes

[1] Following the dissolution of the Union of Soviet Socialist Republics (USSR), Ukraine confirmed its obligations under international treaties signed by the Ukrainian SSR before the announcement of the independence of Ukraine, including the New York Convention. See Law on Legal Succession of Ukraine, No. 1543-XII, 12 September 1991, Article 6.

[2] See, for example, Ukraine-US Trade and Investment Cooperation Agreement (2008); Canada-Ukraine Cooperation Agreement (1994). Other trade agreements with Canada (2016) and Israel (2019), among others, do not contain provisions on investment protection.

[3] Misen Energy AB and Misen Enterprises AB, ICSID Case No. ARB/21/15; Philip Morris Ukraine v. Ukraine, ICSID Case No. ARB/21/3; Emergofin B.V. and Velbay Holdings Ltd. v Ukraine, ICSID Case No. ARB/16/35; Gilward Investments B.V. v. Ukraine, ICSID Case No. ARB/15/33; Poltava Gas B.V. and Poltava Petroleum Company, ICSID Case No. ARB/15/9; Krederi Ltd. v. Ukraine, ICSID Case No. ARB/14/17; City-State N.V., Praktyka Asset Management Company LLC, Crystal-Invest LLC and Prodiz LLC v. Ukraine, ICSID Case No. ARB/14/9; Global Trading Resource Corp. and Globex International, Inc. v. Ukraine, ICSID Case No. ARB/09/11; GEA Group Aktiengesellschaft v. Ukraine, ICSID Case No. ARB/08/16; Bosh International, Inc and B&P Ltd Foreign Investments Enterprise v. Ukraine, ICSID Case No. ARB/08/11; Inmaris Perestroika Sailing Maritime Services GmbH and Others v. Ukraine, ICSID Case No. ARB/08/8; Alpha Projektholding GmbH v. Ukraine, ICSID Case No. ARB/07/16; Joseph Charles Lemire v. Ukraine, ICSID Case No. ARB/06/18; Western NIS Enterprise Fund v. Ukraine, ICSID Case No. ARB/04/2; Tokios Tokelés v. Ukraine, ICSID Case No. ARB/02/18; Generation Ukraine, Inc. v. Ukraine, ICSID Case No. ARB/00/9; Joseph Charles Lemire v. Ukraine, ICSID Case No. ARB(AF)/98/1.

[4] Olympic Entertainment Group AS (Estonia) v. Republic of Ukraine, PCA Case No. 2019-18; PJSC Gazprom v. Ukraine, PCA Case No. 2019-10; Igor Boyko v. Ukraine, PCA Case No. 2017-23; Ministry of Land and Property of the Republic of Tatarstan v. Ukraine; JKX Oil & Gas plc, Poltava Gas B.V. and Poltava Petroleum Company JV v. Ukraine, PCA Case No. 2015-11; OAO Tatneft v. Ukraine, PCA Case No. 2008-8; Laskaridis Shipping Co. LTD, Lavinia Corporation, A.K.Laskaridis and P.K.Laskaridis v. Ukraine, UNCITRAL, ad hoc.

[5] Vnesheconombank v. Ukraine, SCC Case No. 2019/113; Littop Enterprises Limited, Bridgemont Ventures Limited and Bordo Management Limited v. Ukraine, SCC Case No. V 2015/092; Remington Worldwide Limited v. Ukraine, SCC Case No. V116/2008; Limited Liability Company Amto v. Ukraine, SCC Case No. 080/2005.

[6] Skyrizon v. Ukraine; Gilead Sciences Inc. v. Ukraine; DCH Group v. Ukraine.

[7] IA Reporter (2021): "Ukraine on notice of 750+ million USD treaty claim over allegations of government collusion and non-compliance with LCIA award", 30 April 2021, https://www.iareporter.com/articles/ukraine-on-notice-of-750-million-usd-treaty-claim-over-allegations-of-government-collusion-and-non-compliance-with-lcia-award/; "Ukrainian business magnates to lodge second ICSID claim against the USA", 23 February 2021, https://www.iareporter.com/articles/ukrainian-business-magnates-to-lodge-second-icsid-claim-against-the-usa/.

[8] Under the ICSID Arbitration Rules: Artem Skubenko and others v. Republic of North Macedonia (ICSID Case No. ARB/19/9); Eugene Kazmin v. Republic of Latvia (ICSID Case No. ARB/17/5). Under the SCC Arbitration Rules: State Enterprise "Energorynok" (Ukraine) v. The Republic of Moldova (SCC Arbitration V 2012/175). Under the UNCITRAL Rules: NPC Ukrenergo v. Russian Federation; PJSC DTEK Krymenergo v. the Russian Federation; NJSC Naftogaz of Ukraine, PJSC State Joint Stock Company Chornomornaftogaz, PJSC Ukrgasvydobuvannya and others v. The Russian Federation (PCA Case No. 2017-16); Oschadbank v. Russian Federation (PCA Case No. 2016-14); Limited Liability Company Aberon Ltd, Limited Liability Company Libset, Limited Liability Company Lugzor, Limited Liability Company Ukrinterinvest, and Public Joint Stock Company DniproAzot v. The Russian Federation (PCA Case No. 2015-29); Aeroport Belbek LLC and Igor Valerievich Kolomoisky v. The Russian Federation (PCA Case No. 2015-07); Everest Estate LLC et al. v. The Russian Federation (PCA Case No. 2015-36); PJSC CB PrivatBank and Finance Company Finilon LLC v. Russian Federation (PCA Case No. 2015-21); Stabil LLC and Others v. Russian Federation (PCA Case No. 2015-35); PJSC Ukrnafta v. The Russian Federation (PCA Case No. 2015-34); Energoalians TOB v. Republic of Moldova. News reports at the time of writing in the second quarter of 2021 indicate that at least one other dispute has been formally notified by an

Ukrainian investor: IA Reporter (2021), "Ukrainian energy company puts Russia on notice of treaty-based dispute", 28 May 2021, https://www.iareporter.com/articles/ukrainian-energy-company-puts-russia-on-notice-of-treaty-based-dispute/.

[9] Based on the indicative list of "Energy Materials and Products" in Annex EM I of the ECT and UNCTAD's Investment Dispute Settlement navigator (https://investmentpolicy.unctad.org/investment-dispute-settlement), which indicates that 310 out of 1104 know ISDS cases concern investments in or related to these activities.

[10] See IA Reporter (2021), "Ukraine is facing its first renewables arbitration; respondent's counsel may be chosen through negotiated procedure", 28 April 2021, https://www.iareporter.com/articles/ukraine-is-facing-its-first-renewables-arbitration-respondents-counsel-may-be-chosen-through-negotiated-procedure/; Kurylko, V. (2021), "Ukraine faces its first investment arbitration over clampdown on renewable energy sector", *Arbitration Ukraine*, 28 April 2021, https://arbitrationukraine.com/ukraine-faces-its-first-investment-arbitration-over-a-clampdown-on-the-renewable-energy-sector/?fbclid=IwAR1DUe_T9D1JRsRCXdFoo5iXmzOx4XA_k78J0brRa3qCwVGg9FU-hfxZk8Y.

[11] Based on publicly available information, at least five Ukrainian BITs contain no reference to fair and equitable treatment at all (see BITs with Armenia (1994), the Russian Federation (1998), Azerbaijan (1997), and Tajikistan (2001)) or refer to it only in the preamble (see Turkey-Ukraine BIT (1996): "*Agreeing that fair and equitable treatment of investment is desirable in order to maintain a stable framework for investment and maximum effective utilisation of economic resources*"). Most Ukrainian treaties refer to "fair and equitable" treatment but some refer to "fair and equal" treatment (e.g. Ukraine-Bulgaria BIT (1994), Ukraine-Georgia BIT (1995)) and others only to "equal" treatment (e.g. China-Ukraine BIT (1992)) or only to "fair" treatment (e.g. Ukraine-Kyrgyzstan (1993), Ukraine-Uzbekistan (1993), Ukraine-Viet Nam (1994)).

[12] See Tokios Tokelés v. Ukraine, ICSID Case No. ARB/02/18; Western NIS Enterprise Fund v. Ukraine, ICSID Case No. ARB/04/2; Limited Liability Company Amto v. Ukraine, SCC Case No. 080/2005; Joseph Charles Lemire v. Ukraine, ICSID Case No. ARB/06/18; Alpha Projektholding GmbH v. Ukraine, ICSID Case No. ARB/07/16; Inmaris Perestroika Sailing Maritime Services GmbH and Others v. Ukraine, ICSID Case No. ARB/08/8; Bosh International, Inc and B&P Ltd Foreign Investments Enterprise v. Ukraine, ICSID Case No. ARB/08/11; GEA Group Aktiengesellschaft v. Ukraine, ICSID Case No. ARB/08/16; OAO Tatneft v. Ukraine, PCA Case No. 2008-8; City-State N.V., Praktyka Asset Management Company LLC, Crystal-Invest LLC and Prodiz LLC v. Ukraine, ICSID Case No. ARB/14/9; Krederi Ltd. v. Ukraine, ICSID Case No. ARB/14/17; JKX Oil & Gas plc, Poltava Gas B.V. and Poltava Petroleum Company JV v. Ukraine, PCA Case No. 2015-11. The number of actual FET claims against Ukraine may be higher on account of confidential pending claims. Based on publicly available information, arbitral tribunals found FET breach in at least five cases (City-State N.V., Praktyka Asset Management Company LLC, Crystal-Invest LLC and Prodiz LLC v. Ukraine, ICSID Case No. ARB/14/9; OAO Tatneft v. Ukraine, PCA Case No. 2008-8; Inmaris Perestroika Sailing Maritime Services GmbH and Others v. Ukraine, ICSID Case No. ARB/08/8; Alpha Projektholding GmbH v. Ukraine, ICSID Case No. ARB/07/16; Joseph Charles Lemire v. Ukraine, ICSID Case No. ARB/06/18).

[13] See France-Ukraine BIT (1994), Article 3: "[…] In particular, although not exclusively, any restriction on the purchase and transport of raw and auxiliary materials, energy and fuels, as well as on the means of production and exploitation of any kind, any hindrance to the sale and transport of products within the country and abroad, and any other measures having a similar effect, shall be regarded as de jure or de facto obstacles to fair and equitable treatment". Unofficial translation from French by the authors: "En particulier, bien que non exclusivement, sont considérées comme des entraves de droit ou de fait au traitement juste et équitable, toute restriction à l'achat et au transport de matières premières et de matières auxiliaires, d'énergie et de combustibles, ainsi que de moyens de production et d'exploitation de tout genre,

toute entrave à la vente et au transport des produits à l'intérieur du pays et à l'étranger, ainsi que toute autre mesure ayant un effet analogue."

[14] Multiple references to FET occur in preamble text and substantive provisions in some treaties: see, for example, Ukraine's BITs with Denmark (1992), Egypt (1992), Netherlands (1994), the United States (1994), Sweden (1995), Georgia (1995), Turkey (1996), Japan (2015), Turkey (2017) and Qatar (2018)). Other treaties refer to FET in several different substantive provisions: see, for example, Ukraine's BITs Hungary (1994), Lithuania (1994), Czech Republic (1994), Sweden (1995), Estonia (1995), Indonesia (1996), Slovenia (1999), Congo (2000), Gambia (2001), Panama (2003), Equatorial Guinea (2005), and Singapore (2006)). Other formulations of FET in Ukrainian treaties may also leave scope for broad interpretations by arbitral tribunals. For example, the Belgium/Luxembourg-Ukraine BIT (1996) refers to FET as "in no case… less than [that] recogni[s]ed under international law". Such a formulation creates a "floor" for FET, rather than a "ceiling" that would limit FET to the protections already afforded under international law. There is no guidance in this BIT or any other Ukrainian BIT about the extent to which protections may exceed those under international law.

[15] (Gaukrodger, 2016[41]) (Reviewing the applicable law on joint interpretations of investment treaties without express provisions on the issue); (Gordon and Pohl, 2015[40]). For a recent example of a joint interpretation, see the Joint Interpretative Declaration between Colombia and India (2018) regarding the Colombia-India BIT (2009).

[16] Treaty shopping is a phrase used broadly herein to describe the power for a beneficial owner of an investment to choose between investment treaties or between provisions of different investment treaties. See further detail on treaty shopping below.

[17] For a recent discussion of the uncertainty surrounding the interpretation of MFN clauses in ISDS, see (Batifort and Heath, 2017[43])

[18] See, for example, United States-Mexico-Canada Agreement (2018), Article 14.5(4) ("For greater certainty, whether treatment is accorded in 'like circumstances' under this Article depends on the totality of the circumstances, including whether the relevant treatment distinguishes between investors or investments on the basis of legitimate public welfare objectives"); CPTPP (2018), "Note on Interpretation of 'In Like Circumstances'", www.mfat.govt.nz/assets/Trans-Pacific-Partnership/Other-documents/Interpretation-of-In-Like-Circumstances.pdf.

[19] Some agreements contain more detailed sector-specific exclusions, e.g. Ukraine-United States BIT (1994); EFTA-Ukraine FTA.

[20] See the EFTA-Ukraine FTA, Turkey-Ukraine BIT (2017), Japan-Ukraine BIT (2015), Kuwait-Ukraine BIT (2002), Slovenia-Ukraine BIT (1999), Turkey-Ukraine BIT (1996); Israel-Ukraine BIT (1994), Canada-Ukraine BIT (1994), Ukraine-United States BIT (1994).

[21] Some treaties use the phrase "in like situations" (e.g. EFTA-Ukraine FTA), while other rather use the phrase "in like circumstances" (e.g. Turkey-Ukraine BIT (2017)) or "in similar situations" (e.g. Turkey - Ukraine BIT (1996)), "in similar cases" (e.g. Israel-Ukraine BIT (1994)), or "under similar conditions" (e.g. Canada-Ukraine BIT (1994)).

[22] Turkey-Ukraine BIT (2017), Article 4(c); Japan-Ukraine BIT (2015), Article 5(4); Ukraine-United Arab Emirates BIT (2003), Protocol, Paragraph (5): "With respect to Article 3 – It is agreed by both contracting parties that the most favourable treatment shall not apply to any investment disputes".

[23] Ukraine-United Arab Emirates BIT (2003), Protocol, Paragraph (2).

[24] See, for example, the China-Ukraine BIT (1992), Article 10(1), which provides that "any dispute between a Contracting Party by an investor of the other Contracting Party concerning the amount compensation in case of expropriation can be submitted to an arbitral tribunal" (unofficial translation from Ukrainian by the authors).

[25] See Article 9(3) of the Ukraine-United Arab Emirates BIT (2003) ("the dispute relating to the amount of compensation and any other dispute agreed upon by both parties may be submitted to an international Arbitral Tribunal including the ICSID only after the written consent of both contracting parties.") See also Article 10(2) of the Poland-Ukraine BIT (1993) ("If the consultation is not completed by a decision within six months from the date of the written proposal to start consultations, the parties to the dispute may proceed as follows:(a) if the dispute concerns an obligation under Article 5 [transfers] and Article 6 [Withdrawal and reimbursement] of this Agreement, it is, at the request of investors, transferred to the decision to arbitration court; b) a dispute not specified in paragraph 2, paragraph a) of this Article shall be transferred with the consent of both parties to the dispute for arbitration court.")

[26] See Ukraine's BITs with China (1992), Armenia (1994), Canada (1994), Argentina (1995), Belgium-Luxembourg Economic Union (1996), Latvia (1997), Spain (1998), North Macedonia (1998), India (2001), Morocco (2001), Albania (2002), Kuwait (2002) United Arab Emirates (2003), Jordan (2005), and Turkey (2017).

[27] For example, Article 11(6) of the Jordan-Ukraine BIT (2005) provides that "the arbitral tribunal shall reach its decision in virtue if the present Agreement and pursuant to the rules of international law." Article 9 of the Ukraine-United Arab Emirates BIT (2003) provides that "the arbitral Tribunal shall reach its award based upon the provisions of this Agreement, the relevant domestic laws, the agreements both Contracting States have concluded and the generally recognised principles of international law." Article 10(6) of the Turkey-Ukraine BIT (2017) states "the arbitral tribunals shall take its decisions in accordance with the provisions of this Agreement, the laws and regulations of the Contracting Party involved in the dispute on which territory the investment is made (including its rules on the conflict of laws) and the relevant principles of international law as accepted by both Contracting Parties."

[28] For example, the Oman-Ukraine BIT (2002) only provides for arbitration by the ICSID (Article 10), and the Iran-Ukraine BIT (1996) only provides for access to an international ad hoc arbitral tribunal established under UNCITRAL Arbitration Rules (Article 8(2)).

[29] For example, under the Turkey-Ukraine BIT (2017), covered investors may choose to submit a dispute to international arbitration to "an *ad hoc* tribunal established under the Arbitration Rules of Procedures of UNCITRAL, any other arbitration institution or any other arbitration rules, including though not exclusively Istanbul Arbitration Centre (ISTAC) or any relevant Ukrainian Institution if the disputing parties so agree". See also the Japan-Ukraine BIT (2015), under which investors may choose to submit a dispute to arbitration in accordance with the ICSID Convention and Arbitration Rules, ICSID's Additional Facility Rules, the UNCITRAL Rules or any other arbitration rules agreed by the disputing parties.

[30] See, for example, Finland-Ukraine BIT (2004), preamble.

[31] See, for example, Japan-Ukraine BIT (2015), Article 25; EU-Ukraine Association Agreement, Article 296.

[32] See also Summary of 19th FOI Roundtable, October 2013, pp. 12-19; Summary of 18th FOI Roundtable, March 2013, pp. 4-9.

# Annex 4.A. Overview of Ukraine's investment treaties

### Annex Table 4.A.1. Ukraine's bilateral investment treaties – in force as of July 2021

| No | Treaty partner | Date of signature | Date of entry into force |
|---|---|---|---|
| 1 | Qatar | 20-03-2018 | 09-04-2019 |
| 2 | Turkey | 09-10-2017 | 06-09-2018 |
| 3 | Japan | 05-02-2015 | 26-11-2015 |
| 4 | Israel | 24-11-2010 | 20-11-2012 |
| 5 | Saudi Arabia | 09-04-2008 | 18-02-2009 |
| 6 | Slovakia | 26-02-2007 | 20-08-2009 |
| 7 | Singapore | 18-09-2006 | 14-07-2007 |
| 8 | San Marino | 13-01-2006 | 15-10-2008 |
| 9 | Jordan | 30-11-2005 | 17-04-2007 |
| 10 | Finland | 07-10-2004 | 07-12-2005 |
| 11 | Brunei Darussalam | 18-06-2004 | 26-04-2006 |
| 12 | Panama | 04-11-2003 | 13-06-2007 |
| 13 | United Arab Emirates | 21-01-2003 (UAE)<br>22-01-2003 (Ukraine) | 09-03-2004 (UAE)<br>09-04-2004 (Ukraine) |
| 14 | Albania | 25-10-2002 | 30-04-2004 |
| 15 | Syrian Arab Republic | 21-04-2002 | 16-03-2003 |
| 16 | Bosnia and Herzegovina | 13-03-2002 | 22-01-2004 |
| 17 | Oman | 14-01-2002 | 12-05-2010 |
| 18 | Kuwait | 12-01-2002 | 11-06-2003 |
| 19 | Morocco | 24-12-2001 | 28-04-2009 |
| 20 | Tajikistan | 06-07-2001 | 27-05-2003 |
| 21 | Libya | 23-01-2001 | 23-04-2003 |
| 22 | Serbia | 09-01-2001 | 14-08-2001 |
| 23 | Portugal | 25-10-2000 | 18-07-2003 |
| 24 | Slovenia | 30-03-1999 | 01-06-2000 |
| 25 | Russian Federation | 27-11-1998 | 27-01-2000 |
| 26 | North Macedonia | 02-03-1998 | 25-03-2000 |
| 27 | Spain | 26-02-1998 | 13-03-2000 |
| 28 | Turkmenistan | 29-01-1998 | 28-09-1999 |
| 29 | Croatia | 15-12-1997 | 05-06-2001 |
| 30 | Latvia | 24-07-1997 | 30-12-1997 |
| 31 | Azerbaijan | 24-03-1997 | 09-12-1997 |
| 32 | Korea | 16-12-1996 | 03-11-1997 |
| 33 | Austria | 08-11-1996 | 01-12-1997 |
| 34 | Islamic Republic of Iran | 22-05-1996 | 05-07-2003 |

| No | Treaty partner | Date of signature | Date of entry into force |
|---|---|---|---|
| 35 | BLEU (Belgium-Luxembourg Economic Union) | 20-05-1996 | 27-07-2001 |
| 36 | Indonesia | 11-04-1996 | 06-08-1997 |
| 37 | Lebanon | 25-03-1996 | 26-05-2000 |
| 38 | Belarus | 14-12-1995 | 11-06-1997 |
| 39 | Chile | 30-10-1995 | 26-07-1997 |
| 40 | Moldova | 29-08-1995 | 20-05-1996 |
| 41 | Sweden | 15-08-1995 | 01-03-1997 |
| 42 | Argentina | 09-08-1995 | 06-05-1997 |
| 43 | Cuba | 20-05-1995 | 04-12-1996 |
| 44 | Switzerland | 20-04-1995 | 21-01-1997 |
| 45 | Estonia | 15-02-1995 | 05-07-1995 |
| 46 | Georgia | 09-01-1995 | 18-12-1996 |
| 47 | Bulgaria | 08-12-1994 | 10-12-1995 |
| 48 | Canada | 24-10-1994 | 24-07-1995 |
| 49 | Hungary | 11-10-1994 | 20-12-1996 |
| 50 | Armenia | 07-10-1994 | 07-03-1996 |
| 51 | Kazakhstan | 17-09-1994 | 04-08-1995 |
| 52 | Greece | 01-09-1994 | 04-12-1996 |
| 53 | Netherlands | 14-07-1994 | 01-06-1997 |
| 54 | Viet Nam | 08-06-1994 | 08-12-1994 |
| 55 | France | 03-05-1994 | 26-01-1996 |
| 56 | Czech Republic | 17-03-1994 | 02-11-1995 |
| 57 | United States of America | 04-03-1994 | 16-11-1996 |
| 58 | Lithuania | 08-02-1994 | 06-03-1995 (Lithuania)<br>27-02-1995 (Ukraine) |
| 59 | Uzbekistan | 20-02-1993 | 26-05-1994 |
| 60 | Germany | 15-02-1993 | 29-06-1996 |
| 61 | United Kingdom | 10-02-1993 | 10-02-1993 |
| 62 | Poland | 12-01-1993 | 14-09-1993 |
| 63 | Egypt | 22-12-1992 | 13-10-1993 |
| 64 | Mongolia | 05-11-1992 | 05-11-1992 |
| 65 | China | 31-10-1992 | 29-05-1993 (China)<br>30-05-1993 (Ukraine) |
| 66 | Denmark | 23-10-1992 | 29-04-1994 |

Note: Listed in descending chronological order based on date of signature. Dates appear in dd-mm-yyyy format. It is difficult to be precise about the exact status of Ukraine's BITs due to some inconsistencies in publicly-available information. Full-text versions of most but not all Ukrainian BITs are available on the Ukrainian Parliament Legislative Database: https://zakon.rada.gov.ua/laws/. Some information with respect to dates of signature and entry into force may nonetheless be inconsistent with information published by Ukraine's treaty partners. For example, information published in Ukraine's Legislative Database indicates that the United Arab Emirates-Ukraine BIT was signed on 22 January 2003 and came into force on 9 April 2004 while the UAE's Ministry of Finance (https://www.mof.gov.ae/) indicates 21 January 2003 and 18 September 2003 for these dates. Similar discrepancies exist with information published by governments of other Ukrainian treaty partners, including Lithuania and China. Online databases of investment treaties maintained by third parties such as UNCTAD and ICSID indicate a range of other conflicting dates that have not been taken into account for the purposes of this Chapter.
Source: OECD investment treaty database (not public); consultations with the Ukrainian government during the preparation of this *Review*.

### Annex Table 4.A.2. Ukraine's bilateral investment treaties – terminated

| No | Treaty partner | Date of signature | Date of entry into force | Effective date of termination | Type of termination |
|---|---|---|---|---|---|
| 1 | India | 01-12-2001 | 12-08-2003 | 22-03-2017 | Unilaterally denounced |
| 2 | Turkey | 27-11-1996 | 21-05-1998 | 06-09-2018 | Replaced |
| 3 | Italy | 02-05-1995 | 12-09-1997 | 12-09-2012 | Unilaterally denounced |
| 4 | Slovak Republic | 27-06-1994 | 03-04-1996 | 20-08-2009 | Replaced |
| 5 | Israel | 16-06-1994 | 18-02-1997 | 20-11-2012 | Replaced |
| 6 | Finland | 14-05-1992 | 30-01-1994 | 07-12-2005 | Replaced |

Source: OECD investment treaty database; Ukrainian government.

### Annex Table 4.A.3. Ukraine's bilateral investment treaties – signed but not in force

| No | Treaty partner | Date of signature | Date of entry into force |
|---|---|---|---|
| 1 | Equatorial Guinea | 15-12-2005 | - |
| 2 | Gambia | 12-07-2001 | - |
| 3 | Yemen | 19-02-2001 | - |
| 4 | Democratic Republic of the Congo | 11-10-2000 | - |
| 5 | Romania | 23-02-1995 | - |
| 6 | Kyrgyzstan | 23-02-1993 | - |

Source: OECD investment treaty database (not public); consultations with the Ukrainian government during the preparation of this *Review*.

### Annex Table 4.A.4. Ukraine's trade agreements containing investment protections, investment liberalisation provisions and/or ISDS

| No | Treaty | Date of signature for Ukraine | Date of entry into force | Date of entry into force for Ukraine |
|---|---|---|---|---|
| 1 | EU-Ukraine Association Agreement | 21-03-2014 | 01-09-2017 | 01-09-2017 |
| 2 | EFTA-Ukraine FTA | 24-06-2010 | 01-06-2012 | 01-06-2012 |
| 3 | Energy Charter Treaty | 17-12-1994 | 16-04-1998 | 27-01-1999 |

Source: OECD investment treaty database (not public); consultations with the Ukrainian government during the preparation of this *Review*.

## References

American Chamber of Commerce of Ukraine (2021), *Ukraine Business Climate Survey Post-Pandemic Horizon*, https://chamber.ua/wp-content/uploads/2021/09/Post-pandemic-horizon_final.pdf (accessed on 22 September 2021). [8]

Baltifort, S. and J. Heath (2017), "he New Debate on the Interpretation of MFN Clauses in Investment Treaties: Putting the Brakes on Multilateralization", *American Journal of International Law*, Vol. 111/4, pp. 973-913, http://dx.doi.org/10.1017/ajil.2017.77. [42]

Batifort, S. and J. Heath (2017), "The New Debate on the Interpretation of MFN Clauses in Investment Treaties: Putting the Brakes on Multilateralization", *American Journal of International Law*, Vol. 111/4, pp. 873-913, http://dx.doi.org/10.1017/ajil.2017.77. [43]

CMS Law Tax (2016), *Ukraine: Cancellation of State Registration for Foreign Investments*, https://www.cms-lawnow.com/ealerts/2016/06/ukraine-cancellation-of-state-registration-for-foreign-investments. [2]

Council of Europe (2020), *Progress Review Report (1 January 2018 - 31 December 2019) GR-DEM (2020)6*, Council. [7]

Energy Charter Secretariat (2021), *Statistics of ECT Cases*, https://www.energychartertreaty.org/fileadmin/DocumentsMedia/Statistics/All_statistics_-_20_March_2021.pdf. [22]

Energy Charter Secretariat (2019), *Decision of the Energy Charter Conference on the Policy Options for Modernisation of the ECT, Document No. CCDEC 2019 08 STR*, http://dx.doi.org/www.energycharter.org/fileadmin/DocumentsMedia/CCDECS/2019/CCDEC201908.pdf. [25]

European Commission (2020), *EU text proposal for the modernisation of the Energy Charter Treaty (ECT)*, https://trade.ec.europa.eu/doclib/docs/2020/may/tradoc_158754.pdf. [26]

European Commission (2020), *Report on the protection and enforcement of intellectual property rights*, Euopean Commission. [5]

European Union Intellectual Property Office (2015), *Ukraine: IP Country Fact Sheet*, European Union Intellectual Property Office. [4]

Fursa, S. (2015), *Mediation in Ukraine: Urgent Issues of Theory and Practice and Necessity of Legislative Regulation*, Springer. [18]

Gaukrodger, D. (2021), "Business responsibilities and investment treaties", *OECD Working Papers on International Investment*, No. 2021/02, OECD Publishing, Paris, https://dx.doi.org/10.1787/4a6f4f17-en. [30]

Gaukrodger, D. (2021), *The Future of Investment Treaties. Background note on potential avenues for future policies.*, https://www.oecd.org/daf/inv/investment-policy/Note-on-possible-directions-for-the-future-of-investment-treaties.pdf. [23]

Gaukrodger, D. (2018), *Appointing Authorities and the Selection of Arbitrators in Investor-State Dispute Settlement: An Overview*, https://www.oecd.org/investment/investment-policy/ISDS-Appointing-Authorities-Arbitration-March-2018.pdf. [27]

Gaukrodger, D. (2017), "Addressing the balance of interests in investment treaties: The limitation of fair and equitable treatment provisions to the minimum standard of treatment under customary international law", *OECD Working Papers on International Investment*, No. 2017/3, OECD Publishing, Paris, https://dx.doi.org/10.1787/0a62034b-en. [24]

Gaukrodger, D. (2017), "The balance between investor protection and the right to regulate in investment treaties: A scoping paper", *OECD Working Papers on International Investment*, No. 2017/2, OECD Publishing, Paris, https://dx.doi.org/10.1787/82786801-en. [28]

Gaukrodger, D. (2016), "The legal framework applicable to joint interpretive agreements of investment treaties", *OECD Working Papers on International Investment*, No. 2016/1, OECD Publishing, Paris, https://dx.doi.org/10.1787/5jm3xgt6f29w-en. [41]

Gaukrodger, D. (2014), "Investment Treaties and Shareholder Claims for Reflective Loss: Insights from Advanced Systems of Corporate Law", *OECD Working Papers on International Investment*, No. 2014/2, OECD Publishing, Paris, https://dx.doi.org/10.1787/5jz0xvgngmr3-en. [32]

Gherasimov, C. and I. Solonenko (2020), "Rule of Law Reform Reform after Zelenskyi's First Year", *German Council on Foreign Relations*, pp. 1-26. [6]

Gordon, K. and J. Pohl (2015), "Investment Treaties over Time - Treaty Practice and Interpretation in a Changing World", *OECD Working Papers on International Investment*, No. 2015/2, OECD Publishing, Paris, https://dx.doi.org/10.1787/5js7rhd8sq7h-en. [40]

Gordon, K., J. Pohl and M. Bouchard (2014), "Investment Treaty Law, Sustainable Development and Responsible Business Conduct: A Fact Finding Survey", *OECD Working Papers on International Investment*, No. 2014/1, OECD Publishing, Paris, https://dx.doi.org/10.1787/5jz0xvgx1zlt-en. [31]

IDLO (2018), *Establishing the High Anti-Corruption Court in Ukraine*, International Development Law Organisation, https://www.idlo.int/fr/what-we-do/initiatives/establishing-high-anti-corruption-court-ukraine. [12]

International Monetary Fund (2017), *Reforming the Judiciary: Learning from the Experience of Central, Eastern, and Southeastern Europe*, International Monetary Fund. [13]

Joubin-Bret, A. (2015), *Establishing an International Advisory Centre on Investment Disputes?*, https://e15initiative.org/wp-content/uploads/2015/09/E15-Investment-Joubin-Bret-Final.pdf. [37]

Jus Mundi (2021), *Ostchem and others v. OPP, Decision of the Supreme Court of Ukraine, 8 June 2021*, https://jusmundi.com/en/document/decision/uk-ostchem-holding-ltd-and-the-state-property-fund-of-ukraine-v-pjsc-odesa-portside-plant-rishennia-verkhovnogo-sudu-ukrayini-tuesday-8th-june-2021 (accessed on 26 October 2021). [9]

Mistura, F. and C. Roulet (2019), "The determinants of Foreign Direct Investment: Do statutory restrictions matter?", *OECD Working Papers on International Investment*, No. 2019/01, OECD Publishing, Paris, https://dx.doi.org/10.1787/641507ce-en. [21]

Nicolas, F., S. Thomsen and M. Bang (2013), "Lessons from Investment Policy Reform in Korea", *OECD Working Papers on International Investment*, No. 2013/2, OECD Publishing, Paris, https://dx.doi.org/10.1787/5k4376zqcpf1-en. [38]

OECD (2020), *OECD Investment Policy Responses to COVID-19*, http://dx.doi.org/www.oecd.org/coronavirus/policy-responses/oecd-investment-policy-responses-to-covid-19-4be0254d/. [29]

OECD (2019), *Istanbul Anti-Corruption Action Plan, Fourth Round of Monitoring of Ukraine*, https://www.oecd.org/corruption/acn/OECD-ACN-Ukraine-Progress-Update-2019-EN.pdf (accessed on 8 September 2021). [15]

OECD (2018), *OECD Investment Policy Review of Southeast Asia*, https://www.oecd.org/fr/daf/inv/politiques-investissement/oecd-investment-policy-review-southeast-asia.htm. [36]

OECD (2017), *Istanbul Anti-Corruption Action Plan Methodology for the 4th monitoring round*, https://www.oecd.org/corruption/acn/OECD-ACN-4th-Round-Monitoring-Methodology-Amendments-2017-ENG.pdf (accessed on 8 September 2021). [14]

OECD (2016), *OECD Business and Finance Outlook 2016*, OECD Publishing, Paris, https://dx.doi.org/10.1787/9789264257573-en. [33]

OECD (2016), *OECD Investment Policy Reviews: Ukraine 2016*, OECD Investment Policy Reviews, OECD Publishing, Paris, https://dx.doi.org/10.1787/9789264257368-en. [20]

Pohl, J. (2018), "Societal benefits and costs of International Investment Agreements : A critical review of aspects and available empirical evidence", *OECD Working Papers on International Investment*, No. 2018/1, OECD Publishing, Paris, https://dx.doi.org/10.1787/e5f85c3d-en. [19]

Pohl, J. (2013), "Temporal Validity of International Investment Agreements: A Large Sample Survey of Treaty Provisions", *OECD Working Papers on International Investment*, No. 2013/4, OECD Publishing, Paris, https://dx.doi.org/10.1787/5k3tsjsl5fvh-en. [39]

Supreme Court of Ukraine (2021), *Supreme Court of Ukraine*, https://supreme.court.gov.ua/supreme/pres-centr/news/1133986/ (accessed on 26 October 2021). [10]

UNCITRAL Commission (2019), *Possible reform of investor-State dispute settlement (ISDS): Shareholder claims and reflective loss. Note by the Secretariat., Document No. A/CN.9/WG.III/WP.170*, http://undocs.org/en/A/CN.9/WG.III/WP.170. [34]

US - Ukraine Business Council (2017), *Ukraine revises its arbitration law, introduces new arbitration rules*, US - Ukraine Business Council. [17]

Verkhovna Rada of Ukraine (1996), *Constitution of Ukraine*. [1]

Wehrle, F. (2015), *High Level Reporting Mechanisms in Colombia and Ukraine*, https://baselgovernance.org/publications/working-paper-19-high-level-reporting-mechanisms-colombia-and-ukraine. [35]

WIPO (2021), *WIPO GREEN – The Marketplace for Sustainable Technology*, https://www3.wipo.int/wipogreen/en (accessed on 19 July 2021). [3]

World Bank Group (2020), *Doing Business Report*, World Bank. [11]

World Bank Group (2019), *Ukraine Growth Study Final Document: Faster, Lasting and Kinder*, World Bak Group, https://documents.worldbank.org/curated/en/543041554211825812/pdf/Ukraine-Growth-Study-Final-Document-Faster-Lasting-and-Kinder.pdf. [16]

# 5 Energy Infrastructure in Ukraine

This chapter examines the current context of energy infrastructure investments in Ukraine. It reviews the recent reforms to boost upstream, midstream and downstream infrastructure investments, including private participation through public-private partnerships. It also proposes recommendations to overcome the remaining obstacles to improving the business environment in Ukraine for private investments in renewable energy and energy efficiency projects..

## Introduction

Ukraine has undertaken a wide range of institutional, economic and regulatory reforms to increase the role of market forces in the energy sector and advance its integration with the European Union. Some of these reforms have been based on the commitments that Ukraine acquired by becoming, in 2011, a Contracting Party to the Energy Community Treaty, namely the legislative frameworks that enable private participation in the electricity and gas sectors. Additionally, in 2017, the government launched the "Energy Strategy of Ukraine until 2035" (ESU 2035) as an overarching policy to increase the share of renewables in the energy mix, and to achieve energy efficiency, security, competitiveness and greater integration with the EU energy space.

The economic recovery from the COVID-19 crisis presents Ukraine with an opportunity to build back better, placing special emphasis on green infrastructure projects. The government can build back better and advance investments that are properly planned for future generations. Moreover, the world is heading towards a consensus in which international investors are interested in projects that phase out carbon-intensive technologies and infrastructure. Therefore, Ukraine must advance policies that foster green investments in the energy sector.

Ukraine has established policies and programmes that ease the availability of finance for energy infrastructure projects. Finance is available through foreign and domestic capital investors, private banks, development entities and financial institutions. Public-private partnerships and concessions have been two important mechanisms to finance energy projects. As a result, the country passed from having 5% of its total energy mix from renewable energy sources (RES) to 12.4% by the end of 2020 and aims to achieve a goal of sourcing 25% of its power from RES by 2035.

Investments in renewable energy generation and integration capacities of RES to the power grid still face regulatory and market obstacles, along with country-specific impediments, technical challenges, and weak policies to level the playing field between RES and hydrocarbon generators. This chapter assesses the policies and programmes that are critical to unlock private investment in renewable energy infrastructure as well as in energy efficiency.

## Financing availability for energy infrastructure projects

Energy infrastructure investments in Ukraine have traditionally relied on the public sector, although the government has had limited fiscal space for advancing them over the past decade. As such, increasing private sector participation in infrastructure investment is an important priority for the development of the country. However, in Ukraine, one of the key difficulties to overcome for the successful implementation of impactful energy infrastructure projects is the availability of financial resources. Not only do energy infrastructure projects require important amounts of financial resources at their inception, but they also often generate return on investment only in the mid to long term and therefore need long-term commitments of stakeholders. Such commitments have the potential to expose stakeholders to important risks, which explains the use of financial schemes ensuring adequate risk sharing among the numerous stakeholders. Both capital and debt are used to finance energy infrastructure projects, with debt usually representing the vast majority of the financial resources. These resources can be scarce if investors perceive the risks as being too high, but the modernisation of the financial sector through increased market depth and liquidity can strengthen the availability and readiness of investors to bring financial resources to upgrade energy infrastructure, especially with respect to developing renewables.

Ukraine has made important progress to enhance its financial sector. However, ensuring adequate implementation of the regulatory framework for local and financial institutions remains a challenge. Ukraine scores poorly in the Financial System pillar of the 2019 Global Competitiveness Report, obtaining only 42.3 points out of 100 and ranking 136th out of 141 countries (World Economic Forum, 2019[1]). The Global

Competitiveness Report identifies low domestic credit to the private sector, limited availability of venture capital and insufficient financing to SMEs as the main obstacles. Moreover, Ukraine is burdened by the highest non-performing loan (NPL) ratio globally and operational costs are elevated at state-owned banks (SOBs) (World Bank, 2020[2]).

Facilitating access to finance is critical to spur investments in innovative and sustainable energy infrastructure. In Ukraine, energy infrastructure is financed by various actors, including foreign and domestic private investors, state-owned enterprises (SOEs), banks and international financing institutions (IFI). However, local banks reportedly offer unfavourable financing conditions to foreign and domestic investors that want to invest in energy infrastructure projects[1]. Local banks face a high share of NPLs – 49% overall and 65% in SOBs – which constrain credit growth to the private sector and hinder equity investments. This situation was aggravated during 2019, when retail loans in Hryvnia grew by 25% (mostly driven by consumer lending), while loans to enterprises declined by 8% (World Bank, 2020[2]).Therefore, resources of international capital markets or IFI are essential to secure financing of energy infrastructure.

Large energy companies have access to capital through the Ukrainian Exchange, which offers trading in a wide range of financial instruments, from equities to futures and options. Out of 41 issuing firms with listed equity securities on the Ukrainian Exchange, eight were energy companies, as of July 2021. This limited number of issuing firms demonstrates the room available to strengthen capital markets in Ukraine. The regulator of Ukraine's capital markets, the National Securities and Stock Market Commission, lacks financial and operational independence barring the country from becoming a signatory of the Multilateral Memorandum of Understanding Concerning Consultation and Cooperation and the Exchange of Information of the International Organisation of Securities Commissions.

To support Ukraine's progress in sustainable finance in line with international good practice, the National Securities and Stock Market Commission, sponsored by the International Finance Corporation, joined the Sustainable Banking Network (SBN) — a community of financial sector regulatory agencies and banking associations from 40 emerging markets committed to advancing sustainable finance. The SBN and IFC will work with the National Securities and Stock Market Commission to design a sustainable finance roadmap, develop a regulatory framework, and provide technical guidance on developing green and climate finance products as well as implementing good ESG standards and practices (IFC, 2020[3]).

To introduce new models of organised markets and financial instruments aligned with EU legislation, in June 2020 Ukraine's parliament adopted Law N. 738-IX "On Amendments to Certain Legislative Acts regarding the Simplification of Investment Attraction and Introduction of New Financial Instruments". The new regulation provides for the creation of green and infrastructure bonds on Ukraine's capital market, which can be used to finance improvements of Ukraine's energy infrastructure. It is expected that this law will increase the issuance of green bonds.

Green Eurobonds were issued in Ukraine for the first time by private Ukrainian energy company DTEK, before the adoption of the Law N.738-IX. In 2019, DTEK Renewables issued Green Eurobonds with a five-year maturity worth EUR 325 million. DTEK Renewables committed to use the proceeds for financing projects that are aimed at increasing the production, connection and distribution of renewable energy and related infrastructure. To ensure transparency and accountability, the company will use a public reporting system that details exactly how these funds are being distributed in relation to particular projects and describes the projects themselves. The RES crisis that has been affecting renewable energy producers in Ukraine since 2020 has raised concerns among investors who have flagged that DTEK Renewables might need to use green bond proceeds to fund its day-to-day operations, but the company declared that this would not be the case.

Project finance has been used to fund the construction of renewable energy projects in Ukraine, in particular for solar and wind power plants. According to the regulatory framework, the registration of the loan agreement contract for an energy infrastructure project between a Ukrainian borrower and a foreign lender is mandatory and should be done with the National Bank of Ukraine (NBU). This could be perceived as an additional obstacle by foreign lenders, and could weigh on the decision to lend, thus restricting access to finance for energy infrastructure projects in Ukraine. State-guaranteed loans and loans provided by IFIs are, however, exempted from this requirement, which facilitates transactions.

Foreign companies interested in investing in Ukraine's energy sector are also particularly sensitive to being able to repatriate their profits in different jurisdictions and in foreign currency. The Law "On Currency and Currency Transactions" that entered into effect in February of 2019 marked an overhaul of Ukraine's currency environment. The NBU abolished all restrictions related to the repatriation of dividends, allowing payments of dividends to a foreign investor's account in Ukraine or abroad without limits. The NBU also cancelled the mandatory sale of currency proceeds by businesses, removed the hryvnia reserve requirement against foreign currency purchases for banks, and allowed unlimited daily purchase of foreign currency by individuals through banks, financial institutions, and online banking. In September 2019, the NBU cancelled the monthly EUR 5 million limit for the repatriation of proceeds received by a foreign investor from selling shares of, or withdrawing investment from a Ukrainian company. These proceeds were previously capped following measures to restrict capital outflows from Ukraine by the NBU in 2014, but the NBU's current road map is aimed at removing currency restrictions starting from 20 July 2021.[2] Additionally, business will be able to purchase foreign currency in the amount of up to EUR 100 000 per day and will not need to present their reasons and commitments nor submit confirmation documents to the bank (National Bank of Ukraine, 2021[4]). The implementation of the Inclusive Framework on Base Erosion and Profit Shifting (BEPS) and the strengthening of general economic conditions should further liberalise currency flows.

As for projects including government or multilateral support, the Export-Import Bank of Ukraine, Ukreximbank provides substantial lending to energy infrastructure, especially to green energy projects. It is a 100% state-owned bank, acting as the sole financial agent of the Government of Ukraine, with respect to foreign loans, from IFIs borrowed or guaranteed by Ukraine. Ukreximbank was the first bank in the country to introduce energy efficiency and renewable energy financing, starting in 2007. It works closely with IFIs and foreign banks. Ukreximbank has provided financial support to energy investors in partnership with the Global Climate Partnership Fund, Energy Efficiency Fund, Nordic Investment Fund, Nordic Environment Finance Corporation, IBRD, EBRD, IFC, EIB, and KfW. Ukreximbank has executed over USD 500 million from IFIs under sustainable energy facilities and financed over 300 renewable energy and energy efficiency projects.

Sustainable energy credit lines administered by Ukreximbank are similar to more mainstream credit products, particularly on credit assessments and interest rates. The key difference lies in the eligibility criteria and the strict compliance that takes place during the application process. Borrowing from a sustainable energy facility offers the advantages of having access to technical assistance, such as energy audits and business plan support. Green credit lines also offer more generous grace periods, which are essential for the project being able to continue operating during difficult times. They proved, for example, to be particularly useful through the 2020 Renewable Energy crisis (see Chapter 2).

Local commercial banks have an important role to play in providing access to green energy infrastructure, but under the current market conditions in Ukraine, their involvement remains limited. This challenge can be partially explained by the dominant participation of state-owned banks, which account for 55% of banking sector assets. Additionally, lending rates are high, with 16.3% overall in national currency in 2020 (13% to businesses and 34% for households) (World Bank, 2020[2]). Hence, the high cost of funds and unresolved NPLs, at 49% of total loan portfolio at the end of 2019, remain the key impediments for commercial banks to achieve credit growth for the private sector. Having new actors entering the green energy finance market in Ukraine and opening the competition within the sector could possibly lead to better conditions for borrowers and lead to increased demand for green lending. Ukrgasbank provides a particularly good example as a bank that has excelled in granting green energy credit lines and now has the largest green energy investment portfolio in Ukraine (Box 5.1).

**Box 5.1. Ukrgasbank, a key bank to finance green energy infrastructure in Ukraine**

Ukrgasbank, a bank over which the Ministry of Finance has 95% ownership, has positioned itself as the first environmental bank in Ukraine. It provides services to over 46 000 large corporate and SME customers. The bank focuses on financing projects that contribute to the efficient use of resources, the reduction of $CO_2$ emissions and renewable energy development. Ukrgasbank, is currently the leader in financing clean energy facilities in Ukraine, with more than one third of green loans in its portfolio. The green projects financed by the bank contribute to a carbon emissions reduction of more than 1.4 million tons a year.

Since 2016, Ukrgasbank has collaborated with the IFC to develop policies and procedures for green loans and to identify target markets for green finance. Ukrgasbank also incorporated the IFC Performance Standards into green-loan agreements and introduced substantive positive changes to corporate governance practices. On February 2021, the IFC provided a EUR 30 million convertible loan to Ukrgasbank for green investments, including projects on renewable energy and energy efficiency.

Source: IFC, *IFC Supports Ukraine's Ukrgasbank to Boost Financing for Green Energy*, (2021), https://pressroom.ifc.org/all/pages/PressDetail.aspx?ID=26166 and *Ukrgasbank, at a glance*, (2021), /www.ukrgasbank.com/en/about_us/glance/

## Public Private Partnerships and Concessions as mechanisms to spur investments in energy infrastructure

Public-Private Partnerships (PPPs) are viable tools to develop energy infrastructure in Ukraine and their value for energy projects has exponentially increased from USD 24.5 million in 2017 to USD 1.4 billion in 2019. This major increase in the value of energy PPPs is a direct consequence of the 2016 reform to the Law on Public Private Partnerships, which was backed by the EBRD.

According to the EBRD Public-Private Partnership Assessment 2017-18 (EBRD, 2018[5]),which benchmarks the conformity of the local legal framework for PPPs with internationally accepted standards and best practices, Ukraine obtained a "high compliance" score for concession and non-concession PPPs legislation. The evaluation of the institutional framework indicator and the PPP business environment indicator nevertheless resulted in a "low compliance" score. Ukraine scored 68% in the bankability indicator, which serves to establish whether a country's legal framework incorporates fundamental requirements for making PPPs feasible for financing, as seen from a lender's perspective.

Ukraine PPP legislation is extensive, comprising one set of laws and regulations governing non-concession PPS and another set for concession PPPs (Box 5.2). According to the Law on Public-Private Partnerships, PPPs may be executed in four different forms: i) concession agreement, ii) property management agreement, iii) agreement on joint activities, and iv) mixed agreement. The Law on Public-Private Partnership determines that this contractual figure is applicable for the production, transport and supply of heat. Additionally, the law is applicable for the production, distribution and supply of natural gas, production, distribution and supply of electricity and production and implementation of energy-saving technologies. Nevertheless, the Law on PPP includes some burdens for investors. As determined in article 7, PPPs are not possible if a public partner is subject to a privatisation procedure. This limitation affects in practice the potential opportunities for private companies to direct their investments in energy infrastructure, as has been the case with the six SOE oblenergos that have been in the process of privatisation for the past ten years.

**Box 5.2. Concession and non-concession PPP regulatory framework for energy infrastructure projects**

**Non-concessions (governed by the Law on Public Private Partnerships)**

- Relevant regulations for energy infrastructure include: -Resolution of the CMU No. 384 On Certain Issues of Organisation of Public Private Partnership;
- Order of the Ministry of Economic No. 255 On Certain Issues of Carrying out Analysis of Public Private Partnership Effectiveness;
- Resolution of the CMU No. 232 Methodology of Identification, Assessment and Management of Risks related to Public Private Partnership.

**Concessions (governed by the Law on Concessions)**

- Relevant regulations for energy infrastructure include:
  Law on Peculiarities of Lease and Concession of Municipal Heating, Water Supply and Water Drain Facilities;
- Law on Peculiarities of Lease and Concession of State-owned Fuel and Energy Facilities;
- Resolution of the CMU No. 642 Regulation on Concession Tenders, Conclusion of Concession Contracts in Relation to State and Municipal Property.

Source: (EBRD, 2018[5]).

International experience shows that PPP legislation plays a major role in attracting private companies to the infrastructure sector. Although there has been an advancement in the PPP regulatory framework, governmental authorities responsible for implementing PPPs appear to be insufficiently trained and consultations with investors held in the framework of this Review have suggested that local businesses are largely unaware of the advantages and the potential that can come from PPPs, generating low award statistics. Ukraine could follow the example of Costa Rica and Mexico, OECD countries that, in collaboration with the Inter-American Development Bank, provide continuous training to officials involved in PPPs, covering topics from project selection criteria, contract management, prioritisation in infrastructure development and fiscal impacts of the projects (Interfax-Ukraine, 2020[6]). According to central and local authorities in Ukraine, as of January 2020, only ten PPP contracts were being implemented in the energy sector. Eight PPPs were implemented for the production and transport of natural gas and three for the generation of electricity (Figure 5.1).

**Figure 5.1. PPPs in Ukraine's energy sector (as of February 2021)**

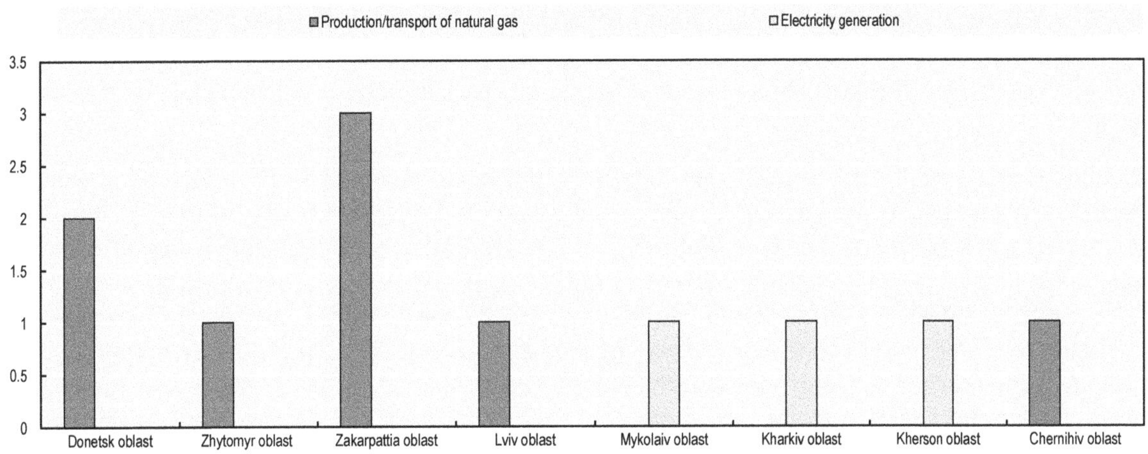


Note: The left axis refers to the number of PPPs.
Source: *Monitoring of PPP implementation in Ukraine*, 2020, (Ministry of Economy of Ukraine, 2021[7])

Ukraine adopted a new Law on Concession N. 155-IX in October 2019 that provides both local and foreign investors with new opportunities, ranging from converting leases into concessions to providing additional guarantees for creditors. The new Law on Concessions establishes a framework based on international best practice to attract private investment in infrastructure and is in compliance with EU standards and regulations pertaining to concessions. Key enhancements of the new Law include: (i) a transparent procedure for selection of the concessionaire on a competitive basis, (ii) clear ownership control, (iii) provisions to enable bankability such as compensation in case of early termination, step-in rights, and direct agreement between project lenders, concessionaires, and grantors, (iv) simplified procedures for licences and permits and for allocating land plots, (v) the possibility of dispute resolution by international commercial or investment arbitration, and (vi) a clear mechanism for monitoring fulfilment of the concession agreement.

The new Law on Concessions is aligned with the PPP Law, including provisions for rigorous economic appraisal of project proposals. An innovative figure of the law is the step-in right, a procedure for changing a concessionaire upon application of the creditor in case of improper fulfilment of obligations. To operationalise the step-in right, in July 2020, the CMU adopted Decree 541 “On approval of the Procedure for replacement of a private partner (concessionaire) under an agreement concluded within a public-private partnership (concession agreement)”. The regulation of step-in rights is a relevant improvement by the government to strengthen the PPP regulatory framework and to incorporate best international practices into the local regulation. In addition, the Concession Law incorporates practices that aim to benefit investors, such as a simplified procedure for obtaining property rights for land plots that are required for concession activities and a tighter deadline within which to conduct the selection of a concessionaire. The Law follows the principles of international law by allowing disputes under a concession agreement to be solved via mediation, non-binding expert assessment, international commercial arbitration or investment arbitration based in Ukraine or abroad (see chapter 4). The Law on Concessions specifies the legal, financial and organisational basis of concession projects aimed at modernisation of infrastructure and improvement of quality of important public services. However, it does not apply to projects on the search of minerals, exploration and extraction of mineral resources.

The Law, which is aligned with EU standards and regulations pertaining to concessions, will enable Ukraine to continue to shift its infrastructure investment toward a more climate-friendly and green path, in line with its commitments to the EU as outlined in its Association Agreement. The new law includes specific provisions that incentivise energy efficiency in concession investments. In particular, Article 8 of the law specifies limits on the amount of losses and thermal energy per unit of service provided for heating, water supply and wastewater disposal facilities, which must be part of the terms of the concessions' agreement. With appropriate strengthening of the environmental assessment system and enforcement mechanisms, foreign and private investors will be expected to increase social responsibility awareness and introduce climate-friendly and environmentally sound technologies and practices that support climate adaptation and mitigation.

Although the efforts of Ukraine to adopt new regulatory frameworks covering PPPs and concessions are commendable, it is important for the country to transpose the EU Regulation 347/2013 through the Law on Projects of Highest National Priority in the Field of Energy and to designate the national competent authority. The draft foresees that the Cabinet of Ministers of Ukraine acts as the national competent authority, with the possibility of transferring its power to the so-called Interdepartmental Commission. By adopting this law, Ukraine will comply with its obligations to adopt the EU acquis as a Contracting Party of the Energy Community and will benefit from EU technical support in the development of strategic infrastructure projects related to the synchronisation of Ukraine with the Continental European power system, as well as oil and gas pipeline projects.

## Property rights for energy infrastructure projects

For the adequate implementation of energy infrastructure projects, it is essential to ensure the availability of relevant construction permits and land ownership rights. To ensure real property rights and the unification of urban planning and land management documentation in one publicly available electronic document, in July 2020, Ukraine's parliament adopted the Law N. 2280 "On Amendments to the Land Code of Ukraine and Other Legislative Acts on Land Use Planning", as mentioned in Chapter 3. The Law, as amended, allows property owners to determine the use of their land as long as the use is relevant to the functional destined purpose of the territory defined by the approved land use planning. Establishing and changing the type of intended use of the land plot by its owner does not require documentation on land management and decision-making by local authorities. In addition, the law determines that during the privatisation of land, communication with local governments shall be done through the interface of the Public Cadastral Map, making the process simpler and more transparent. In April 2021, further amendments to the land code were adopted in order to facilitate access to land resources of the population and business, cancel unnecessary permits and duplication of procedures, introduce an independent control of land management documentation, open and make data publicly available, and reduce the cost and length of procedures related to land management, as well as reduce the risks of bribery and corruption.

Since 2019, the State Cadastre Service has set up an online map showing land use by energy enterprises. It has been improved over 2019 and 2020 to include additional features, such as showing different layers (crops, mineral deposits, and oil and gas wells, among others). Full digitalisation entails every land plot being assessed and stored in an electronic database, thereby enhancing openness and transparency of data. The updated information can be used during the development and approval of land management documentation in terms of determining possible restrictions on the use of land.

To foster the participation of private investors in energy infrastructure projects, the government adopted a reform allowing investors to own the land used for the development of energy projects. The Law "On lands for the energy sector and legal regime of special zones for energy objects" adopted in 2011 foresees that state- and municipally-owned land may be transferred to private owners who develop energy projects. The law is then approved by the state executive bodies or the relevant local authorities, following the procedures described by the Land Code. Moreover, energy objects may be built on all land plots without changing the destined purpose of the land.

Article 116 of the Land Code (version as of May 2021) determines that legal and natural persons may acquire property rights of state and municipal land plots on the basis of auctions, as is set out in the Land

Code. However, the same Code waives the auction requirement for Public-Private Partnership projects for the construction and maintenance of energy infrastructure.

For the construction, location and operation of electricity or heat transmission facilities, land plots of all forms of ownership, under an agreement with the owner or user of the land plot, may also establish permanent or temporary land easements without changing the purpose of these land plots. Therefore, energy investors have the rights to own, lease and use land plots on the basis of the Land Code and the specialised law on land for the energy sector.

Most of the equipment of power plants operating on renewable energy sources can be located only on land plots that have the purpose of "electricity industry land". As an exception, electricity transmission facilities (overhead and cable transmission lines, transformer substations, distribution points and devices) may be located on land of any purpose. Any other use of land plots for electricity production (with a purpose other than "electricity industry lands") is only possible if the land is repurposed. It should be borne in mind that Ukraine has a moratorium on repurposing most agricultural land, which is essential to advance biofuels. Another problem that affects investors, as highlighted in chapter 3 of this *Review*, is that foreign companies (Ukrainian legal entities with foreign investment) are not authorised to own agricultural land. Any acquisition of state and municipal land by foreign legal entities is also subject to approval by the Cabinet of Ministers.

## Transparency in energy infrastructure

In Ukraine, much remains to be done in the field of transparency and anti-corruption in energy infrastructure. Corruption remains an everyday reality in Ukraine's energy sector and this includes infrastructure projects as previously highlighted in this Review. The wide range of institutions and stakeholders involved in every phase of energy infrastructure projects, and their vulnerabilities to different types of misconduct, have exposed projects to acute risks of corruption. To mitigate those risks, fostering a culture of transparency and openness is essential in order to mobilise citizens and stakeholders against corruption practices. In recent years, several initiatives have sought to address this issue.

An example of a private initiative aimed at raising awareness and providing solutions to these issues is the "Infrastructure Transparency Initiative" (CoST), developed in Ukraine with the support of the government and the World Bank. CoST, which has been implemented by Ukraine since 2015, addresses corruption risks in the infrastructure sector. It focuses on four core features that are especially relevant for energy infrastructure in Ukraine: disclosure, assurance, multi-stakeholder working and social accountability. More specifically, it offers a multi-stakeholder approach to strengthening governance in the infrastructure sector through improved transparency, stakeholder engagement and accountability. This approach enables coordinated discussions and decisions related to energy infrastructure, ensuring that private, bilateral or multilateral investors can feel confident about investing in Ukraine and that their perspective is discussed at the adequate level of government. Considering the complexity of energy infrastructure projects, investors typically seek a particularly high level of transparency to minimise risks and select the best value-for-money outcomes. Consequently, private and public infrastructure investments can increase in value and quality with higher transparency, which is particularly useful for stimulating investments in REs and energy efficiency projects.

CoST regularly publishes assurance reports to monitor the achievements and efforts made. As detailed in the CoST Ukraine Sixth Assurance Report (2019)[3], Ukraine is almost fully compliant with the Open Contracting for Infrastructure Data Standard (2018)[4], that is used to guide what data and information should be disclosed at each stage of the project cycle. Ukraine has also enjoyed a successful transition from a paper-based system to a modern one aligned with the Open Contracting Data Standard (2017)[5], which defines a common data model to enable the disclosure of data and documents at all stages of the contracting process. The main gaps identified by the Open Contracting Standards are related to citizen participation and information disclosure. In particular, Ukraine obtains the lowest scores in the indicators assessing the formalisation of citizens' participation opportunities and online mechanisms, as well as the disclosure of information relative to the supervision of infrastructure contract procurement and implementation.

In addition, as further discussed in chapter 7 of this *Review*, the Government of Ukraine has been actively involved in increasing transparency and anti-corruption practices, starting from the elaboration and implementation of strategic plans addressing the issue of corruption in general, that have had positive impacts on the issue of widespread corruption and lack of transparency in the energy infrastructure sector. One of the key milestones in this area includes the launch in June 2020 of the National Anti-Corruption Strategy for 2020-2024 and the adoption at first reading by parliament on 5 November 2020 of the draft Law "On the Principles of State Anti-Corruption Policy for 2020-2024", which at the time of drafting of this *Review* was awaiting its second reading. The draft has been strongly supported by international partners and is seen as filling many gaps identified in the previous National Anti-Corruption Strategy for 2014-2017 (see chapter 7). The government is involved in increasing transparency in the energy sector by working with international partners, such as USAID through the Energy Security Project (2018-2023) and the Energy Sector Transparency initiative (2019-2023)[6]. These initiatives aim to help government agencies and the energy regulator meet EU energy acquis requirements, establish competitive energy markets, and reduce opportunities for corruption in the energy sector. Transposition of EU regulation, such as through the draft Law on Projects of the Highest National Priority in the Field of Energy, which transposes EU regulation 347/2013, also has positive impacts in terms of transparency and anti-corruption practices.

These strategic plans and efforts have led to material outcomes, such as the creation of a comprehensive anti-corruption institutional infrastructure in Ukraine, or the upgrade of procurement processes. As is further discussed in chapter 7 of this *Review*, the anti-corruption system is composed of the National Anti-Corruption Bureau (NABU), the Specialised Anti-Corruption Prosecutor's Office (SAPO), the High Anti-Corruption Court (HACC), the National Agency for Corruption Prevention (NACP) and the National Agency on Recovery and Asset Management (ARMA) that enforce relevant laws, establish preventative mechanisms, investigate, prosecute and adjudicate corruption cases. Separately, and particularly relevant for the infrastructure sector, the government has implemented the ProZorro platform to ensure fair procurement processes (see chapter 2).

Corruption unfortunately exists in all sectors and its consequences are universally negative, but corruption in infrastructure is particularly harmful for transition economies. Despite increasing awareness and decisive steps that have been taken to decrease corruption and improve transparency in Ukraine, including in Ukraine's energy sector, on-the-ground observations point to the persistence of corruption. With the COVID-19 pandemic putting health, social and economic strains on an already fragile global economy, mitigating corruption in infrastructure is more critical now than ever. The perception of corruption also has reputational risks for governments, undermining public trust and disincentivising public-private co-operation with quality contractors.

## Specific infrastructure investment: the example of heat transmission

A key sector where Ukraine would greatly benefit from achieving energy efficiency gains is heating. Heating in Ukraine is mostly centralised, due to the Soviet legacy, and the lack of investment to update or maintain this outdated heating infrastructure generates significant energy and monetary losses. Investment to modernise heating transmission and distribution networks, as well as to improve building insulation would create immediate gains for the government and municipalities in terms of energy efficiency and financial proceeds, while contributing to wider goals such as the decrease of GHG emissions and of energy consumption per capita.

Ukraine has 33 122 kms of heat transmission and distribution networks. Transmission pipelines total 3 500 kms and distribution pipelines are owned by municipalities and total 20 800 km. Additionally, there are 12 400 kms of industrial pipeline networks. Despite the large heating network in the country, district heating is characterised by inefficient and outdated technologies, with assets close to or beyond the end of their design lifespans, considerable energy losses and inadequate maintenance of the infrastructure. As an inheritance of the Soviet era, most boilers have low efficiency factors, resulting in heat losses of 10% to 15%. Losses in the distribution network, mainly due to leaks and lack of pipe insulation, are estimated at around 17%.

Breakdowns are also frequent in Ukraine's district heating systems, estimated at more than 1.6 breakdowns per km of network in operation, which is approximately ten times higher than in well-maintained modern systems. Moreover, 70% of the delivered heat is lost in the end-use phase due to insufficient building insulation and the absence of adaptability of heat delivery to consumer requirements. By the end of December 2017, the installation of heat meters in buildings had increased to 90% from 32% in 2014[7].

Government actions do not always align with the need to modernise heating infrastructure, and the overall energy infrastructure. For example, Naftogaz, which provides gas to district heating companies, indicates in its 2020 annual report[8] that it was forced to pay more than 90% of its profit to the national budget as dividends for two years in a row. This results from a decision by the Cabinet of Ministers of Ukraine to raise the mandatory payment of SOEs to the State from 75% to 90% of their net profit in 2019[9]. Naftogaz perceives this requirement as hampering its investment capabilities because it prevents the company from using retained profits to invest, and obliges it to raise external finance not necessarily on the most favourable terms.

## Outlook and policy recommendations

Investment in energy infrastructure is essential for providing the country with reliable, green and affordable supply of energy. The Energy Strategy of Ukraine until 2035 envisions that the government shall invest by itself, from the State Budget to develop energy infrastructure, not more than 5-10% of the general amount of investments. Hence, there is a gap in energy infrastructure investment that can only be filled with the participation of private investors.

Energy infrastructure is financed from different sources: by private investors like foreign and domestic corporations investing in renewable energy power plants, by SOEs, for example, Naftogaz in hydrocarbons extraction, storage, transport, and supply, or Energoatom building and reconstructing NPPs. In Ukraine, companies, both public and private, have access to capital via banks by means of loans or guarantees, IFIs, or capital markets, by means of bonds issue. However, foreign and domestic investors of energy infrastructure project still face challenges in accessing domestic long-term financing at affordable rates.

- **Improve market conditions for commercial banks to finance a higher share of energy infrastructure** by adopting policies that enable competition between commercial and state-owned banks. Reinforce projects' screening by lenders to avoid the very high proportion of non-performing loans that in turn increase banks' profitability and widen access to affordable credit.
- **Foster the development of green and climate financial products**, such as green bonds, that comply with best environmental, social and governance standards and practices.
- **Strengthen institutional capacity of the governmental agencies that participate in** PPPs by providing training to officers and develop awareness-raising tools directed at investors.
- **Establish prioritisation of PPP projects by the government** in order to send clear signals to investors and outline long-term relevant goals in PPP area. In addition, Ukraine should evaluate

the possibility of allowing PPPs in SOEs that are in the process of being privatised, in order to mobilise private capital in energy infrastructure.

- **Finalise the pending reform on land and evaluate the restriction on foreign companies to acquire agricultural land**, especially if Ukraine would like to activate the biofuel industry.
- **Continue implementing measures to enhance transparency and tackle corruption in the energy sector** by using technological tools in infrastructure energy projects such as CoST, and align citizen participation and information disclosure with the Open Contracting and Open Data Standards.
- **Advance the efforts to upgrade district heating and open investment opportunities to private companies** by scaling up the capital available for energy efficiency and DH modernisation projects with further potential to attract FDI.
- **Transpose EU Regulation 347/2013** through the Law on Projects of Highest National Priority in the Field of Energy.
- In collaboration with IFIs or development agencies, **create and offer continuous trainings to officials involved in PPPs**, covering topics from project selection criteria, contract management, prioritisation in infrastructure development and fiscal impacts of infrastructure projects, focusing on energy efficiency and renewable energy.

## Notes

[1] IPR Questionnaire, answers provided by the Government of Ukraine.

[2] Resolution of the Board of the National Bank of 13 July 2021 No 80 on Approval of Amendments to the Regulations on protection measures and determination of the procedure for carrying out certain operations in foreign currency.

[3] CoST Ukraine Sixth Assurance Report, 2019, https://infrastructuretransparency.org/resource/cost-ukraine-sixth-assurance-report/.

[4] The Open Contracting Data Standard (OCDS) has many stakeholders: governments (procuring entities, monitoring & oversight authorities, project managers and policy makers), the private sector, and civil society organisations. The needs and interests of these stakeholders, as publishers and users of the data, are varied. As OCDS develops over time, with updated versions and new features, it is important that a diverse group of stakeholders are engaged in the process. See more at https://standard.open-contracting.org/latest/en/.

[5] The Open Contracting Partnership, CoST - the Infrastructure Transparency Initiative - and Open Data Services Co-operative are working together to document how the Open Contracting Data Standard, and additional standardised data models, can be used to represent, share and analyse all the information required under the CoST Infrastructure Data Standard. See more at https://standard.open-contracting.org/infrastructure/latest/en/.

[6] www.usaid.gov/ukraine/energy-energy-security.

[7] www.iea.org/reports/ukraine-energy-profile/energy-security.

[8] Naftogaz 2020 Annual Report, www.naftogaz.com/files/Zvity/Annual_report_Naftogaz_2020_EN_28_04_2021_3.pdf.

[9] https://interfax.com.ua/news/economic/583737.html (Russian).

## References


EBRD (2018), *PPPs/concessions sector assessment 2017/2018*, https://www.ebrd.com/what-we-do/sectors/legal-reform/ppp-concessions/sector-assessment.html. [5]

IFC (2020), *IFC Partners with Ukraine's National Securities and Stock Market Commission to Boost Green Finance*, https://pressroom.ifc.org/all/pages/PressDetail.aspx?ID=24687. [3]

Interfax-Ukraine (2020), *"Investors in renewable energy to be forced to sue Guaranteed Buyer for non-payments under feed-in tariffs – market player"*, https://en.interfax.com.ua/news/press-conference/667637.html. [6]

Ministry of Economy of Ukraine (2021), *Public-private partnership projects, Monitoring of PPP implementation in Ukraine 2020*, https://www.me.gov.ua/Documents/Detail?lang=en-GB&id=6aab1657-215d-46f8-8d93-46961e76fd6f&title=MonitoringOfPppImplementationInUk. [7]

National Bank of Ukraine (2021), *NBU to Lift Gradually the Restriction for Businesses to Purchase FX against Commitment*, https://bank.gov.ua/en/news/all/natsionalniy-bank-postupovo-rozshiryuvatime-mojlivosti-biznesu-z-kupivli-valyuti-ne-lishe-pid-zobovyazannya. [4]

World Bank (2020), *Ukraine - First Economic Recovery Development Policy Loan*, https://www.worldbank.org/en/news/loans-credits/2020/06/26/ukraine-first-economic-recovery-development-policy-loan. [2]

World Economic Forum (2019), *The Global Competitiveness Report*, http://www3.weforum.org/docs/WEF_TheGlobalCompetitivenessReport2019.pdf. [1]

# 6 Investment Promotion and Facilation

This chapter analyses investment promotion and facilitation measures and policies in Ukraine, particularly those aiming to foster private sector participation in the energy sector. It examines the overarching institutional framework for investment promotion and facilitation, with a specific focus on the role and activities of UkraineInvest, and highlights key reforms and measures implemented by the government to attract foreign investment in the energy industry. It also identifies remaining challenges and provides recommendations to address them.

## Introduction

Investment Promotion Agencies (IPAs) play an essential role in promoting and facilitating investments in specific sectors. IPAs typically support the attraction of foreign investors through their core functions of image building, investment generation, facilitation and aftercare (including dedicated MNE-SME matchmaking programmes), and policy advocacy. Since 2016, the Ukraine Investment Promotion Office "UkraineInvest" has been a key tool of the government's efforts to attract MNEs to the energy sector, providing foreign companies with relevant information on market access and promoting investment bringing advanced technologies in the power, heating and hydrocarbons domestic industries.

Since its inception in 2016, UkraineInvest has implemented a sector-specific work programme to unlock investment opportunities in natural gas, renewable energy and oil & gas. This programme has been aligned with the national objective to strengthen Ukraine's energy security and to improve the investment climate in the country. In this context, the country has launched programmes to facilitate investments and to advance administrative facilitation to retain investors in the country, including recently the 2021 National Strategy to Increase Foreign Direct Investment in Ukraine, which was elaborated with support from the USAID Competitive Economy Program. The renewable energy sector crisis has nevertheless posed challenges to the government and to Ukraine's attractiveness to investors.

## Investment Promotion

### *The institutional set-up: UkraineInvest and the consolidation of an investment promotion agency (IPA)*

As discussed earlier in this *Review*, Ukraine's legal framework for investment is conducive to a general openness to foreign investments. In Ukraine, the 1958 Convention on the Recognition and Enforcement of Foreign Arbitral Awards (New York Convention) entered in force in 1961, as did the 1965 Convention on the Settlement of Investment Disputes between States and Nationals of Other States (ICSID) in 2000. Despite some restrictions mainly in the agriculture, transport and real estate sectors, Ukraine guarantees protection from expropriations in its Constitution, and defined as early as 1996 the conditions and procedures associated with it in the Foreign Investment Regimes Act. Over the years, Ukraine has signed 17 free trade agreements with a total of 47 countries, as well as additional international investment agreements with partner countries, to provide substantive protection to foreign investors.

Recently, the 2016 Association Agreement between the EU and Ukraine, including the Deep and Comprehensive Free Trade Area (DCFTA), has provided an anchor for strengthening the institutional framework and modernising activities, including with respect to investment promotion. This impulse has also been supported by the OECD *Declaration on International Investment and Multinational Enterprises*, which, as noted earlier, Ukraine joined in 2017.

Amid the modernisation effort, Ukraine established its Investment Promotion Agency (IPA), UkraineInvest, in 2016. Initially formed as a consultative body reporting to the Prime Minister, UkraineInvest has been transformed into an independent state body led by a supervisory board in 2018 (OECD, 2020[1]). UkraineInvest has a dedicated board to supervise its operations, which includes public sector representatives and independent experts. As part of its mission to help identify investment opportunities, guide investors and provide support to resolve systemic issues investors may face, the agency recognises the particular importance of Ukraine's energy independence and therefore emphasises its support towards the development of oil, gas and renewable energy sources (UkraineInvest, 2020[2]). Energy is designated by UkraineInvest in its 1+4 sector strategy as one of the top priority sectors in terms of investment promotion and facilitation efforts, along with innovation technologies, agribusiness, manufacturing and infrastructure (UkraineInvest, 2020[3]). Investment promotion and facilitation measures are conducted in coordination with UkraineInvest and executive authorities, such as the Ministry of Economy and the Ministry of Energy. Currently, UkraineInvest actively participates in the development of sector-specific programmes to attract, retain and incentivise private investors in the energy sector.

While UkraineInvest offers services to potential investors, e.g. licence and construction approval, assistance with utilities and legal issues, business match-making and cluster programmes, as well as aftercare services, it does not function as an effective one-stop service centre since it does not provide a window into several administrative procedures that are necessary to start and run a business (OECD, 2021[4]). Agencies that serve as one-stop-shop for foreign investors play a key role in facilitating investments. Ukraine may in this regard follow the example of agencies such as the Nigerian Ministry of Power and the Investment Promotion Commission, as these government agencies are in the process of establishing a Green Energy Investment Platform that will function as a one-stop-shop for renewable energy and energy efficiency investment projects. It is worth mentioning that Ukraine already has an easily accessible online investment platform"UAMAP"[1], which is an online interactive map providing up-to-date information on opportunities in Ukraine's energy sector and promoting energy efficiency and renewable investment.

The investment promotion activities implemented by UkraineInvest in the energy sector are aligned with the Energy Strategy of Ukraine until 2035 (ESU), which explicitly stipulates investment attractiveness as a key objective to achieve the objectives of the ESU as part of the overall strategy to build a technically reliable, safe, economically efficient and environmentally friendly energy sector to guarantee the improvement of social well-being[2].

The ESU articulates the objective of improving investment attractiveness as hinging on the fulfilment of six priorities. Namely, it mentions:

- The implementation of EU acquis requirements in the legislation regulating activities;
- The alignment of transparent and strategic decision-making processes with established long-term goals;
- The creation of conditions for the development of innovative solutions and technologies;
- The promotion of a competitive environment and uninterrupted access to markets and existing infrastructure;
- The stability and predictability of the investment attraction policy;
- The targeting of new international investors through a communication policy promoting their entrance to the national market.

As a result, UkraineInvest's investment promotion activities are designed to contribute to enhancing efficiency in the domestic energy sector, as well as to improving its safety and competitiveness. For example, UkraineInvest actively promotes new investment opportunities enabled by recent reforms in the energy sector, that are aimed at increasing the role of renewable sources of energy or at deregulating the hydrocarbon sector, with the launch of open auctions of special permits for oil and gas (UkraineInvest, 2020[3]).

With the launch in July 2021 of the National Strategy to Increase Foreign Direct Investment in Ukraine elaborated with support from the USAID Competitive Economy Program, Ukraine continues to affirm its commitment towards the international investment community. This Strategy, developed at the request of the government by Ernst and Young (EY) in consultation with the Office of the National Investment Council, the Ministry of Economy of Ukraine, and UkraineInvest, provides recommendations to attract investments into promising sectors of the Ukrainian economy. It is built around both cross-sectoral (such as privatisation, export promotion, education, and digital transformation) and sectoral incentives to increase foreign direct investments through the relocation of production facilities or the start of new activities in Ukraine. Moreover, the Strategy is divided into 3 sections: a macro view of the state of affairs regarding FDI, sectoral analytical documents and the proposed Action Plan and Vision until 2030 (EY, 2021[5]).

### *UkraineInvest's contribution to enhancing the overall investment climate*

Ukraine has substantially improved its investment climate over the past few years, climbing 48 places to 64th out of 190 countries in the World Bank's Ease of Doing Business ranking between 2014 and 2020 (World Bank, 2020[6]). The Association Agreement and the Deep and Comprehensive Free Trade Area with the EU also benefit the overall investment climate through the gradual alignment of national laws and regulations to European legislation.

In 2015, the OECD was already warning about the number of public monopolies in Ukraine that restrict private investment in oil and gas pipeline transport, distribution and transmission of electricity, railways, supply and distribution of water and heating, the burial of domestic waste and the production of ethyl alcohol (OECD, 2015[7]). However, the progress made by the government in addressing the concern of public monopolies has supported more openness regarding FDI. Ukraine still applies some restrictions on foreign investments but its overall OECD FDI Regulatory Restrictiveness Index (a measure of statutory restrictions on foreign direct investment) as of December 2019 was higher than the OECD average, and slightly higher than the average of non-OECD countries (OECD, 2018[8]), although Ukraine scored better than the OECD average in the electricity sector.

The investment climate has particularly benefitted from laws addressing specific issues ranging from technical barriers to trade (Law on authorised economic at customs, Law on the joint transit regime and introduction of the national electronic transit system operator) to obstacles to investment such as in the energy (Law on unbundling of Naftogaz), infrastructure (Concession law) or financial services sectors ("Split" law, Law on protection of the rights of financial services consumers). In addition, Ukraine is set to privatise more than one thousand state-owned entities in the coming years, which creates opportunities for investors. Among the key clauses stipulated in the Privatisation Law, the possibility of dispute settlement by means of international arbitration and the possibility of concluding sales agreement under English law demonstrate the efforts made by Ukraine to improve its business climate and attractiveness to foreign investors (UkraineInvest, 2020[3]).

Ukraine has been promoting its openness to attract foreign investment through a number of recent bilateral actions and reforms. Notably, the Law on State Support of Investment Projects with Significant Investments signed by the President in February 2021 will provide investment project incentives amounting to over EUR 20 million and creating at least 80 jobs, the incentives of which will include state support for up to 30% of the investment made or exemption from taxes and import duties relief. Projects in the energy sector are, however, not specifically targeted by this Law, which primarily targets the manufacturing, mining, recycling of minerals, waste recycling and transport sectors, among others.

Examples of recent promotion actions implemented at the bilateral level include the Memorandum of Understanding signed between UkraineInvest and German institutions in March 2021 to establish the "Ukrainian German Digital Partnership" to facilitate greater investment into Ukraine's tech industry. In January 2021, UkraineInvest's Executive Director and the French MEDEF International's CEO also signed a MoU to strengthen and diversify the existing co-operation between Ukraine's IPA and the French private business association.

Despite reforms and the promotion of a positive image, the existence of corruption and vested interest that has characterised Ukraine over the past few years undermines investment promotion efforts. The government attitude towards foreign investment has been varying between a business-friendly agenda encouraged by international partners and the reluctance of local oligarchs and resistance from some key national institutions. The issue of widespread corruption and perceived corruption represents another key obstacle to investment promotion through its direct deterrence effects for foreign investors, but also through the political instability it creates, as was demonstrated by the constitutional obstacles faced by the President when seeking to consolidate anti-corruption institutions.

Ukraine is also the sole member of the Eastern Partnership without special economic zones (SEZ), following their closure in 2016. Ukraine established a legal regime for SEZs in 1998; but a 2005 law abolished both the customs and tax preferences granted to these zones, and zones were formally closed in 2016 (OECD, 2020[9]). Over 50 industrial parks are operating in Ukraine under the 2012 Law on Industrial Parks, which sets out the legal framework without providing special fiscal treatment to residents.

### *National image-building*

Supported by international lenders and partners, Ukraine has made considerable efforts to break with the bureaucratic and opaque culture that has characterised its national business environment. Despite setbacks often illustrating the resistance of local elites who use their inner circles of influence to weaken the pace of modernisation, Ukraine's actions have followed an overall positive trend, strengthening its image as an attractive destination for investment.

Aware of the perception of high risks among foreign investors who seek to enter the Ukrainian market, UkraineInvest has focused its communication strategy on building a positive national image. regular report updates and guides for investors highlight success stories and name the large companies that have already made the decision to invest in Ukraine as a way to crowd in additional investors of all sizes. The government's aspiration to advance the reform agenda in co-operation with international partners often supports the strategic investment promotion activities undertaken by UkraineInvest, which are reinforced by the guidance of its supervisory board.

However, the reality faced by foreign investors when prospecting or entering the Ukrainian market is often challenging. As highlighted earlier in this *Review*, the legal environment and rule of law remain rather weak in Ukraine, marked by the low capacity of the legal system, lengthy and costly arbitration processes to settle commercial disputes and political interference in courts. This is particularly true in the energy sector, which has historically represented a large source of revenues for the state and where modernisation has been hampered by the prevalence of internal power struggles, non-existent competition and an opaque culture.

Among the main reforms, the implementation of Naftogaz unbundling, the Law on Electricity Market and the privatisation drive launched by the government aim to strengthen the business climate for investors by promoting competition and lowering corruption, which is particularly widespread in state-owned enterprises. UkraineInvest emphasises the importance of these reforms and their positive expected outcomes such as the creation of jobs, the attraction of investment and the generation of additional revenues for the state through direct sale proceeds and future tax revenues from new businesses (UkraineInvest, 2021[10]). As described in Box 6.1, an effective communication strategy is crucial for ensuring the success of the reforms.

### Box 6.1. Communication strategy as a mechanism to deploy major energy reforms

International experience has shown that communication is critical to the success of major energy reforms. If an effective communication programme is not implemented before, during, and after reform measures go into effect, it is difficult to earn the public's trust and foster understanding of the political decisions that underpin the reform. A well-researched communication programme with informational, attitudinal, and behavioural objectives can enhance the effectiveness of reform.

An effective communication campaign involves mapping key stakeholders, using outreach and two-way dialogue with citizens, conducting opinion research, consulting with stakeholders, creating and testing compelling messages that build awareness of reform benefits, assigning credible messengers, identifying good channels of communication, coordinating within government, setting strategic goals, and communicating consistently with evidence-based messages. Public reactions to reform programmes are highly contextual and dynamic. A well-informed public understands the rationale for reform and greatly improves the likelihood of success.

Ukraine rolled out a communication strategy in support of stiff tariff hikes. The rollout included a 30-second public service announcement that aired on 19 TV stations across Ukraine and appeared on 15 government websites. The announcement was rooted in a detailed understanding of public perceptions; the key messages reflected the public's concern. The effort included involving local media in major cities and making them aware of the energy sector status.

Source: (Heather Worley et al., 2018[11])

### Box 6.2. Chile's National Green Hydrogen Strategy and Diplomacy to attract foreign investment

In November 2020, the Government of Chile published its National Green Hydrogen Strategy (Strategy). The Strategy aims at positioning Chile as a global leader in hydrogen production and export. To attain this goal, the Strategy delineates three phases: (i) 2020-2025 for a domestic ramp up and export preparation; (ii) 2025-2030 to consolidate domestic market and develop the export markets; and (iii) 2030 and beyond to export to global markets. The Strategy builds upon the country's commitment to become a carbon-neutral country, the high-quality and abundant renewable resources available in the country, and its demonstrated capability of enabling private investment to deploy large-scale clean energy projects on a competitive basis.

The comparative advantages of Chile for the development of a green hydrogen economy are evident throughout the hydrogen value chain, and offer multiple opportunities for lessons learned and replicability in Latin America. Chile has substantial renewable energy sources and a vast potential to continue expanding them, which strongly complements the development of green hydrogen. Chile has a vast potential for green hydrogen production, of over 160 million tons per year, which correlates with over 1.75 TW of untapped renewable electricity generation potential mapped in the country. The country also has strong potential to develop green hydrogen for complex industrial sectors, including mining, transport, maritime and fishery, transport and heating sectors, which can additionally support a reduction in pollution levels. Developing green hydrogen in Chile can become a leading reference for other countries, as well as becoming an entry point for private investment in the Latin American region.

The government considers the development of the green hydrogen industry a critical enabler to reach its goal of carbon neutrality by 2050 and deliver a socially just energy transition. In 2020, Chile updated its Nationally Determined Contribution and set a firm commitment to achieve Carbon Neutrality by 2050. The government is strongly committed to developing the green hydrogen industry as a critical enabler to reach its goal of carbon neutrality, because green hydrogen could help reduce up to 21% of the country's GHG emissions. The Chilean High-Level Advisory Committee for Green Hydrogen has noted that green hydrogen has the potential to provide for 18% of energy demand, represent a market of USD 2.5 trillion and create about 30 million jobs by 2050. As an example, Chile considers green hydrogen to be a strategic industry that can foster a just transition in the context of the planned closure of coal-fired thermal plants.

Chile's nascent green hydrogen industry could also contribute to a more resilient and sustainable post-COVID-19 economic recovery. Developing green hydrogen infrastructure and projects in Chile could help to stimulate the economy in the post-COVID-19 recovery period, as it would enable new green local employment opportunities and building back better.

In a bid to tap the potential that green hydrogen development represents for Chile, the Ministry of Foreign Affairs and the Ministry of Energy have launched the "green hydrogen diplomacy" strategy, an initiative that, through openness to foreign investment, seeks to transform Chile into a global centre for green hydrogen research, development, production and export. According to the authorities, the initiative aims to boost Chile's promising position with respect to the so-called "fuel of the future", taking advantage of the country's natural potential in terms of renewable energy – particularly solar and wind energy – and the institutional potential that has earned the country international recognition for its political stability, legal certainty and equal treatment of local and foreign investment.

The "green hydrogen diplomacy" strategy will mobilise the Foreign Ministry's human and material resources to publicise the initiative and will work with the Energy Ministry and the government's Economic Development Agency on various key aspects: the definition of appropriate regulatory frameworks, facilities for investments such as the setting aside of public land for projects, the articulation of collaboration in scientific research, the exchange of information about cutting-edge technologies and innovation, the design of financing proposals, and the harmonisation of certification processes and regulation for the production and export of green hydrogen.

Not surprisingly, the implementation of Chile's Green Hydrogen Strategy and Diplomacy has successfully positioned Chile as a major player in the green hydrogen industry and consolidated a pipeline of 40 projects in the country.

Source: (InvestChile, 2020[12]) and (InvestChile, 2020[13])

### *Investment generation in the energy industry*

Between 2015 and 2020, Ukraine has attracted USD 6.9 billion worth of FDI. After the manufacturing sector, which received USD 2.5 billion worth of FDI, the energy sector is the second biggest recipient of FDI with USD 1.9 billion. Within the energy sector, wind and solar energy have particularly benefited from FDI with USD 960 million and USD 900 million respectively invested in Ukraine by foreign investors. FDI in the energy sector has created 500 jobs and 30 new production facilities since 2015 (UkraineInvest, 2021[14]).

In Ukraine, eleven countries have invested more than EUR 2 billion of FDI. Among key investors in the energy industry, Norway accounted for 19% of FDI in Ukraine's renewable energy in 2020, and companies such as Scatec Solar, Norsk and NBT have invested in solar and wind energy generation (Kyiv Post,

2021[15]). There are companies, such as TIU Canada, which declared that Ukraine's energy reforms, as well as the free-trade agreement signed between Canada and Ukraine, were drivers of its decision to invest, which demonstrates that investment promotion efforts yield positive results (UkraineInvest, 2021[14]).

More specifically, energy projects represent an important part of the overall value of announced greenfield FDI projects. Between 2003 and 2017, it was estimated that a total of 15% announced greenfield FDI projects were in the energy sector, with 7% in the coal, oil and natural gas industries, and another 8% pertaining to renewable energy (OECD, 2020[9]).

The aforementioned data shows that FDI has been essential to unlocking private capital for the renewable energy industry. However, if Ukraine wishes to promote investments in disruptive energy technologies, as green hydrogen, it is necessary to retain and attract RES investors because this specific type of hydrogen can only be produced with renewable energy sources. Moreover, in 2020, the EU named Ukraine among its priority partners in the implementation of the European Hydrogen Strategy. Ukraine's gas transmission system is the second largest in Europe and one of the largest in the world, while the pipelines could be used to transport green hydrogen to the EU. Considering Ukraine's ambition to develop renewable energy resources, as well as its potential in solar and wind generation, its potential in the field of green hydrogen is significant (East European Association for the Development of the Hydrogen Economy, 2020[16]).

As a result, Ukraine is currently being supported by international partners such as the EU and the United Nations Economic Commission for Europe in a study of the feasibility of developing a green hydrogen industry in Ukraine. Current barriers to the development of this sector include the outdated and non-harmonised regulatory and technical safety regulations, as well as the lack of awareness of businesses and officials in this area, but the development of the hydrogen industry could generate substantial investments in Ukraine while reducing Ukraine's carbon footprint (UNECE, 2021[17]).

## Investment facilitation and administrative simplification efforts

### *Success with investment climate reforms but challenges remain*

Ukraine has implemented a wide range of reforms aimed at facilitating investment and simplifying its administrative framework, which is often seen as overly bureaucratic by foreign investors. The progress of Ukraine in terms of rankings illustrates the rapid pace of reforms that should benefit companies and investors. The improvement of the business climate has been supported by the policy advocacy activities that UkraineInvest undertakes, although companies' operations and investors' sentiment remain affected by a challenging institutional environment slowly adjusting to new realities.

Policy advocacy consists of actions to monitor the investment climate (through international rankings, surveys, or meetings with business) and formal or informal feedback to the government on how to improve the investment climate (such as meetings with high ranking officials, participation in taskforces and councils, reports or public awareness campaigns). Through their interactions with foreign investors, IPAs are best placed to understand their challenges and expectations, and can accordingly provide invaluable insights and feedback that enriches the policy-making process and contributes to enhancing the overall investment climate. UkraineInvest is particularly active in this domain, as demonstrated by its EaP-beating range of policy advocacy activities, from meetings with heads of state to public awareness campaigns and the production of reports (Table 6.1).

**Table 6.1. Policy advocacy activities of IPAs**

| Activity | % of OECD IPAs | Azerbaijan | Belarus | Georgia | Ukraine |
|---|---|---|---|---|---|
| Meetings with the private sector or business associations | 97% | ✓ | ✓ | ✓ | ✓ |
| Informal feedback to the government on investment climate | 97% | ✓ | ✓ | ✓ | ✓ |
| Tracking of rankings (e.g., WEF, WB) | 94% | ✓ | ✓ | ✓ | ✓ |
| Meetings with the prime minister / president / other agencies | 90% | | ✓ | | ✓ |
| Participation in a taskforce on investment climate reforms | 90% | ✓ | ✓ | ✓ | ✓ |
| Production of reports or position papers | 87% | ✓ | | | ✓ |
| Consultation with foreign offices, embassies, consulates | 84% | ✓ | ✓ | ✓ | ✓ |
| Public awareness campaigns or events | 74% | ✓ | ✓ | | ✓ |
| Surveys of foreign investors | 65% | ✓ | | | |
| Inputs on Regulatory Impact Assessment | 42% | ✓ | | | ✓ |
| Surveys of domestic firms investing at home/abroad | 35% | ✓ | | | |
| Surveys of expats | 19% | ✓ | | | |

Source: (OECD, 2020[18])

As measured by the OECD *FDI Regulatory Restrictiveness Index* that was calculated in December 2019, Ukraine energy sector often scores better than the average of OECD countries. Focusing on the energy sector, the electricity sector measured by openness in both electricity generation and distribution is particularly open to FDI compared to OECD average. Oil refinery and chemicals industries, as well as mining and quarrying industries (excluding oil extraction) are, however, more restrictive to FDI than the average of OECD countries.

The improvement of Ukraine's rank as part of the World Bank *Doing Business* assessment should also be mentioned. Ukraine ranked 64th out of 190 countries in the overall ranking in 2020, up 48th places since 2014, but important disparities between indicators must be noted. Ukraine ranks well in terms of dealing with construction permits (20th) or getting credit (37th), whereas getting electricity and resolving insolvency seem to be particularly complex in Ukraine with a respective rank of 128th and 146th. This reflects the difficult situation in the energy sector and a constrained legal system suffering from capacity limitations and delays. Despite recent reforms targeting the energy industry, and the electricity market specifically, as well as the judiciary, the *Doing Business* ranking shows that additional issues need to be addressed to create greater practical impacts for companies (World Bank, 2020[6]).

These issues hamper the enhancement of Ukraine's competitiveness. As measured by the World Economic Forum's *Global Competitiveness* report, Ukraine ranked 85th out of 141 countries in 2019, sliding two places compared to 2018. The WEF report identifies the financial system, macroeconomic stability and the institutional environment as being among the key impediments to Ukraine's competitiveness (World Economic Forum, 2019[19]).

Indeed, investors face challenging realities on the ground, experiencing obstacles that range from poor enforcement of legal obligations in a constrained legal system to the complexity of tax system and corruption interfering in judicial processes. Transparency and predictability of government actions represent another challenge for investors that weigh on their decisions to invest or reinvest in the country. The modification of the green feed-in tariffs, the obstacles faced by the executive power to establish independent anti-corruption bodies and the resistance of local elites are examples of increasing uncertainty and the perception of risk among investors, which creates a challenging environment to attract and maintain investment.

### *Promotion tools designed for foreign investors*

UkraineInvest makes available to investors analytical materials with the latest regulatory policy, institutional and strategic developments and statistics, which serve as useful tools to showcase its investment promotion activities. In the latest version of the "Ukraine Invest Guide: Explore your opportunities" published on March 2021, UkraineInvest provides data on key indicators that are relevant to investors, including GDP growth, FDI flow, average exchange rate, consumer price index and macroeconomic trends. The Guide also contains a regulatory overview of the country and sectoral investment opportunities, from energy and infrastructure to mining and manufacturing. It also explains the government to business services offered to foreign companies and outlooks of the investment climate. To demonstrate the government's policy coherence efforts, the Guide has introductory notes by the President of Ukraine, the Prime Minister and key Ministers illustrate the mobilisation of the Government to improve Ukraine's investment attractiveness. The description of the UkraineInvest Supervisory Board and CEO gives a practical and strategic dimension to this objective (UkraineInvest, 2021[10]).

In this Guide, UkraineInvest provides a broad overview of the recent and expected policy developments aimed at improving the business climate, while advertising its competitiveness as an investment destination, such as comparatively low labour costs associated with available and skilled workforce. It also expands on Ukraine's endowment of natural energy resources and the number of years of reserves of traditional energy resources, such as gas, oil, uranium, and coal. Here, UkraineInvest could consider readjusting the focus of its promotion and attraction efforts from coal-generated power to renewable energy.

The Guide dedicates one section to describing the investment promotion achievements and initiatives specifically targeting the energy sector. Such achievements include the 2019 Law on Electricity Market improving competition in the sector, the unbundling of Naftogaz operations and the development in 2020 of a wholesale short-term market allowing gas transmission system operator to exchange products on a trading platform. UkraineInvest also advertises the plans to increase energy efficiency through an origin warranties system, improve wood market regulation through tender processes, and stimulate waste management investments through transparent regulation and coherent waste disposal system. In addition, the Guide categorises investment energy projects by forms of investment allocation – privatisation, concession, equity investment, debt financing – while listing investment energy projects' status, key financial indicators, estimated amount of investments, and type of investment opportunity.

It is important to note that the energy sector is not expected to directly benefit from investment advantages and incentives under the 2021 Law of Ukraine on State Support for Investment Projects with Significant Investments in Ukraine. Advantages include notably fiscal incentives that can amount to up to 30% of the investment value and the so-called "investment nanny" programme to provide custom advice to investors committing at least EUR 20 million and creating over 80 jobs (Verkhovna Rada of Ukraine, 2020[20]). The energy industry can, however, expect indirect benefits, considering that this incentive programme covers projects in the transport, waste management or enrichment of minerals sectors, among others.

Separately, UkraineInvest has been specifically involved in promoting and facilitating investment in Ukraine's oil and gas sector, with the publication in July 2021 of the Ukraine Oil & Gas Industry Guide 2021 in collaboration with the Association of Gas Producers of Ukraine, the Ministry of Energy of Ukraine, the Naftogaz Group, the Ukrainian Geological Survey and the law firm CMS. This Industry Guide provides analytical information to international investors about the oil and gas sector, including a presentation of reforms implemented over the past five years, a description of the sector's legal, tax and fiscal framework, as well as investment opportunities for foreign investors (Association of Gas Producers of Ukraine, 2021[21]).

### *Investor servicing*

Besides efficient communication relative to legal changes and to the improvement of the overall business climate, investors are often attentive to the services they could receive as part of their investment. An important concern for investors is being able to submit their queries to the right interlocutors, which is significantly facilitated by one-stop shops to access all government services available to investors in a given country. These services generally include information, assistance and clearances necessary for establishing and operating a company. A one-stop shop allows investors to navigate more easily through administrative procedures and requirements by centralising the processes and hosting officials from different government agencies and ministries under the same roof.

In Ukraine, UkraineInvest assumes this role, but the range of services offered in terms of facilitating administrative procedures are not as comprehensive as those of other IPAs with dedicated one-stop services centres. While Ukraine's IPA offers licences and construction approvals, as well as assistances with utilities, legal issues and other business matters, it does not provide tax registration and work permits (OECD, 2020[9]).

UkraineInvest also advertises the convenience and transparency of the online platform *Diia* that is expected to include all government to business services by 2024, such as the registration of LLCs within 24 hours and free or charge, the obtention of permits and licences for transport, water use and other, the submission of waste declarations, the access to government data on land use, companies register and the provision of custom support on administrative procedures (UkraineInvest, 2021[10]).

So-called aftercare or retention measures are also influential in companies' decisions to stay in the country and reinvest. UkraineInvest provides existing investors with such services aimed at triggering reinvestments or at least maintaining existing investments. UkraineInvest undertakes a wide range of aftercare activities compared with other EU Eastern partner countries such as Azerbaijan, Belarus or Georgia, but could further improve its offer to align with OECD practices (Table 6.2) (OECD, 2020[9]).

**Table 6.2. Aftercare services of IPAs**

| Activity | % of OECD IPAs | Azerbaijan | Belarus | Georgia | Ukraine |
|---|---|---|---|---|---|
| Structured trouble-shooting with individual Investors | 81% | ✓ | | ✓ | ✓ |
| Database of local suppliers | 65% | ✓ | ✓ | ✓ | |
| Matchmaking service between investors and local firms | 65% | ✓ | | | ✓ |
| Linkage programmes | 58% | ✓ | | | ✓ |
| Cluster programmes | 48% | | | | ✓ |
| Mitigation of conflicts (e.g. between investors & authorities/ communities) | 45% | ✓ | | | ✓ |
| Capacity-building support for local firms | 39% | ✓ | | | |
| Assistance in recruiting local staff | 39% | | | | |
| Ombudsman Intervention | 26% | | | | ✓ |
| Personnel recruitment programmes | 23% | | | | |
| Training or educational programmes for local staff | 19% | | | | |

Source: (OECD, 2020[18])

### *Investment incentives and tax systems for energy companies*

#### *Inventory of incentive regimes*

In order to modernise the energy infrastructure, it is essential to focus on sustainable alternatives and attract low-carbon FDI in accordance with EU approaches. Hence, the Ministry of Energy of Ukraine was, as of July 2021, developing the Integrated National Plan for Energy and Climate 2021-2030, which would combine agreed goals, policies and measures for energy efficiency, environmental protection and renewable energy. As part of this plan, the Ministry of Energy would determine the volume of annual support quotas and auctions schedules for 2021 and indicative forecasts of annual support quotas for 2022-2025. Pursuant to Article 9-3 of the Law of Ukraine "On Alternative Energy Sources", proposals on annual support quotas are prepared taking into account Ukraine's international commitments on renewable energy development, Ukraine's Energy Strategy, and the Generation Capacity Assessment Report and Transmission System Development Plan (see Chapter 2).

Broadly speaking, the main investment incentives provided in the energy sector pertain to renewable energy. The establishment of an auction system is seen as central to supporting the development of renewable electricity, as defined in Law of Ukraine № 2712-VIII "On Amendments to Certain Laws of Ukraine on Ensuring Competitive Conditions of Electricity Production from Alternative Energy Sources". Key provisions include: (i) mandatory participation in the auction from 2020 for solar power stations with a capacity of at least 1 MW and wind farms with a capacity of at least 5 MW; (ii) receipt by the winners of the auction of state support for the sale of "green" energy for 20 years under PPA agreement; (iii) provision of the opportunity to participate in auctions for all types of renewable generation; (iv) possibility to receive a surcharge of up to 10% of the auction price for the use of Ukrainian equipment.

Heat production from renewable energy sources is incentivised through the 2017 Law of Ukraine №1959-VIII "On Amendments to the Law of Ukraine "On Heat Supply" to stimulate heat production from alternative energy sources". This law provides for the establishment of tariffs for thermal energy from alternative sources set at 90% of the current tariff level for thermal energy generated from gas.

Over the course of 2018-2019, a number of laws and regulations of NEURC were adopted to create incentives for investment in renewable energy and to facilitate the construction of new generation capacities. Most notably, Law №2517--VIII "On amending some laws regarding investment attractiveness of construction of renewable energy objects" eased regulatory requirements for the construction of wind farms and other renewable energy generation objects; and Law №2628--VIII further eased regulatory requirements for the construction of renewable energy generation objects and allow the construction on different types of land plots without legal change of purpose (OECD, 2020[22]).

In terms of tax incentives, investments made in renewable energy can benefit from 100% corporate income tax exemption over a defined period (tax holiday) and a permanent exemption on trade taxes, such as import duties, VAT on imports, or exports taxes. The acquisition of renewable power sources or energy saving equipment for own-use of electricity production is also exempt from customs duties (OECD, 2020[9]), and companies can benefit from 75% land tax discount for land that is used for the generation of energy from renewable energy sources (OECD, 2020[22]).

Energy companies are also expected to benefit from programmes aiming at increasing energy efficiency of households and industrial facilities through attractive loan conditions ("Warm loans"). However, the feed-in tariffs introduced in 2009 and anticipated to last until 2030 were among the most attractive in Europe and were expected to be one the main instruments to attract investors into the renewable energy sector, but they were abandoned by the government.

A legal regime for special economic zones (SEZ) was established in Ukraine in 1998, but a 2005 law abolished both the customs and tax preferences granted to these zones, and zones were formally closed in 2016 (OECD, 2016[23]). Similarly, the 2012 Law on Industrial Parks set out the legal framework for industrial parks of which over 50 are currently in operation in Ukraine, excluding special fiscal treatment for residents (OECD, 2020[9]).

### Ongoing tax reform

In order to align its legislation with OECD recommendations and ensure the attraction of quality investment, Ukraine passed a major tax reform in 2020. The new law[3] clarifies or simplifies a number of elements, and contains important provisions affecting cross-border transactions based on the OECD base erosion and profit shifting (BEPS) project. As such, the tax reform influences non-residents activities in Ukraine quite significantly by amending the definition of permanent establishment, establishing a general anti-avoidance rule and defining a mutual agreement procedure (Deloitte, 2019[24]). Other positive developments for foreign investors include the lifting of restrictions relative to interest rates for borrowing in foreign currency.

Concerns by investors about the overly complicated tax system in place in Ukraine are also being addressed, albeit less energetically, considering the need to consolidate fiscal revenues and the current high level of tax avoidance. For instance, a law passed in 2020[4] introduced simplification or redefinition of procedures for individual entrepreneurs, such as procedures relative to penalties as part of the non-compliance with submission deadlines or in case of technical failure or mistakes (Deloitte, 2020[25]).

## Ukraine's regulatory policy to improve the investment climate in the country

### Administrative simplification efforts

As mentioned earlier, an important element of administrative simplification and investment facilitation that greatly benefit investors is the establishment of a one-stop shop to access all government services. UkraineInvest performs this function as part of its mandate but this excludes the provision of tax registration and work permits. Nevertheless, it offers licences and construction approvals, as well as assistance with utilities and legal issues, which can significantly reduce transaction costs for businesses. The use of a Customer Relationship Management system by UkraineInvest covering all organisational units also enables the tracking of investors at each stage of the investment process, which ensures better and targeted support (OECD, 2020[1]).

Besides UkraineInvest, other entities also support investment facilitation by providing businesses established in Ukraine with advantages, which could indirectly attract foreign investors willing to use their business in Ukraine as a strategic location to export their products. For example, the creation of Ukraine's Export Credit Agency in 2019 intends to boost Ukraine's export competitiveness and is particularly important in terms of providing Ukrainian exporters with affordable financing instruments and insurance together with the country's State Export-Import Bank (Ukreximbank). Ukraine Investment & Trade Facilitation Centre (ITFC) also advertises its role in supporting deregulation efforts, fiscal reforms, currency control liberalisation and financial sector development, which can all benefit foreign investors. ITFC lists electric power and the oil and gas industries as its priority sector of intervention (Ukraine Investment & Trade Facilitation Center, 2016[26])

The adoption of the Law of Ukraine No. 2314-VIII on "Deregulation of the Oil and Gas Industry" in 2018 has simplified regulatory procedures relating to oil and gas exploration and production activities, and reduced the number of permits and approvals. Notably, the Law eased land use and the construction of wells outsides cities. The Law also stipulates that approval of state authorities is no longer required for the exploration and commercial development of oil and gas fields, and that there is no mandatory registration and approval of transfer of geological information.

In early 2019, Ukraine launched a series of licensing rounds in the oil and gas sector with the opening of a public tender for 12 blocks under a PSA covering a total area of 15 600 square km, and 38 onshore blocks under royalty/tax terms. The terms of the PSAs have been improved with a simplification of the permitting system, and adjusted rules for access to gas aimed at increasing the attractiveness of Ukraine as a destination for foreign investments. Foreign investors could also participate in the block offering under royalty/tax terms via a local subsidiary company. However, results from the different rounds highlighted a lack of foreign involvement.

In the energy sector, NEURC is particularly attentive to administrative simplification, as is shown by the reduction in documents required to obtain a licence, which now ranges from 1 to 6 documents required to constitute the whole package necessary for submission. The digital platforms, from which businesses can get information on licensing and submit documents to obtain licences, also facilitate their operations, as in the case of the Unified State Portal of Administrative Services and the websites of NEURC and the State Service of Geology and Subsoil of Ukraine (OECD, 2020[22]).

In addition, Ukraine is taking steps to ease the regulation for small energy producers that do not pose risks to the balance of the energy system. For example, the Law of Ukraine "On the Electricity Market" stipulates the right for household consumers to install solar or wind generating installations in their private households with a capacity not exceeding 50 kW without a licence. Other types of consumers, such as energy co-operatives, are now also allowed to generate electricity from solar, wind, biomass, biogas, hydro, or geothermal energy with a capacity of up to 150 kW without licence (OECD, 2020[22]).

### *Regulatory policy-making and quality*

To ensure quality policy-making that takes into account investors' concerns, the authorities have developed several initiatives aimed at enabling investors to communicate their complaints through different channels. UkraineInvest acts as the first interlocutor by providing investors with one-stop support where they can find reliable, current information as well as advice on doing business in Ukraine. As part of this mandate, UkraineInvest also guides investors through government agencies at all levels and helps to resolve systemic issues that investors may face (UkraineInvest, 2020[2]). Through its central position interacting with executive, advisory and legislative bodies, UkraineInvest is able to identify the main issues and inform policy-making.

The Temporary Special Commission on Protecting Investors' Rights, which was created in 2020 by the Parliament, is another regulatory channel aiming to reform and develop Ukrainian investment legislation, and deal with business complaints. Created in the context of the Covid-19 crisis, it acknowledges the competition existing between countries to attract investors and the interference of individual government officials in business operations in Ukraine. As a result, this special commission envisions the creation of simple and clear investment legislation that could be a source of competitive advantage, and the use of parliamentary control to support businesses in a timely manner (Interfax, 2020[27]).

As part of the Law "On State Support for Investment Projects with Significant Investments in Ukraine", the government has created an "Investment Nanny" programme for investments worth over EUR 20 million creating at least 80 jobs. This programme provides investors with custom assistance by a dedicated investment manager, enabling large investors to navigate the complex administrative environment more easily and communicate the issues they are facing. The communication of issues at the micro level could then inform decision-making regarding the most common issues faced by large investors, with a view to offering solutions by filling legislative gaps or change regulations.

Moreover, international partners and lenders assist Ukraine in developing high-quality policies and reforms. Alignment of national legislation with EU acquis and norms boosting liberalisation and modernising the legal framework, as well as compliance with conditionality and technical assistance associated with IMF lending, improve the overall regulatory and institutional environment in Ukraine. Meanwhile, the application in Ukraine of OECD best practices and recommendations contained in the *OECD Declaration on International Investment and Multinational Enterprises* and the *OECD/G20 Inclusive Framework on base erosion and profit shifting* (BEPS) provides Ukraine with useful tools to solve regulatory and policy challenges.

## Outlook and policy recommendations

Ukraine has been able to attract investors through a series of policies that allow investors to participate in the energy market. UkraineInvest has promoted opportunities to invest in the renewable energy sector, the electricity market and the oil and gas industry.

Ukraine has stimulated investments in the energy sector by introducing tax, customs and land use incentives, which have led to the creation of investment opportunities. Nevertheless, the country is still promoting investment opportunities and the privatisation of power generation with coal. This is a major challenge as it could create stranded assets that will limit the green energy potential of the country.

- **Further align the promotion and attraction of investment efforts with Ukraine's international commitments on decarbonisation and reduction of greenhouse gas emissions**. Ukraine has the opportunity to foster the attraction of green and renewable energy sources, as well as energy efficiency companies, to consolidate its pathway as a green economy and to attract investors that generate positive environmental impacts to the country.
- **National image-building should strike a balance between promoting Ukraine's attractiveness and addressing foreign investors' needs and expectations through realistic targets and a pragmatic agenda of reforms**.
- **Implement a CRM system allowing customer feedback and regular evaluation**. These services should be offered to foreign investors as part of aftercare activities, as they would enable UkraineInvest to gather information on the success and shortcomings of its investment promotion and facilitation actions. Such information would then help improve foreign investors' satisfaction with regards to the services that UkraineInvest provides.
- **Ensure predictability and certainty of government actions by maintaining the conditions offered to investors over time**. A history of honouring long-term government commitments, such as feed-in tariffs, special economic zones, without alteration of initial conditions would lower investors' perception of risks and enable the increase of FDI flows to the country.
- **Evaluate the incorporation of a one-stop-shop investment platform for renewable energy and energy efficiency projects that encompasses all the information and procedures to de-risk projects and scale up investments in the sector**.

## Notes

[1] See https://uamap.org.ua.

[2] Energy Strategy of Ukraine until 2035, 2017, https://razumkov.org.ua/uploads/article/2018_Energy_Strategy_2035.pdf.

[3] Draft Law "On Amendments to the Tax Code of Ukraine on Improving Tax Administration, Removing Technical and Logical Mismatches in the Tax Legislation".

[4] Law of Ukraine No. 786-IX "On amending the Tax Code of Ukraine as regards taxpayers' accounts functioning and simplification of procedures for individual entrepreneurs".

## References

Association of Gas Producers of Ukraine (2021), *Ukraine Oil & Gas Industry Guide 2021: Embracing investment opportunities*, https://agpu.org.ua/images/pdf/guide21-web.pdf. [21]

Deloitte (2020), *Tax Reform 2020: Changes in Law No.466-IX*, https://www2.deloitte.com/ua/en/pages/press-room/tax-and-legal-alerts/2020/2020-08-11-tax-reform-2020.html. [25]

Deloitte (2019), *Ukraine tax reform 2020: BEPS legislation is adopted in the first reading*, https://www.taxathand.com/article/13673/Ukraine/2020/President-signs-BEPS-tax-reform-into-law. [24]

East European Association for the Development of the Hydrogen Economy (2020), *Ukraine Hydrogen Valley Pilot Project: Development of a Hybrid Park of Wind & Solar Power Plants*, https://ec.europa.eu/regional_policy/rest/cms/upload/26092020_035002_green_hydrogen_ukraine.pdf. [16]

EY (2021), *National Strategy to Increase Foreign Direct Investment in Ukraine, Section 1: The View from Above*, https://ukraineinvest.gov.ua/wp-content/uploads/2021/08/FDI-Strategy-Section-1-The-View-from-Above-ENG.pdf. [5]

Heather Worley, E. et al. (2018), "Designing Communication Campaigns for Energy Subsidy Reform", https://documents1.worldbank.org/curated/en/939551530880505644/pdf/ESRAF-note-10-Designing-Communication-Campaigns-for-Energy-Subsidy-Reform.pdf. [11]

Interfax (2020), *The Verkhovna Rada of Ukraine has Created a Special Commission for Investors Protection. What will it work on?*, https://en.interfax.com.ua/news/blog/668157.html. [27]

InvestChile (2020), *Government presents "green hydrogen diplomacy" to attract foreign investment*, https://blog.investchile.gob.cl/government-presents-green-hydrogen-diplomacy-to-attract-foreign-investment (accessed on 25 October 2021). [12]

InvestChile (2020), *Green hydrogen will create 100 000 jobs and generate US$200,000 million in investment over the next 20 years*, https://blog.investchile.gob.cl/green-hydrogen-will-create-100000-jobs-and-generate-us200000-million-in-investment-over-the-next-20-years. [13]

Kyiv Post (2021), *Ukraine-Norway business overview: corruption no-go for Norwegian investors - KyivPost - Ukraine's Global Voice*, https://www.kyivpost.com/business/ukraine-norway-business-overview-corruption-no-go-for-norwegian-investors.html. [15]

OECD (2021), *Sustainable Infrastructure for Low-carbon Development in the EU Eastern Partnership: Hotspot Analysis and Needs Assessment*, Green Finance and Investment, OECD Publishing, Paris, https://dx.doi.org/10.1787/c1b2b68d-en. [4]

OECD (2020), *Investment Perspectives in Eastern Partner Countries*, https://www.oecd.org/investment/Investment-perspectives-in-Eastern-Partner-countries.pdf. [9]

OECD (2020), *Investment Promotion in Eurasia: A Mapping of Investment Promotion Agencies*, https://www.oecd.org/eurasia/competitiveness-programme/Investment-Promotion-in-Eurasia-A-Mapping-of-Investment-Promotion-Agencies-ENG.pdf. [1]

OECD (2020), *Investment Promotion in Eurasia: A Mapping of Investment Promotion Agencies*, https://www.oecd.org/eurasia/competitiveness-programme/investmentpromotionineurasia.htm. [18]

OECD (2020), *Policy Framework for Investment questionnaire. OECD Investment Policy Review Ukraine´s Energy Sector.* [22]

OECD (2018), *FDI Regulatory Restrictiveness Index*, https://www.oecd.org/investment/fdiindex.htm. [8]

OECD (2016), *OECD Due Diligence Guidance for Responsible Supply Chains of Minerals from Conflict-Affected and High-Risk Areas: Third Edition*, OECD Publishing, Paris, https://dx.doi.org/10.1787/9789264252479-en. [23]

OECD (2015), *Assessment of Ukraine's Investment Policy Framework: An Overview*, https://www.oecd.org/eurasia/competitiveness-programme/eastern-partners/Overview_2IPR_Ukraine_ENG.pdf. [7]

Ukraine Investment & Trade Facilitation Center (2016), *What We Do*, http://tradecenter.org.ua/eng/about. [26]

UkraineInvest (2021), *FDI in Ukraine in 2015-2020*, https://uae.mfa.gov.ua/storage/app/sites/80/2-foreign-investors-success-stories-presentation.pdf. [14]

UkraineInvest (2021), *UkraineInvest Guide: Explore Your Opportunities. March - May 2021*, https://ukraineinvest.gov.ua/guide/. [10]

UkraineInvest (2020), *About UkraineInvest*, https://ukraineinvest.gov.ua/services-team/about-ukraineinvest/. [2]

UkraineInvest (2020), *Invest in Ukraine NOW*, https://ukraineinvest.gov.ua/wp-content/uploads/2020/04/UkraineNOW_b.pdf. [3]

UNECE (2021), *Draft Roadmap for Production and Use of Hydrogen in Ukraine*, https://unece.org/sites/default/files/2021-03/Draft%20Roadmap%20for%20production%20and%20use%20of%20hydrogen%20in%20Ukraine_Final%20.pdf. [17]

Verkhovna Rada of Ukraine (2020), *Adopted the Law of Ukraine "On State Support for Investment Projects with Significant Investments" - Verkhovna Rada of Ukraine*, https://www.rada.gov.ua/en/news/News/201157.html (accessed on 25 October 2021). [20]

World Bank (2020), *Doing Business 2020*, https://www.doingbusiness.org/en/doingbusiness. [6]

World Economic Forum (2019), *The Global Competitiveness Report*, http://www3.weforum.org/docs/WEF_TheGlobalCompetitivenessReport2019.pdf. [19]

# 7 Public Governance – Reducing Corruption and Mitigating Risk in the Energy Sector

This chapter provides an overview of the level of corruption in Ukraine, including in the energy sector, assesses Ukraine's recent advances in the fight against corruption, and highlights remaining challenges relating to Ukraine's public governance and judicial system.

## Introduction

The quality of public governance significantly affects the business and investment climate in all economic sectors, including energy. Ukraine's economy, and in particular its energy sector, have suffered for decades from systemic corruption that has reached the highest layers of Ukraine's executive, legislative and judicial systems. Since Ukraine's independence in 1991, corruption in the energy sector has had a central role in most of the political crises in the country (Kuzio, 2008[1]).

Ukraine's "Revolution of Dignity" in 2014 has played the role of a "wake-up call" for Ukraine, urging the country to make concrete institutional and legislative changes to fight corruption and to increase Ukraine's energy independence. With the support of the international community, notably the EU, the International Monetary Fund and the OECD, Ukraine has adopted a broad range of reforms aimed at establishing a well-functioning public governance and judiciary system and reinforcing public trust.

These efforts notwithstanding, corruption continues to plague Ukraine's energy sector and affects its attractiveness for foreign and domestic investment. Misappropriation of public funds for energy projects, corruption, and – as described earlier in this *Review* – a weak judiciary have all affected Ukraine's energy sector attractiveness. Corruption in Ukraine happens through different channels such as procurement, privatisation of state assets, infrastructure development, and management of SOEs, to name a few. Unless Ukraine addresses these challenges, it will continue to face issues with respect to its attractiveness for foreign and domestic investors in its energy sector (OECD, 2019[2]).

## Reforms positively affecting Ukraine's energy sector public governance have advanced

The 2014 Euromaidan events created an impulse for the government to reform the energy sector and strengthen the fight against corruption. Since then, Ukraine has continued to reform the country's energy sector to promote security and sustainability while attracting investors, as is discussed in previous chapters of this *Review*. For instance, as highlighted in chapter 2 of this *Review*, in 2015, Ukraine adopted the Natural Gas Market Law[1], which is aligned with the unbundling requirements of the EU Directive 2009/73/EC and established an independent system operator model. Notably, the law reformed the SOE Naftogaz and liberalised gas prices, which until 2015 were regulated and heavily subsidised, resulting in major financial losses for Naftogaz (Chatham House, 2018[3]). As is also discussed earlier in this *Review*, in 2016, with the support of the international community, Ukraine developed a modern regulatory framework and established an independent energy regulator – the National Energy and Utilities Regulatory Commission (NEURC). In October 2018, Ukraine raised natural gas tariffs for regulated markets and started reforming some of its state-owned enterprises. The year before, Ukraine adopted the Electricity Market Law[2], which called for the establishment of an independent and certified transmission system operator (TSO) integrated into the ENTSO-E. In 2018, the Ukrainian government introduced an open auctions practice for granting licences for natural resource extraction which increased transparency of actors in oil and gas production.

Another important step forward for Ukraine, as is discussed in chapter 2 of this *Review*, has been the establishment of the ProZorro platform for public procurement procedures that has enhanced transparency of public procurement procedures and reduced risks for corruption, including in the framework of energy sector infrastructure investment projects.[3] The reliability and good reputation of ProZorro made it an easy choice to be part of the Open Contracting Partnership with the World Bank and the World Trade Organisation (Open Government Partnership, 2019[4]).

In March 2018, Ukraine adopted the Law On Privatisation of State-Owned and Municipal Property[4] which changed the process of large-scale privatisation[5], replaced numerous and often contradictory regulations, reduced the privatisation timeline, and made the online ProZorro[6] electronic system mandatory for the privatisation of small SOEs. In addition, the Law On Privatisation of State-Owned and Municipal Property gave additional guarantees to investors by introducing the option of referring disputes to international commercial arbitration (Article 26, para. 12, Law On Privatisation of State-Owned and Municipal Property) as well as the obligation to employ international advisers for the sale of larger SOEs.

More generally, since the 2014 Revolution of Dignity, Ukraine has undertaken several legislative reforms to strengthen its anti-corruption legal and institutional framework. The establishment of the National Anti-corruption Bureau of Ukraine (NABU) in 2015 and the High Anti-Corruption Court (HACC) in 2019 have been one of the most important recent achievements (Gerasimov and Solonenko, 2020[5]). In 2014, Ukraine introduced the obligation for public officials to submit electronic asset declarations with all property and interests an official may have.

To further fight high-level corruption and improve its financial asset declaration legislation, in June 2021 Ukraine adopted amendments to the Code of Ukraine on Administrative Offences and its Criminal Code, introducing criminal liability for declaring inaccurate information and for failing to submit a financial asset declaration. Strengthening Ukraine's financial asset declaration legislation was very much needed, given that 99% of asset declarations audited in 2017-2019 contained false information.[7]

Measures have also been taken to improve public governance and reduce corruption risks at sub-national level (OECD, 2018[6]), notably by creating new opportunities for citizens to hold local authorities accountable for managing local public resources (Chatham House, 2018[3]). In January 2020, a new law[8], which establishes additional protections and provides financial incentives for whistle-blowers who report alleged cases of corruption or corruption-related offenses, also entered into force. In addition, the introduction of new rules for tax administration and judicial system reforms, as well as the establishment of a Business Ombudsman Council in 2015, have improved Ukraine's overall investment climate with regards to the fight against corruption and misconduct in the public sector.

These developments illustrate the willingness of the Ukrainian government to acknowledge the problem of widespread corruption and to implement practical measures to address it. As a result of these measures, Ukraine gained three points in the Transparency International's Corruption Perceptions Index 2020 (CPI) compared with 2019, ranking 117$^{th}$ in the 2020 Corruption Perceptions Index out of 180 countries. Despite Ukraine's efforts to combat corruption, however, the country still suffers from negative perceptions of corruption remaining widespread. This perception is reflected when Ukraine is compared with other economies. For instance, in the 2020 edition of the World Justice Project Rule of Law Index, Ukraine ranked 72$^{th}$ out of 128 in the rule of law category, performing below countries such as Belarus (68$^{th}$) and Kazakhstan (62$^{nd}$). The World Justice Project Rule of Law Index also measures countries' performance with regards to the absence of corruption by considering different forms of corruption, notably bribery, the improper influence of public or private interests, and the misappropriation of public funds or other resources. In this category, the Government of Ukraine ranked 110$^{th}$ out of 128 countries worldwide and 7$^{th}$ out of 14 in Eastern Europe and Central Asia in 2020.

## Ukraine has established an institutional and legal anti-corruption framework but anti-corruption agencies' work and law enforcement remain a challenge

The institutional setting of the law enforcement system has been a focus of reform as well. For the past seven years, Ukraine has implemented important reforms to establish a more effective anti-corruption institutional architecture, including establishing the National Agency on Corruption Prevention, the National Anti-corruption Bureau of Ukraine, and the Specialised Anti-corruption Prosecutor's Office, and the Asset Recovery and Management Agency (Box 7.1). These specialised agencies were empowered to detect and investigate high-profile corruption, including cases involving sitting-in-office high-level officials. Since October 2016, Ukrainians have been able to examine public officials' asset declarations. In 2019, Ukraine established the High Anti-Corruption Court (HACC) as a way to address the ineffectiveness of Ukraine's regular courts in dealing with high-level corruption. The first year of activity of the HACC resulted in 16 verdicts in high-level corruption cases, in some cases leading to long prison sentences (European Commission, 2020[7]). Along with these institutions, in 2018, Ukraine established the State Bureau of Investigation (SBI) to investigate crimes committed by high-ranking officials. In addition, the National Agency for the Prevention of Corruption (NAPC) became operational in 2016 to develop and implement anti-corruption policies with the overall objective of making corruption prevention stronger. However, the framework in which these bodies operate remains weak, and the enforcement of many anti-corruption safeguards meets resistance and stalling, thereby putting the success of other anti-corruption efforts at risk. In October 2020, the Constitutional Court of Ukraine (CCU) found the practice of holding officials criminally liable for false asset declarations to be unconstitutional and stripped the NACP of many of its key functions, including its powers to control and verify declarations.[9] The CCU also called into question the constitutionality of a NABU senior management appointment. Major donors, including the G7 countries and the IMF, have called on the government to counter efforts to roll back anti-corruption reforms. The IMF also notably withheld from Ukraine a scheduled tranche of USD 700 million due to the Court's actions.[10]

### Box 7.1. Main public bodies leading Ukraine's anti-corruption investigations and prosecutions

**The National Anti-Corruption Bureau of Ukraine** (NABU), established in 2015, is an anti-corruption law enforcement agency that investigates corruption in Ukraine and prepares cases for prosecution. It has investigatory powers but cannot indict suspects.

**The Specialised Anti-Corruption Prosecutor's Office** (SAPO), established in 2015, is an independent structural sub-division of the General Prosecutor of Ukraine and is primarily responsible for supporting and overseeing criminal investigations launched by the NABU.

**The High Anti-Corruption Court of Ukraine** (HACC), established in 2019, is responsible for corruption-related cases in the country that are to be brought directly to this court. It has nationwide jurisdiction over high-level corruption cases entailing a damage in excess of a monetary threshold.

**The National Agency for Prevention of Corruption** (NAPC), established in 2015, is responsible for the verification (audit) of financial declarations of public officials. It has a preventive function. It was established by the Law on Prevention of Corruption of 2014 and implements anti-corruption policy while creating an environment conducive to the prevention of corruption that includes the electronic declaration of assets.

**The Recovery and Management Agency** (ARMA), established in 2015, is a central executive body with a special status, responsible for finding, tracing, and managing assets derived from corruption and other crimes. ARMA is authorised to formulate and implement state policy in the sphere of tracing, finding of assets that are subject to seizure and that are aimed to be seized, as well as management of seized assets in criminal proceedings.

Source: Multiple sources including (NABU, n.d.[8]), (Ukraine Specialised Anti-Corruption Prosecutor's Office, n.d.[9])

While the jurisdiction of NABU and SAPO are set out in law, in practice some cases falling under their jurisdiction have been investigated by other agencies, which has led to their mandate being undermined. For instance, in April 2018 the court acquitted the Security Service of Ukraine officer who had been charged with an abuse of influence, because the case had fallen under the jurisdiction of NABU but had been investigated by the Military Prosecution Office. Attacks on anti-corruption agencies, and especially NABU, have continued throughout their existence. Another major obstacle to NABU's work is that the agency is not habilitated to do independent wiretapping, which often leads to information leaks about NABU investigations to the Security Service (OECD, 2019[10]).

## Risks of corruption and policy capture of Ukraine's energy sector remain an issue from investors' perspective

As discussed in Chapter 5 of this *Review*, the importance of Ukraine's energy sector, as well as the complexity regarding the management of large energy infrastructure projects involving different state bodies, create additional risks of corruption. As confirmed by previous OECD studies, corruption continues to challenge actors in Ukraine's energy sector. This is especially true in the oil, gas, and energy sector, where corruption appears to be most widespread in Ukraine (OECD, 2018[11]). Corruption has been detected in many of the leading SOEs of the energy sector, such as Naftogaz, Energoatom, Ukrnafta, Ukrgazvydobuvannya, and Centerenergo (OECD, 2018[11]). To this day, oligarchs continue to dominate key sectors for Ukraine, such as energy, and exert an influence on the state through their representation in Parliament (World Bank, 2020[12]).

### Box 7.2. Example of cases of corruption offences and abuses in Ukraine's energy sector revealed by NABU

Over the years, NABU has investigated key SOEs, including the subsidiaries of Naftogaz such as Ukrgasvydobuvannya (which may have suffered UAH 3 billion in losses due to corruption) and Ukrzaliznytsia (nearly UAH 500 million in potential losses), as well as the Ukrainian Seaports Authority (UAH 247 million in potential losses) and Oschadbank (UAH 500 million in potential losses). While these cases have often been hampered in courts, NABU has continued investigating cases and collaborating with other institutions, including the Specialised Anti-corruption Prosecutor's Office (SAPO). During the first half of 2020, NABU and SAPO were investigating the heads of nineteen SOEs. They also detained three individuals who were looking to bribe the head of the State Property Fund in appointing the CEO of the Odessa Port Plant.

In addition, in 2020, NABU and SAPO's investigations revealed an organised corruption scheme under which the gas company did not pay for obtaining a special permit to use the subsoil of the Svistunkivsko-Chervonolutsky gas condensate field. This corruption scheme resulted in a state budget loss of UAH 196.8 million.

Another case of corruption exposed in 2020 concerned a scam to complete the construction of a nuclear power plant storage with the participation of a former member of Parliament, who is also involved in the scheme of seizure of property of the National Guard (to the tune of UAH 81.64 million).

Note: This list of examples is not exhaustive and focuses on more recent cases of corruption in Ukraine's energy sector.
Source: (NABU, 2020[13]), (OECD, 2021[14])

This finding is also aligned with the investigations of cases of corruption of Ukraine's anti-corruption bodies – the NABU and the SAPO. Since its establishment in 2015, in co-operation with SAPO, NABU has launched 986 pre-trial investigations in high-level corruption cases. In addition, NABU has submitted a total of 265 cases to courts, resulting in 41 convictions, as the vast majority of cases were blocked in Ukraine's ordinary courts (European Commission, 2020[7]). An important part of NABU's investigation and findings of corruption abuses concern Ukraine's energy sector, which according to NABU remains the most corrupt in Ukraine's economy.[11] NABU's investigations of Ukraine's energy sector have revealed corruption schemes such as bid-rigging, the purchase of goods and services by state-owned enterprises at inflated prices, bribery and tender purchases at unsolicited or superfluous prices (Box 7.2). In terms of the volume of corruption abuses, Ukraine's fuel and energy complex occupies the first place, causing financial losses of more than UAH 3 billion (NABU, 2020[15]).

## Judicial reform has advanced but important challenges need to be addressed

As discussed in previous chapters of this *Review*, Ukraine has undertaken significant reforms over the past five years to improve its judiciary. In 2016, Ukraine's judicial reform advanced with the creation of a new Supreme Court and the reduction of the number and levels of courts from four to three. Following constitutional amendments in 2016, the authority to appoint judges was transferred from the Ukrainian Parliament to the High Council of Justice (HCJ). Other more recent reforms took place in 2019, notably strengthening the independence of the National Agency on Corruption Prevention (NACP)[12] and reforming the Public Prosecutor's Office of Ukraine.[13]

Despite these encouraging developments, the public perception of judicial independence has improved only marginally. In 2021, almost 80% of Ukrainians did not trust courts and judges, according to a survey conducted by the think-tank Razumkov Centre in March 2021. According to a survey on Ukraine's investment climate released in September 2021 by the American Chamber of Ukraine, 93% of surveyed businesses stated that implementation of real and effective judicial reform, the rule of law, fair justice, and the eradication of corruption constitute the government's primary objectives in order to deliver economic growth, improve the business climate, and attract FDI (American Chamber of commerce of Ukraine, 2021[16]). The integrity and independence of Ukraine's judiciary are still seen by domestic and international investors as hampering Ukraine's ability to fight corruption. An important issue remains the independence and the integrity of the High Judicial Council of Justice, which is a collective, independent judicial self-government entity responsible for the appointment or dismissal of judges. Further evidence suggests that the HCJ exercises pressure over independent judges through disciplinary investigations and has taken part in corruption schemes involving judges and public officials (Box 7.3). In April 2021, the President of Ukraine initiated the liquidation of the Kyiv District Administrative Court (KDAC), frequently referred to as the epitome of alleged judicial corruption in Ukraine.[14]

To further address the aforementioned issues, in July 2021 Ukraine adopted the Law "On amendments to certain legislative acts of Ukraine concerning the procedure for selection (appointment) to the positions of members of the High Council of Justice and the activities of disciplinary inspectors of the High Council of Justice" (No. 1635-IX, in force as of August 5, 2021). It provides for the establishment of an Ethics Council with a mandate of six years to assist the bodies selecting the members of the High Council of Justice (HCJ) in determining whether the applicants for the position of member of the HCJ and the current members of the HCJ meet the criteria of professional ethics and integrity. The new law envisages that the first composition of the Ethics Council will comprise three active or retired judges appointed by the Council of Judges and three appointed by international organisations with experience of working with Ukraine on anti-corruption and judicial reform issues. For the approval of any decision of the first Ethics Council, the decision must be supported by at least two international experts.

Of particular importance for Ukraine's judiciary has been the issue of there being a shortage of judges. As of June 2021, there were approximately 1977 vacancies for judicial posts, a shortage that has resulted in an increase of the length of time that is required to resolve cases. The main reason for this shortage is that at the end of 2019 with the adoption of law No. 193-IX, the High Qualification Commission of Judges, which is responsible for the selection of judges, ceased functioning. In response to this problem, in July 2021, Ukraine adopted two laws aimed at rebooting the High Qualification Commission of Judges (HQCJ) (Law No 1629-IX) and reforming the High Council of Justice (HCJ) (Law No 1635-IX), which entered in force on 5 August 2021.

**Box 7.3. The case of the Kyiv District Administrative Court (KDAC), a case of judiciary corruption**

In July 2019, NABU and the Special Investigations Directorate of the PGO investigated the Kyiv District Administrative Court (KDAC) judges and revealed that the chief judge, his deputy, and a court judge knowingly organised unlawful decision-making and interfered in the work of judicial agencies to obstruct the work of the HQCJ. The suspects allegedly wanted to avoid the mandatory qualification assessment. The KDAC is endowed with exclusive powers to consider all lawsuits against central public authorities located in Kyiv.

In July 2020, the NABU revealed criminal organisations including the Head of the KDAC, which includes judges of the KDAC, the Head of the State Judicial Administration of Ukraine (SJA), former members of the High Qualification Commission of Judges of Ukraine (HQCJ) and others. The NABU Detectives exposed the entire system of administered justice, which contributed to the personal enrichment of judges and was used by the KDAC Head as a tool for seizing power in the judiciary.

Source: (Transparency International, 2019[17]) (NABU, 2020[18])

In addition, according to Article 95, para. 5 of the Law "On the judiciary and the status of judges" (Law № 1402-VIII), a Competition Commission will be established to select candidates for the position of a member of the High Qualification Commission of Judges of Ukraine who meet the criteria of integrity and professional competence. More recently, on September 17, 2021, the Acting Chairman of the HCJ signed an order appointing the first members of the Competition Commission, which will elect the members of the HQCJ.

Ukraine's flawed judicial system is widely regarded as a major obstacle for both domestic and foreign business, and distrust of the judiciary is one of the reasons why foreign investors may be deterred to invest in Ukraine's Energy sector. Ukraine needs to continue working on judicial reform, ensuring consistency between different laws and strengthening the integrity and independence of its judiciary.

## Public procurement in the energy sector continues to be perceived as vulnerable to corruption and collusion

For the past five years, significant progress has been made in modernising and increasing transparency of public procurement in Ukraine. For example, in 2016, the Law on Public Procurement[15] was aligned with the 2014 EU-Ukraine Association Agreement.[16] More recently, the latest amendments to the law "On Public Procurement" that entered into force in April 2020 introduced more social and environmental aspects related to RBC practices.

Notwithstanding this new environment, the proportion of businesses that regard corruption in public procurement as very or fairly widespread in Ukraine's public opinion is high. Anecdotal evidence abounds that powerful private operators exert pressure on public administration to channel public procurement to major companies linked through circles of influence to them. Investors report that bribes and diversion of public funds due to corruption and favouritism in decisions of government are still challenging their businesses in Ukraine's energy sector. A forthcoming OECD Typology of Corruption Schemes in the Energy Sector in Ukraine will document cases of corruption in the energy sector and will show that an important share of them involve corruption schemes in the public procurement process (Box 7.4).

Echoing these concerns, the legislation governing public procurement has been amended on several occasions, with each amendment enhancing transparency and control. Bid rigging is an administrative offence in Ukraine and has long been an enforcement priority for the Ukrainian Competition Authority (AMCU). In a 2021 assessment of procurement practices of Ukrenergo against the OECD *Recommendation on Fighting Bid Rigging in Public Procurement* (OECD, 2012[19]), the OECD found that procurement at Ukrenergo is already highly professional although more could be done to target the problem of bidder collusion in tender design and preparation and to detect bidder collusion. The report proposed several ways of achieving this objective (OECD, 2021[20]). The *Recommendation on Fighting Bid Rigging in Public Procurement* (OECD, 2012[19]) as well as the OECD 2015 *Recommendation on Public Procurement* (OECD, 2015[21]), which is the overarching OECD guiding principle that promotes the strategic and holistic use of public procurement, could be used by other SOEs in Ukraine as well as public procurement agencies to benchmark their own practices and adjust them accordingly.

**Box 7.4. Typology of Corruption and Collusion Schemes in the Energy Sector**

Some of the typical corruption and collusion schemes in the procurement processes have the following characteristics (this list is non-exhaustive):

- Tenders and purchases of unsolicited or superfluous services and goods.
- Schemes for the purchase of equipment, works or services, which were carried out with a significant excess of the planned cost without justification and without prior agreement on the conditions for a lawful and justified contract modification (such as unforeseen increase of the cost of raw materials, change of applicable tax or labour laws etc.). The winner's product as a result is "expensive" in every sense of the word and the winner itself is usually a favoured supplier.
- Prior agreement on the price between the bidders or participation of fictive competitors (usually companies whose beneficial owners are family members/ friends from the circle of political elite or energy companies' leadership).
- Suppliers rigging the procurement process to ensure the winner is predetermined, with a large payment made in advance to the selected winner. The bid winner can be a shell company that immediately transfers the money to an offshore company or one that does not deliver on its contractual obligations.

Source: OECD (forthcoming), OECD Typology of Corruption Schemes in the Energy Sector

## Outlook and policy recommendations

The impact of the COVID-19 outbreak on Ukraine's economy, including on the energy sector, the ongoing conflict in eastern Ukraine, and the high perception of corruption and of a weak justice system in the country have been challenging for investors interested in Ukraine's energy sector. Despite significant governance and judicial system reforms, as well as in the area of public procurement, trust in the government's combat against corruption remains low.

- **Continue ongoing reforms to prevent and combat corruption**, with a special focus on high-level corruption.
- **Ensure the independence of the anti-corruption agencies**, NABU, SAPO, and the High Anti-Corruption Court, and that these agencies are sufficiently resourced, staffed, and empowered to conduct investigations, as well as shielded from political and other improper interferences.
- **Pursue a holistic approach** for reforming Ukraine's judiciary in line with international standards and good practices. Continue judicial reforms to strengthen Ukraine's judicial independence and

effectiveness and increase public confidence; address inconsistencies in legal and regulatory frameworks.

- **Continue actions to simplify and make more transparent public procurement** proceedings in line with the findings of the forthcoming OECD *Typology of Corruption Schemes in the Energy Sector* in Ukraine, including ensuring clear and accessible policies on procurement in SOEs and encouraging the establishment of specialised board committees on procurement when appropriate. Given that the public procurement system in Ukraine still suffers from low trust by businesses and citizens alike, the country could make further use of the OECD *Recommendation on Fighting Bid Rigging in Public Procurement* and of the OECD *Recommendation on Public Procurement.* Ukraine should also continue to seek international assistance, which can provide capacity-building training that is focused on the fight against corruption and conflicts of interest in the procurement system.

## Notes

---

[1] The Natural Gas Market Law of Ukraine (2015), https://zakon.rada.gov.ua/laws/show/329-19#Text.

[2] The Electricity Market Law No 4493 of 2016 was adopted in June 2017 coming into full effect in July 2019. The Law aligns Ukraine's national legislation with the European Union's regulation embodied in the Third Energy Package on the European gas and electricity markets liberalising the country's national electricity market, available at: https://zakon.rada.gov.ua/laws/show/2019-19.

[3] ProZorro has been integrated with the unified state register of legal entities and individual entrepreneurs which allows for automatic verification of a tenderer's data.

[4] Available at https://zakon.rada.gov.ua/laws/show/2269-19.

[5] The law divides companies into three categories: those to be privatised, liquidated, or retained.

[6] See ProZorro website: https://prozorro.gov.ua/en.

[7] See www.kyivpost.com/ukraine-politics/zelensky-signs-law-improving-criminal-liability-for-inaccurate-declaring-of-assets.html.

[8] See Law of Ukraine "On Amendments to the Law of Ukraine On Prevention of Corruption" concerning whistleblowers, https://zakon.rada.gov.ua/laws/show/198-20#Text.

[9] On 27 October 2020, Ukraine's Constitutional Court by decision no. 13-r/2020 invalidated as unconstitutional NACP's mandate to verify the accuracy of financial declarations submitted by public officials as well as Article 366-1 of the Criminal Code of Ukraine, which provides criminal liability for submitting false declarations (or for failure to submit a declaration). Due to this decision, the mechanism of asset declarations has become largely ineffective and over 100 pending corruption cases at the time were closed.

[10] See www.ukrinform.net/rubric-polytics/3126275-g7-ambassadors-on-constitutional-court-decision-ukraine-must-not-go-back-to-past.html, https://www.intellinews.com/nbu-says-no-imf-tranche-for-ukraine-this-year-196579/.

[11] See www.kyivpost.com/ukraine-politics/nabu-largest-corruption-energy-sector-among-economic-sectors.html.

[12] Law “On amendments to certain legislative acts of Ukraine on ensuring the effectiveness of the institutional mechanism for corruption prevention“ (No. 140-IX, 2 February 2019) aims at replacing the management structure of the National Agency on Corruption Prevention (NACP), strengthening NACP’s capacity and guaranteeing of its independence.

[13] In September 2019, Ukraine adopted the Law of Ukraine No. 113-IX “On amendments to certain legislative acts of Ukraine on priority measures for the reform of the prosecution authorities“, reforming the Public Prosecutor’s Office of Ukraine into the Prosecutor General’s Office (PGO) that started working in February 2020.

[14] See www.kyivpost.com/ukraine-politics/kyiv-court-epitomizes-corruption-impunity.html.

[15] Available in Ukrainian at: https://zakon.rada.gov.ua/laws/show/922-19#Text.

[16] Association Agreement between the European Union and its Member States, of the one part, and Ukraine, of the other part, 21 March 2014, Article 153, https://trade.ec.europa.eu/doclib/docs/2016/november/tradoc_155103.pdf.

## References


American Chamber of commerce of Ukraine (2021), *Ukraine Business Climate Survey Post-Pandemic Horizon*, https://chamber.ua/wp-content/uploads/2021/09/Post-pandemic-horizon_final.pdf. [16]

Chatham House (2018), *Are Ukraine’s Anti-corruption Reforms Working*, https://www.chathamhouse.org/2018/11/are-ukraines-anti-corruption-reforms-working. [3]

European Commission (2020), *Association Implementation Report on Ukraine*, https://eu-ua.org/sites/default/files/inline/files/ar_aa_implementation-2019-4_eng.pdf. [7]

Gerasimov, C. and I. Solonenko (2020), *Rule of Law Reform after Zelenskyi’s First Year*, https://dgap.org/sites/default/files/article_pdfs/DGAP-Analysis-2020-4-EN.pdf. [5]

Kuzio, T. (2008), “Ukrainian Politics, Energy and Corruption under Kuchma and Yushchenko”, http://www.taraskuzio.com/conferences2_files/Ukrainian_Politics_Energy.pdf. [1]

NABU (2020), *Abuse of office by the KDAC judges: new episodes (video decoding) | National Anti-Corruption Bureau of Ukraine*, https://nabu.gov.ua/en/novyny/abuse-office-kdac-judges-new-episodes-video-decoding. [18]

NABU (2020), *National Anti-Corruption Bureau of Ukraine Report: January to June 2020*, https://nabu.gov.ua/en/report/report-first-half-2020. [15]

NABU (2020), *National Anti-Corruption Bureau of Ukraine Report: July to December 2020*, https://nabu.gov.ua/en/report/report-second-half-2020. [13]

NABU (n.d.), *National Anti-Corruption Bureau of Ukraine Website*, https://nabu.gov.ua/en. [8]

OECD (2021), *Fighting bid rigging in public procurement in the energy sector in Ukraine*, https://www.oecd.org/daf/competition/fighting-bid-rigging-in-public-procurement-in-the-energy-sector-in-ukraine.htm. [20]

OECD (2021), *OECD Review of the Corporate Governance of State-Owned Enterprises: Ukraine*, https://www.oecd.org/corporate/soe-review-ukraine.htm. [14]

OECD (2019), *Istanbul Anti-Corruption Action Plan, Fourth Round of Monitoring of Ukraine*, https://www.oecd.org/corruption/acn/OECD-ACN-Ukraine-Progress-Update-2019-EN.pdf. [10]

OECD (2019), *Snapshot of Ukraine's Energy Sector: Institutions, Governance and Policy Framework*, https://www.oecd.org/eurasia/competitiveness-programme/eastern-partners/Snapshot-of-Ukraines-Energy-Sector-EN.pdf. [2]

OECD (2018), *Fighting Corruption in Eastern Europe and Central Asia Anti-Corruption Reforms in Ukraine: Prevention and Prosecution of Corruption in State-Owned Enterprises 4 th round of monitoring of the Istanbul Anti-Corruption Action Plan*, https://www.oecd.org/corruption/acn/OECD-ACN-Ukraine-4th-Round-Bis-Report-SOE-Sector-2018-ENG.pdf. [11]

OECD (2018), *Maintaining the Momentum of Decentralisation in Ukraine*, OECD Multi-level Governance Studies, OECD Publishing, Paris, https://dx.doi.org/10.1787/9789264301436-en. [6]

OECD (2015), *OECD Recommendation on Public Procurement*, https://www.oecd.org/gov/public-procurement/OECD-Recommendation-on-Public-Procurement.pdf. [21]

OECD (2012), *OECD Recommendation on Fighting Bid Rigging in Public Procurment*, https://www.oecd.org/daf/competition/RecommendationOnFightingBidRigging2012.pdf. [19]

Open Government Partnership (2019), *Global Report on Open Contracting: Anti-Corruption Initiatives*, https://www.opengovpartnership.org/wp-content/uploads/2019/05/Global-Report_Open-Contract.pdf. [4]

Transparency International (2019), *Best-Known Cases of the High Anti-Corruption Court | Transparency International Ukraine*, https://ti-ukraine.org/en/news/best-known-cases-of-the-high-anti-corruption-court/. [17]

Ukraine Specialised Anti-Corruption Prosecutor's Office (n.d.), *Ukraine Specialised Anti-Corruption Prosecutor's Office Website*, https://nabu.gov.ua/en/tags/specialized-anti-corruption-prosecutors-office. [9]

World Bank (2020), *What Is the Cost of Crony Capitalism for Ukraine?*, https://www.worldbank.org/en/news/opinion/2018/03/15/what-is-the-cost-of-crony-capitalism-for-ukraine. [12]

# 8 Responsible Business Conduct in Ukraine's Energy Sector

This chapter provides an overview of the responsible business conduct (RBC) landscape in Ukraine and outlines steps taken by the government to promote and enable responsible business practices in the energy sector. It proposes policy recommendations to further enhance RBC practices applicable to the sector and promote sustainable development.

## Introduction

Responsible business conduct (RBC) helps attract and retain quality investments, and ensures that business activities contribute to broader value creation. RBC centres on the expectation that all businesses – regardless of their status, size, ownership structure or sector – avoid and address negative impacts of their activities. A core element of RBC is ensuring that businesses carry out due diligence to mitigate potential and actual adverse impacts throughout their operations, supply chains and relationships. Moreover, enhancing RBC is integral for attracting quality investments, as outlined in the OECD Policy Framework for Investment. Ukraine's energy sector has been associated with important RBC-related challenges, including social, environmental and governance risks, and creating an enabling environment for RBC has been particularly relevant for ensuring the sustainability of upstream, midstream and downstream activities in the sector. Further to mitigating adverse impacts and attracting quality investments, promoting RBC policies has been significant for meeting international commitments, particularly under the EU-Ukraine Association Agreement.

To create an enabling environment for RBC, Ukraine has adopted laws and regulations on environmental and social protection, and anti-corruption measures, which are applicable to its energy sector. In 2017, the country also became an adherent to the Declaration on International Investment and Multinational Enterprises, which entails promoting policies and practices outlined under the *OECD Guidelines for Multinational Enterprises* (MNE Guidelines) and establishing a National Contact Point, which was set up in 2018. It has also adopted RBC-related policies, including the National Strategy on Human Rights and an action plan, and a concept and an action plan on corporate social responsibility (CSR), while joining the Extractive Industries Transparency Initiative (EITI). Despite these efforts, further steps are needed to enhance RBC in Ukraine's energy sector, including strengthening policy frameworks and enforcement to advance anti-corruption efforts, as well as environmental, labour and human rights protections. Other areas include improving transparency and disclosure practices in the sector, as well as strengthening the role of the National Contact Point, as further elaborated below.

## Scope and importance of RBC

Following the adoption of the 2030 Sustainable Development Agenda, many businesses, governments, and stakeholders have sought to enhance responsible business conduct (RBC). Related concepts include corporate social responsibility (CSR) and Business and Human Rights (BHR), which are often used interchangeably with RBC. Collectively, these concepts reflect the expectation that businesses should consider the impact of their operations and supply chains on people, the planet and society. A key characteristic of these concepts is that they call on businesses to contribute positively to sustainable development by going beyond domestic requirements, while managing risks and harms that may result from their operations, as well as throughout their supply chains and relationships. These concepts are not and should not be understood as philanthropy. To help enhance responsible conduct, there has been convergence on RBC across international instruments, as further outlined under Box 8.1.

## Box 8.1. Key International Instruments on RBC

The three main instruments that have become key reference points for RBC and outline how companies can act responsibly include the OECD *Guidelines for Multinational Enterprises*, the ILO *Tripartite Declaration of Principles concerning Multinational Enterprises and Social Policy*, and UN *Guiding Principles on Business and Human Rights*. These instruments are aligned with and complement each other.

The OECD *Guidelines for Multinational Enterprises* (MNE Guidelines) are recommendations from governments to businesses on how to act responsibly and represent a part of the OECD Declaration on International Investment and Multinational Enterprises. The Guidelines cover all areas of business responsibility, including labour and human rights issues, environment, disclosure, bribery, consumer interests, science and technology, competition, and taxation. The MNE Guidelines also include a unique non-judicial grievance mechanism known as the National Contact Points (NCPs).To date, 50 countries, including OECD and non-OECD members, have adhered to the Guidelines and have established NCPs. In addition, the OECD *Due Diligence Guidance for Responsible Business Conduct* provides practical support for enterprises in implementing the Guidelines and helps them operationalise RBC instruments. It introduces a due diligence and risk management mechanism, which includes embedding RBC practices within the core of company operations, identifying, preventing and mitigating adverse impacts, engaging in monitoring and evaluation, communicating results, and providing access to remedy, as needed. In addition to a cross-sectoral instrument, the OECD has developed guidance to provide tailored recommendations across sectors, including agriculture, minerals, extractives, garments and footwear, and finance.

The ILO *Tripartite Declaration of Principles concerning Multinational Enterprises and Social Policy* (the ILO Declaration) provides guidance to encourage positive contributions companies can make to advance economic and social progress, and to minimise and resolve adverse impacts in their operations. The ILO Declaration also provides policy guidance to governments, as well as employers' and workers' organisations, which play central and distinctive roles in creating an enabling environment for responsible business. Its recommendations on employment, training, conditions of work and life, and industrial relations are based on international labour standards, including the fundamental Conventions underpinning the ILO Declaration on Fundamental Principles and Rights at Work (1998) which addresses forced labour, child labour, non-discrimination and freedom of association, and collective bargaining. The ILO Declaration was updated in 2017 to include new labour standards and policy outcomes, and to make references to developments, such as the adoption of the UN Guiding Principles and the 2030 Agenda.

The UN Guiding Principles on Business and Human Rights (UN Guiding Principles) focus on avoiding and addressing adverse business-related human rights impacts. They are founded on three pillars: 1) the state duty to protect against human rights abuses by third parties, including businesses, 2) the independent responsibility of businesses to respect human rights, which means that they should avoid infringing on human rights and should address adverse human rights impacts with which they are involved, and 3) the need for those harmed by business-related activities to have access to effective remedy. These principles were unanimously endorsed in 2011 by the UN Human Rights Council. Both the Office of the UN High Commissioner for Human Rights (OHCHR) and the UN Working Group on Business and Human Rights (UN Working Group) are to promote the UN Guiding Principles and their implementation, including by unpacking what the principles mean in practice with respect to different human rights issues, sectors and types of actors.

Source: (OECD, 2019[1])

The main OECD instrument for promoting and enabling RBC is the OECD *Guidelines for Multinational Enterprises* (the MNE Guidelines). To support the implementation of the MNE Guidelines, the OECD has developed due diligence guidance, which provides practical recommendations for businesses on how to identify and respond to risks and adverse impacts throughout company operations, supply chains and business relationships. While adopting a cross-sectoral *Due Diligence Guidance for Responsible Business Conduct*, specific instruments have also been adopted for agriculture, extractives, minerals, garment and footwear, and financial sectors.[1]

The MNE Guidelines have an implementation mechanism known as the National Contact Points (NCPs), which are agencies established by governments to fulfil a twofold mandate: (i) to promote the MNE Guidelines and related due diligence guidance, and (ii) to handle cases (referred to as "specific instances") as a non-judicial grievance mechanism. Governments adhering to the MNE Guidelines have an obligation to establish an NCP, which, to date, has been achieved across all 50 adhering economies.

Considering that the MNE Guidelines provide a comprehensive coverage across thematic aspects to promote responsible conduct, their provisions and recommendations can also be used to improve RBC within the energy sector, including with regard to addressing environmental, social and governance issues.[2] More specifically:

- *Environmental.* Energy company operations often contribute to pollution and challenges in waste management, and greenhouse gas emissions, and can have a negative impact on land, water and biodiversity, as well as on human well-being. For example, companies operating in the hydrocarbons sector can witness improper drilling, extraction and resource management, which could lead to environmental degradation. In addition, producers of nuclear power may face hazards due to processing and storing radioactive waste, while hydro power plant operations may negatively impact rivers, reservoirs and communities. Moreover, a lack of energy efficiency measures often result in wasteful energy consumption, leading to excess emissions and high levels of pollution.
- *Social.* Key social risks faced by energy companies relate to employee and industrial relations, and human rights. This is particularly relevant in facing hazardous working conditions, such as grid operations, exposure to toxic substances, and a lack of protective equipment. Certain sectors also carry higher risks of human rights violations, e.g. through forced and child labour. Moreover, activities carried out by energy companies (such as mining, drilling and infrastructure development) may negatively impact local communities and violate stakeholder rights. For example, energy company operations and infrastructure development without stakeholder consultation may result in the triggering of disputes, which could result in stalling operations.
- *Governance.* Energy companies often face risks related to transparency and disclosure, and the presence of vested interests, and may experience corruption, bribery and extortion, particularly in the hydrocarbons sectors. Further governance risks, including conflicts of interest, can stem from improper separation of ownership, regulatory and policymaking functions, particularly among state-owned enterprises. More broadly, an absence of a risk assessment and mitigation mechanism in corporate governance frameworks may raise challenges in identifying and mitigating aforesaid risks not only in operations, but throughout business relationships and supply chains.

The aforementioned energy sector-related risks, however, are not exhaustive, and additional factors may need to be taken into consideration. These include potential or actual adverse impacts associated with low-carbon transition and efforts to promote digitalisation, among others (OECD, 2021[2]).

## Efforts to promote policy coherence on RBC in Ukraine

As highlighted in this *Review*, Ukraine became the 47th country to adhere to the OECD *Declaration on International Investment and Multinational Enterprises* in 2017. In May 2018, Ukraine also adhered to the *Recommendation of the Council on the OECD Due Diligence Guidance for Responsible Business Conduct* that aims to provide practical support to enterprises on the implementation of the MNE Guidelines and seeks to promote a common understanding among governments and stakeholders on due diligence practices applicable to businesses. Moreover, to meet requirements as an adherent to the declaration and to further the effectiveness of the MNE Guidelines, Ukraine established a National Contact Point (NCP) under its Ministry of Economy. The NCP reports to the government and has an advisory body, and engages in awareness raising on RBC through events and information dissemination. However, the NCP currently has only part-time staff and remains under-resourced. Moreover, while the NCP engages with businesses, it does not currently engage with NGOs, trade unions, or other advisory bodies (OECD, 2020[3]).

### *National Human Rights Strategy and Action Plan*

Over the years, Ukraine has sought to enhance RBC through its policy framework. In 2015, the country adopted a National Strategy on Human Rights and its Action Plan for the period 2015-2020. The National Strategy and the Action Plan covered 25 sectors and included almost 200 actions (Government of Ukraine, 2015[4]). In March 2021, the President of Ukraine approved a new National Strategy on Human Rights, which aims to improve the framework governing responsible business conduct in the country. In particular, the new strategy has introduced Strategic Direction 16 that ensures respect for human rights when engaging in business activities. (This provision was proposed by the working group set up by the Ministry of Justice and was supported by Ukraine's Business Ombudsman, the National Contact Point, and civil society organisations.) The new strategy also includes sections on labour rights protection and anti-discrimination practices, as well as on environmental protection (Ukrinform, 2021[5]) (Government of Ukraine, 2021[6]) (Danish Institute for Human Rights, 2021[7]).

To implement the National Strategy on Human Rights, in June 2021 the Ukrainian Government approved an action plan, which includes approximately 100 actions to be implemented in the next three years.[3] The action plan cover areas related to preventing discrimination in the workplace, ensuring equal rights and opportunities for men and women, creating conditions for freedom of entrepreneurship and ensuring the right to work. It also contained a reference on strengthening social responsibility of businesses and incorporating CSR-related practices into their operations. However, the action plan includes limited aspects with regard to environmental and consumer protection, and anti-corruption measures (Ukrainian Helsinki Human Rights Union, 2020[8]).

In addition, in January 2019, the Ministry of Justice announced it would start developing a National Action Plan on Business and Human Rights. As part of the process, the Yaroslav Mudryi National Law University, in co-operation with the Ministry of Justice, prepared and published a National Baseline Assessment in mid-2019 (Danish Institute for Human Rights, 2021[7]) The assessment revealed that while Ukraine has ratified core international treaties on human rights,[4] there is currently no guidance on how businesses can appropriately ensure protection of human rights, and determine social and environmental impacts of their operations. The assessment also revealed that the mining sector continued to witness significant human rights violations (as further examined in the following sections) (Yaroslav Mudryi National Law University, 2019[9]). While this action plan is still being developed, the provision on protecting human rights when carrying out business activities was incorporated under the current National Strategy on Human Rights, as mentioned above.

### Concept on Corporate Social Responsibility

In January 2020, the Cabinet of Ministers of Ukraine approved the Concept for the Implementation of State Policy in the Field of Promoting Corporate Social Responsibility (CSR) for the period until 2030. The Concept references the MNE Guidelines, and it aims to promote CSR and sustainable practices in the country (Government of Ukraine, 2020[10]). The Concept and a subsequent action plan for implementation were developed by the Ministry of Economy, and they set the basis for creating policies and implementing actions that would advance RBC in Ukraine (European Business Association, 2020[11]). Moreover, the strategy and action plan have introduced specific targets, which include decreasing wage gaps and work-related accidents, and increasing minimum wage, while attracting FDI, among others. (Government of Ukraine, 2020[10]). While these indicators are RBC-related, the Concept does not integrate the full scope of RBC principles outlined in the MNE Guidelines, or related instruments and standards.

### Linking RBC with Ukraine's energy strategies

Further to adopting broader policies, Ukraine has sought to translate RBC-related measures in strategies applicable specifically to the energy sector. While the 2035 Energy Strategy of Ukraine (ESU), the Low Emission Development Strategy, and the Green Energy Transition Concept until 2050 do not directly reference RBC, they include provisions, such as improving disclosure and environmental protection. For example, the ESU seeks to enhance transparency in the extractives sector and to align with the Extractive Industries Transparency Initiative (EITI). It also requires all energy resources to be produced and supplied with high levels of environmental responsibility, while looking to promote energy efficiency and reduce greenhouse gas (GHG) emissions. Moreover, the Government of Ukraine has also sought to restructure the coal sector and avoid adverse social and environmental impacts by looking to develop mitigation plans for coal mines and generation plants (Government of Ukraine, 2017[12]).

## RBC policy frameworks applicable to Ukraine's energy sector

Further to the aforementioned initiatives, broader RBC-related legal and regulatory frameworks are applicable to Ukraine's energy sector. While the country has taken steps towards improving laws and regulations related to environmental protection, human and labour rights, anti-corruption and disclosure, it continues to witness challenges across these areas, as further examined below.

### Anti-corruption efforts in Ukraine's energy sector

#### Corruption in Ukraine's energy sector

According to the National Anti-Corruption Bureau of Ukraine (NABU), Ukraine's energy sector has been subject to one of the highest volume of corruption-related abuses, with estimated losses in the sector reaching UAH 3 billion in 2020 (NABU, 2021[13]). Challenges often stem from Ukraine's weak institutional and governance structures, large rents from extractive activities, and market concentration among specific groups (Extractive Industries Transparency Initiative, 2019[14]) (Flaker, Sergi and Teichmann, 2021[15]). Enforcement is often constrained due to a lack of resources and undue interference with anti-corruption agencies through vested interests. For example, high levels of secrecy surrounding the extraction of oil and gas production create an impression that politically connected actors are affecting licensing processes (Chatham House, 2018[16]). Other challenges are related to conflicting legal and regulatory requirements, as well as issues related to the corporate governance of state-owned enterprises, which are heavily concentrated in the energy sector (Chatham House, 2018[16]) (Centre for Economic Strategy, 2020[17]) (OECD, 2021[18]). Previous OECD studies have also outlined corruption-related challenges in Ukraine's energy sector, and a forthcoming Typology of Corruption Schemes is expected to document specific cases of (alleged) corruption (see Box 8.2).

**Box 8.2. Typology of Corruption Schemes in the Energy Sector**

A forthcoming report on the OECD Typology of Corruption Schemes in the Energy Sector in Ukraine will document cases of (alleged) corruption in the energy sector. Some of the typical schemes have the following characteristics (this list is non-exhaustive):

- A system of kickbacks at which the price of goods and services is increased at least several times in order to pay bribes to lobbyists, politically connected individuals and relatives, including in SOEs.
- Tenders and purchases of unsolicited or superfluous services and goods (or via intermediaries).
- Schemes for the purchase of equipment, works or services, which are carried out with a significant excess of the planned cost. Suppliers that offer a lower price are simply "thrown out" of the tender on artificial, pre-set formal grounds. The winner's product as a result is "expensive" in every sense of the word and the winner itself is usually a favoured supplier.
- Prior agreement on the price between the bidders or participation of fictive competitors (usually represented by the companies whose beneficial owners are family members/ friends from the circle of political elite or energy companies' leadership).
- Bid rigging the procurement process to ensure the bidder is predetermined, with a large payment made in advance to the selected supplier. The bid winner can be a shell company that immediately transfers the money to an offshore company or one that does not deliver on its contractual obligations.
- Outsourcing services previously carried out by an energy SOE to an external provider, who then bribes the SOE officials to use the company's own resources (equipment and staff) to carry out the outsourced services.

Source: (OECD, 2021[18])

### *Anti-corruption efforts*

Ukraine has taken important steps to enhance its institutional capacity to fight corruption through the creation of specialised agencies. These include Special Anti-Corruption Prosecutor's Office (SAPO); the National Agency for the Prevention of Corruption (NAPC), responsible for the development of anti-corruption policy and the prevention of corruption; and the National Anti-Corruption Bureau of Ukraine (NABU), responsible for preventing, exposing, stopping, investigating and solving corruption-related offences committed by high-level officials. The establishment of the High Anti-Corruption Court in 2018, and the launch of its operations in 2019 as a specialised judicial body with nationwide jurisdiction over high-level corruption cases helped improve efficiency in addressing corruption-related cases.

Ukraine has also introduced the Law on "On Prevention of Corruption", which mandates companies to assess corruption risks and implement anti-corruption measures. Although the Law prohibits bribery by officials of legal entities, it does not impose liability on corporations. Further to the Law on Prevention of Corruption, the Criminal Code of Ukraine establishes that legal entities, as well as employees and officers, may face sanctions for corruption offences. Efforts have also been made to strengthen whistleblower protection and to remove liability for disseminating information related to criminal offences.

Moreover, as indicated in the previous chapter of this *Review,* in order to strengthen anti-corruption measures and as a follow up to the 2014-2017 Anti-Corruption Strategy, in June 2020 the National Agency for the Prevention of Corruption (NAPC) released the National Anti-Corruption Strategy for the period 2020-2024. The new strategy seeks to fill the gaps identified in the previous version, particularly since NAPC considered that it was unable to achieve its objectives due to constraints on its operations (Government of Ukraine, 2020[19]). Despite improvements, concrete results in reducing corruption in the energy sector remain to be achieved (International Monetary fund, 2020[20]).

### *Anti-corruption and public procurement in the energy sector*

The adoption of the Law on Public Procurement in 2015 and the introduction of ProZorro, an e-procurement platform, helped improve transparency of public procurement contracts in Ukraine's energy sector (Synyutka, 2019[21]). Public procurement requirements generally apply to state agencies and majority-owned commercial SOEs that engage in certain activities, including gas transportation, though many other SOEs use ProZorro as a procurement platform (OECD, 2021[18]). As mentioned in Chapter 2, energy SOEs, including Ukrenergo and Naftogaz, were some of the first entities in Ukraine that started using ProZorro, allowing them to generate savings (Ukrenergo, 2019[22]) (Naftogaz, 2020[23]).

Despite these improvements, corruption in public procurement still remains prevalent. For instance, NABU uncovered a scheme involving three state-owned coal companies that took place between 2016 and 2018 and resulted in UAH 51.2 million in losses. NABU identified that tenders were organised on behalf of the Selydivvuhilya, Myrnohradvuhilya, and Shakhtopravlinnya state-owned mines and 70 tender contracts were established with a single company, in which the organisers had vested interests. Tenders included the supply of mining equipment, metal products and mining cables. The company re-sold products to the state-owned mines at inflated prices after purchasing them on the open market (Government of Ukraine, 2020[24]). Another case was related to the embezzlement of UAH 14.33 million, which was allocated by the CMU in 2018 to coal mines located in Luhansk to introduce technology for preventing accidents (NABU, 2020[25]).

### *Efforts to combat corruption in energy SOEs*

State-owned enterprises (SOEs) in the energy sector have continue to face particular challenges with regard to corruption, and have sought to take steps to mitigate corruption-related risks. Notably, they report to the NAPC and, depending on their activities and number of employees, are required to develop anti-corruption programmes that evaluate corruption risks, resolve conflicts of interest, protect whistle-blowers and ensure due diligence in procurement processes. Some SOEs, including Naftogaz, Energoatom, Ukrenergo, and Ukrhydroenergo have developed such programmes, while adopting ethics codes and implementing anti-corruption policies. Compliance with ISO standards relative to anti-bribery management systems is also gaining foothold among companies (OECD, 2021[2]). However, conflicting legal and regulatory provisions have contributed to weakening anti-corruption efforts in SOEs. For example, legislation stipulates that the CEO of an SOE needs to appoint an anti-corruption officer, which creates potential conflicts of interest and could hamper anti-corruption efforts. Moreover, the NAPC lacks resources, capacity and mandate to effectively monitor implementation of anti-corruption programmes across the SOE portfolio (OECD, 2021[18]).

## ***Environmental issues in Ukraine's energy sector***

### *Environmental risks in Ukraine's energy sector*

Ukraine continues to witness environmental challenges stemming from its energy sector, not least because its energy consumption is nearly three times the OECD average per unit of GDP (OECD, 2019[26]). Considering the composition of Ukraine's energy mix and dependence on hydrocarbons, companies engaged in oil, gas, and coal sectors are often responsible for air pollution, greenhouse gas emissions, decreased quality of water resources and land degradation, as well as human health issues associated with environmental risk factors (World Bank, 2016[27]) (International Finance Corporation, 2017[28]). The operation of coal mines in Ukraine has often resulted in challenges due to water pollution, wastewater treatment and flooding, and air pollution and emissions due to the burning of waste heaps (including in both government and non-government controlled territories). Further to extraction, risks are also posed by the operation of thermal power plants (TPP) and combined heat and power plants (CHP) that require coal and/or gas as inputs (International Finance Corporation, 2008[29]). As of December 2020, Ukraine had a total installed capacity of the power system reaching 54 498 megawatts (MW), of which, 21 842 MW were generated by TPP and 6 069 MW were produced by CHP plants (STATISTA, 2020[30]). In 2019, two-thirds of greenhouse gas emissions in the country were energy-related, of which power and heat generation represented 47% (Government of Ukraine, 2020[31]).

The main operators of coal and gas-fired power plants are DTEK and Centrenergo. In 2019, their total GHG emissions amounted to 9.6 million tonnes and 5.2 million tonnes in $CO_2$ equivalent, respectively (DTEK, 2020[32]) (Centrenergo, 2019[33]). In 2020, Burstyn power plant (operated by DTEK) was responsible for emitting 123 000 tonnes of sulphur dioxide, 26 000 tonnes of dust and 11 000 tonnes of nitrogen oxides, while its fuel efficiency and sulphur dioxide emissions per kWh were 1.5 times higher compared to Polish and German counterparts (BOELL, 2020[34]). As indicated in Chapter 2 of this *Review*, to decarbonise its electricity mix and reduce the adverse environmental impacts of coal, Ukraine is planning to increase its share of renewables and to align policies with the European Green Deal (See Box 8.3).

### Box 8.3. The European Green Deal: an opportunity to decarbonise Ukraine's economy

The European Green Deal (EGD) is a roadmap to transform Europe into the world's first climate-neutral continent by 2050, while stimulating economic development, improving health and quality of life, and transforming climate and environmental challenges to opportunities. The Green Deal was approved by the European Commission in December 2019. Strategies, plans, and legal framework to implement the EGD will be drafted and approved during 2020-2021. Currently, the pace of implementing EGD has slowed due to Covid-19. However, the European Commission reiterated that the recovery will focus on ensuring sustainability and digitalisation, and introducing solutions with positive economic and environmental outcomes.

A key target of the EGD is further decarbonisation of the energy system, which is currently responsible for 75% of GHG emissions in the EU. To reach climate neutrality by 2050, EGD sets the following targets for energy industry: 1) RES as a basis for electrical energy industry (rejection of coal, transition to decarbonised gas, unlocking the potential of offshore wind energy); 2) energy efficiency, particularly in buildings; 3) just energy transition (engaging consumers as beneficiaries and combating energy poverty); 4) development of infrastructure through integration and digital transformation.

In Ukraine, the energy sector is responsible for over two-thirds of GHG emissions. Though the country shows an active development of RES, Ukraine falls behind the EU average in terms of RES as a share of electricity generation. Over 2019, in Ukraine and the EU, variable RES-based generation accounted for 3.6% and 23.8%, respectively. Moreover, according to the most optimistic scenario of the 2050 Strategy for Low Carbon Development of Ukraine, greenhouse gas emissions in 2050 will account for 31% of the 1990 levels, while the EU intends to reach a full climate neutrality by that time. As part of promoting decarbonisation, in 2020 the State Agency on Energy Efficiency and Energy Saving of Ukraine announced that an agreement was being prepared between Ukraine and the EU regarding the implementation of the Green Deal, though details remain to be confirmed.

Source: International Renaissance Foundation (2020) European Green Deal: Opportunities and Threats to Ukraine (International Renaissance Foundation, 2020[35]) and (Ukrinform, 2020[36])

Further environmental risks may be affiliated with low-carbon sources, including potential discharges from nuclear plants, as well as the construction and operation of hydro power plants, which may negatively impact water resources and biodiversity (OECD, 2021[2]). In addition, solar and wind power plants can pose risks to biodiversity derived from land clearing and operation of turbines (International Finance Corporation, 2008[29]). In Ukraine, RES producers have substantially increased their generation capacity, reaching 12% of the total installed capacity of the power system. As of June 2021, renewable projects built and operating in Ukraine had not reported negative environmental impacts (State Statistics Service of Ukraine, n.d.[37]). (However, as further outlined in Box 8.4, this may result from the classification of certain renewable projects, some of which may be exempt from examination).

### *Environmental Impact Assessment*

Following the recommendations of the Secretariat of the Energy Community on improving environmental performance and meeting international obligations, Ukraine adopted the Law "On Environmental Impact Assessment (EIA)", which entered into force in December 2017. The Law on EIA is aligned with the obligations under the EU-Ukraine Association Agreement. More specifically, it transposed the requirements of Directive 2011/92 on the assessment of the effects of individual public and private projects on the environment, as well as the relevant provisions of Directive 2003/4 on access to environmental information (Energy Community, 2016[38]). By setting legal and organisational policies for environmental impact assessments, the Law on EIA seeks to avoid and prevent environmental damage, while ensuring environmental protection, rational use and restoration of natural resources, and taking into account public and private interests.

Since the introduction of the Law on EIA, it has become mandatory to perform environmental impact assessments to obtain permits authorising all types of energy projects, including construction, modernisation and operation of facilities (Verkhovna Rada, 2017[39]). This Law groups activities in two categories. The first category includes gas and oil refineries, thermal power stations, extraction of oil and natural gas on the continental shelf, construction of gas pipelines with a diameter of 0.8m or greater and over 40 km in length, and aerial electricity lines with a voltage of 220kV or more and over 15 km in length. The second category includes deep drilling, certain agriculture and infrastructure projects, certain mining and extraction industries, hydropower plants, wind power plants with two or more turbines or where their height is 50m or more. For activities falling under the first category, the Ministry of Environmental Protection and Natural Resources (MEPR) is responsible for issuing opinions on EIA. For the second category, environmental departments of local state administrations are responsible for issuing opinions on the EIA. Temporary suspension or termination of business activity can be ruled by court in case of failure to comply with the Law on EIA (Verkhovna Rada, 2017[39]).

To improve transparency, a unified EIA register was developed, which is administered by the Ministry of Environmental Protection and Natural Resources of Ukraine (Government of Ukraine, 2021[40]). The registry is aimed at simplifying the process of conducting the EIA procedure for new projects, raising public awareness of potential projects and related risks, and ensuring transparency in the decision-making process. It records and discloses the assessment of the potential environmental effects of the project, as well as decisions and measures taken to reduce potential negative environmental impacts of planned activities (OECD, 2021[2]). Further to disclosing EIA-related filings online, the overall process involves mandatory consultations with local communities. While completion of the EIA and consultations are required, in July 2020 Ukraine amended the Law on EIA to temporarily suspend public discussions of the EIA reports with local communities due to Covid-19 and substitute them with written comments and suggestions from the public until the end of quarantine (Verkhovna Rada of Ukraine, 2020[41]).

**Box 8.4. Applicability of Environmental Impact Assessment (EIA) to wind and solar projects in Ukraine**

In October 2018, the Law "On Investment Attractiveness of the Construction of Renewable Energy Facilities" entered into force to stimulate the development of renewables, focusing on electricity production from wind and solar energy. According to this law, solar and wind projects subject to environmental impact assessment can be categorised as CC1 for obtaining construction permits.[1] The construction of objects falling under classification CC1 requires a notification (Declaration on the commencement of construction works) to be submitted in order to commence construction works, but they are exempt from expert examination of design documentation and do not require construction permits and commissioning certificates.

Note:
1. According to the Ukrainian legislation, all buildings and structures are classified in three categories determined by their complexity, which consequently influences the procedure for obtaining construction permits: (i) CC1 – lower class of consequences / insignificant consequence class; (ii) CC2 – medium class of consequences and (iii) CC3 – high class of consequences.
Source: Environmental Impact Assessment (EIA) for wind & solar projects in Ukraine, (EUEA, 2018[42]).

While the introduction of EIA has contributed to improving environmental protection, challenges remain. In particular, air pollution is still a major issue in Ukraine, with energy generation from fossil fuels contributing to almost one third of the total air pollution in the country (State Statistics Service of Ukraine, 2019[43]). Coal-fired power plants release particularly high levels of sulphur dioxide and nitrous oxide, which makes Ukraine one of the top air polluters in Europe (Environmental Performance Index, 2020[44]). The reported sulphur dioxide emissions of 20 Ukrainian coal power plants in 2019 were 589 557 tonnes, which was close to emissions by 16 power plants operating across Western Balkans that emit more sulphur dioxide than all power plants in the EU combined (Bankwatch Network, 2020[45]).

### *Environmental inspections*

State Environmental Inspection Agency carries out environmental inspections in Ukraine's energy companies. Its activities are directed and co-ordinated by the MCU through the MEPR, and its tasks include supervising environmental protection and ensuring rational use, recovery and protection of natural resources (Government of Ukraine, 2018[46]). Based on the Law "On the State Ecological Inspection of Ukraine" and the Law "On Basic Principles of State Supervision", it has the mandate to evaluate if entities comply with legislation (i) on environment safety, including the fulfilment of conditions prescribed by EIA opinions; (ii) on use and protection of lands and subsoil; (iii) on the availability of permits, limits and quotas for special use of natural resources; and (iv) on waste management. Further to carrying out inspections and checking legal and regulatory compliance, the Agency has the ability to issue fines (Extractive Industries Transparency Initiative, 2020[47]). Since 2020, discussions have been held regarding the draft law "On State Environmental Control", which aims to strengthen the role of the State Environmental Inspection Agency. According to the head of the Agency, the adoption of this draft law would increase fines for non-compliance and refusal to conduct inspections.

However, moratoria imposed by Ukrainian authorities have prevented environmental inspections across energy companies, particularly between 2014-2019. The rationale for exempting businesses from inspections was to minimise requirements for investors to operate in the country, increase investment attractiveness and facilitate entrepreneurship (World Bank, 2016[27]) (OECD, 2021[2]). To remove the moratorium on environmental inspections, in early 2020, the State Environment Inspection Agency was explicitly tasked by the Prime Minister to tackle environmental pollution by conducting a comprehensive inspection of entities suspected of pollution, including thermal power plants (Vasil Kisil & Partners, 2020[48]). As a result, in early 2020, the Inspection Agency performed more than 30 000 inspections, for which 28 500 people faced administrative responsibility and 508 criminal proceedings were opened. The overall damages caused by violation of the legislation estimated by the Inspection Agency amounted to more than UAH 2 billion (Government of Ukraine, 2021[49]). For instance, in August 2020, the Inspection Agency fined Darnytsia Heating Plant in Kiev for UAH 1 million for violating environmental laws. However, in mid-2020, a new moratorium on inspections was introduced for the duration of the COVID-19 measures, which also suspended planned inspections (EU4Climate, 2020[50]).

### *Disclosure and transparency in Ukraine's energy sector*

#### *Transparency and disclosure requirements in Ukraine's energy sector*

In the 2016 IPR, the OECD recommended that Ukraine enhance transparency and clarify (non-financial) disclosure requirements for companies. Since then, Ukraine has strengthened transparency and disclosure requirements, which are applicable to its energy sector. These requirements are outlined under the Law on Accounting and Financial Reporting, and supplementary regulations and recommendations. Disclosure requirements are more strictly applicable to large companies or those operating in specific sectors, including extractives (see Table 8.1). Moreover, companies required to submit consolidated financial statements are also required to issue consolidated annual reports, though the coverage of non-financial information is often voluntary. Based on the recommendations issued by the Ministry of Finance, non-financial reports should cover information related to environmental liabilities, social issues, personnel policy, risks, development prospects and corporate governance structure (OECD, 2021[18]).

### Table 8.1. Summary of reporting and disclosure requirements in companies by type

| Enterprise type | Financial statements | Mandatory IFRS reporting | Auditor's report | Disclosure | Reporting deadline [2] |
|---|---|---|---|---|---|
| Enterprises of public interest [4] | Yes | Yes | Yes | Yes | April 30 |
| Public joint stock companies | Yes | Yes | Yes | Yes | April 30 |
| Natural monopolies | Yes | No | Yes | Yes | April 30 |
| Companies operating in the extractives sector | Yes | Yes | Yes | Yes | April 30 |
| Large enterprises (non-issuers of securities) [3] | Yes | Yes | Yes | Yes | June 1 |
| Holding companies [1] | Yes | No | Yes | Yes | April 30 |
| Financial institutions belonging to micro and small enterprises | Yes | No | Yes | Yes | June 1 |

[1] Consolidated statements to be submitted by holding companies where two of the following conditions are met: book value is below EUR 4 million, net income is below EUR 8 million, and number of employees is below 50 individuals. They are required to prepare and submit consolidated financial statements in accordance with national accounting standards or IFRS, as well as non-financial statements.
[2] Deadlines for audited statements are together with financial statements
[3] Large enterprises are entities that meet at least two of the following criteria: (i) employ over 250 individuals, (ii) have a book value of over EUR 20 million, or (iii) have a net income of EUR 40 million)
[4] Enterprises of public interest include issuers of securities admitted to trading on stock market (or if a public offer has been made), banks, insurers, private pension funds, other financial institutions (except other financial institutions and non-governmental pension funds belonging to micro-enterprises and small enterprises) and large enterprises, as defined above.
Source: (OECD, 2021[18])

Further to general transparency and disclosure requirements applicable to companies, those operating in the extractives sector are also expected to meet requirements under the Law on Ensuring Transparency in Extractive Industries (EITI Law), which was adopted in November 2018 (see Figure 8.1). The law has been regarded as a milestone for promoting transparency and accountability in the country's oil, gas and mining sectors (DiXi Group, 2018[51]). It is aligned with requirements under the EU and the Extractive

Industry Transparency Initiative, and outlines requirements for the collection, disclosure and dissemination of data on Ukraine's extractive industries. Despite its adoption, secondary legislation remains to be introduced to ensure implementation.

One of the key aspects of the law focuses on the disclosure of payments, as well as the ultimate beneficial owners of companies and material elements related to the extractive industry, such as social obligations, building infrastructure and barter arrangements (Extractive Industries Transparency Initiative, 2018[52]). With regard to payments, EITI identified that companies operating in oil and gas extraction in Ukraine contributed 85.14% of revenues received by the government, while 6.6% of revenues came from coal mining companies (Extractive Industries Transparency Initiative, 2020[47]). EITI also recognises that Ukraine has made progress on the beneficial ownership disclosure requirement, as the government improved verification procedures through the Unified State Register of Legal Entities, Individual Entrepreneurs, and Public Organisations (Extractive Industries Transparency Initiative, 2021[53]). However, real owners are often unknown because they are hidden through shell companies and involve vested interests (Extractive Industries Transparency Initiative, 2019[14]).

**Figure 8.1. Disclosure responsibilities in accordance with the EITI Law in Ukraine**

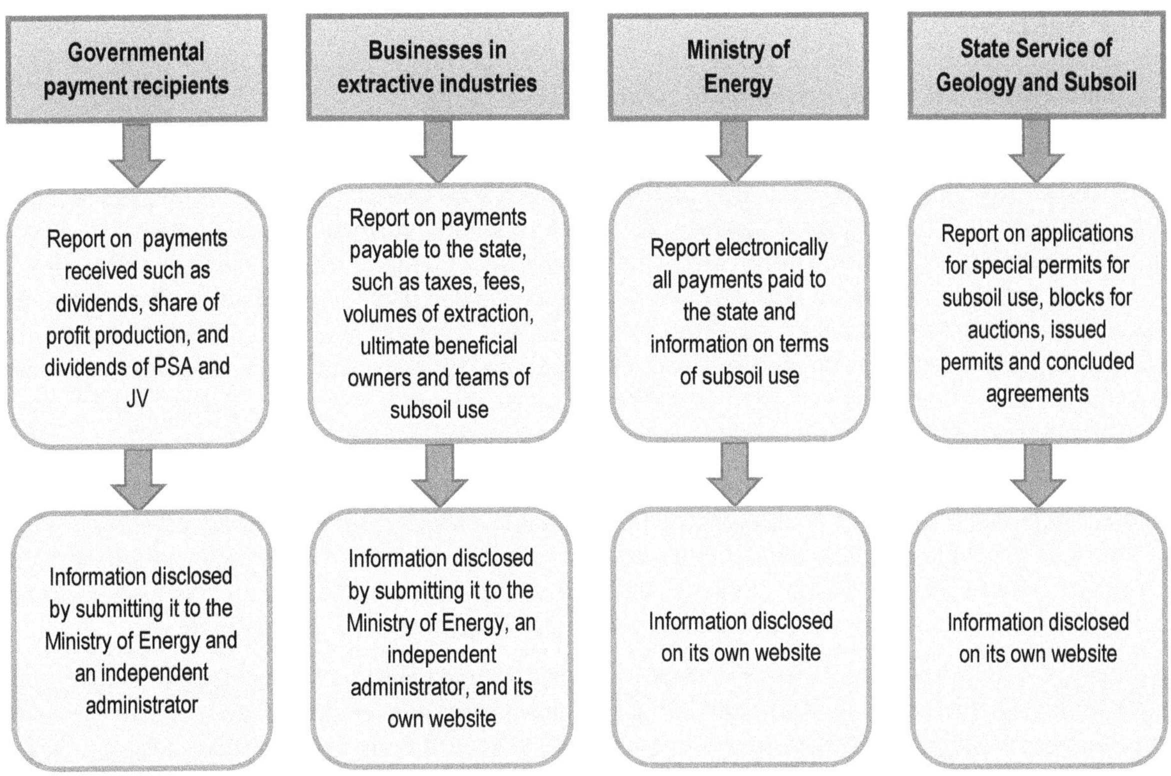


Source: (DiXi Group, 2018[51])

Furthermore, an EITI working group began collaborating with the governments of Ukraine and Germany in 2019, and, for the first time, pilot communities in extractive regions were identified where companies in the extractives sector would disclose their contributions, as part of meeting requirements under Ukraine's budget code on rent payments (Extractive Industries Transparency Initiative, 2020[47]). Some of the rent payments are affiliated with production, non-production and transport-related royalties, as well as with fees for water use.

### Disclosure practices in Ukraine's energy companies

On a broader scale, energy companies in Ukraine have yet to improve transparency and disclosure practices, particularly in terms of non-financial reporting. Some of the key energy companies, including Naftogaz, Ukrhydroenergo, Ukrenergo, Energoatom and DTEK, among others, have significantly improved their non-financial reporting practices, as they issue annual reports containing RBC-related information. In addition, these companies have also started using frameworks, such as GRI, in presenting their non-financial performance. However, according to the Ukraine Company Transparency Index developed by the Corporate Governance Professional Association (CGPA) and the Centre for CSR Development Ukraine, such practices still remain limited. For example, in 2018, only 13% of companies in Ukraine across all sectors produced reports showing indicators of corporate social responsibility (CGPA, 2020[54]). Moreover, where they exist, the publication of non-financial reports can often be intermittent, including among both private and state-owned companies (OECD, 2021[2]). Moreover, while companies in the extractives sector are subject to disclosures based on EITI, practices vary and remain to be enforced on a broader scale. For example, Naftogaz is strictly required to ensure transparency and accountability regarding its operations in the oil and gas sector. While similar requirements are applicable to state-owned coal companies, information is often not fully disclosed or accessible (OECD, 2021[18]).

## Labour rights

### Challenges in enforcing legislation to protect labour rights

Ukraine has developed legal and regulatory frameworks to protect labour rights, which is applicable to the energy sector. The country's Labour Code has been the main legal basis for employer-employee relations. Along with outlining labour rights, it contains provisions regarding collective agreements, trade unions, employee contracts, occupational health and female employment, among others. In addition, the rights of trade unions and associations are outlined in the Constitution and in other normative acts. The unions may conduct inspections, demand information from companies and communicate with employees. Employees belonging to trade unions may engage in collective bargaining and disciplinary action. Moreover, Ukraine has introduced sector-specific legislation regarding occupational safety measures, particularly in nuclear and hydrocarbons sectors, and the operation of specialised equipment (OECD, 2021[18]).

Despite these requirements, there have been challenges in ensuring implementation and protecting workers' rights due to existing contradictions in the legal framework. Notably, while the Labour Code provides for the right to strike "to defend one's economic and social interests", the Mining Law prohibits strikes (Verkhovna Rada of Ukraine, 1999[55]). Regardless of these contradictions and, as further outlined in the subsequent section, in recent years coal miners have held strikes due to wage arrears.

The State Labour Service, under the supervision and control of the Ministry of Social Policy, is responsible for implementing the regulatory framework on labour inspection and enforcing laws relating to labour conditions, employment, safety and health. It is a central executive body established in accordance with the requirements of the Resolution of the CMU of September 10, 2014 "On optimising the system of central executive bodies" as a result of merging the State Mining Supervision Service and Industrial Safety with the State Labour Inspectorate. However, due to moratoria on state inspection of activities in coal mines, there have been challenges in ensuring workplace safety (ILO, 2018[56]) (US Department of State, 2020[57]).

### Labour rights challenges in the energy sector

According to the National Baseline Assessment on Business and Human Rights, mining sector in Ukraine continues to witness significant health and safety challenges. Specific problems in coal mining include workplace accidents, deriving from coal miners often lacking protective equipment and operating in hazardous conditions (OECD, 2021[2]) (Yaroslav Mudryi National Law University, 2019[9]). In addition, state-owned mines do not provide timely payments of salaries, which has resulted in protests due to considerable wage arrears (Yaroslav Mudryi National Law University, 2019[9]). In June 2020, coal miners, in co-ordination with the Independent Trade Union of Miners of Ukraine, held strikes due to wage arrears amounting to UAH 1.2 billion. While the Ministry of Energy allocated UAH 340 million to repay debts owed to miners of state-owned mines, challenges have continued (Industriall Global Union, 2020[58]). Special attention should be also paid to forced labour and child labour in coal mines, including in loading, transporting and sorting coal (Yaroslav Mudryi National Law University, 2019[9]). In addition, coal mines in non-government controlled territories have witnessed cases of forced labour and exploitation, especially of internally displaced persons (OECD, 2021[2]).

In addition to challenges witnessed across coal mines, Ukrainian energy unions have expressed concerns about financial imbalances in the energy sector, which worsened during the Covid-19 pandemic due to drop in energy demand. In an event organised by IndustriAll, representatives from different Ukrainian energy unions, participants (i) called for an inclusive dialogue to achieve the goals of decarbonisation, (ii) agreed on the need to develop a common position, and (iii) stood in favour of an updated strategy to defend workers' rights (IndustriAll, 2020[59]). Union representatives also noted a lack of state control and co-ordination within the energy sector and transparency in decision-making. These issues were also identified in the National Baseline Assessment on Business and Human Rights, which stated that coal miners are normally not consulted by their employers before making important management decisions (Yaroslav Mudryi National Law University, 2019[9]).

### *Opportunities for achieving a just transition*

The Government of Ukraine, in collaboration with the European Commission, is looking to implement an initiative to help coal regions in Ukraine and in the Western Balkans to transition from coal towards a carbon-neutral economy (Box 8.5). The initiative aims to alleviate socioeconomic consequences of transition, while promoting the development of new, future-oriented economic activities. The funding and technical assistance will come from the European Commission, the World Bank, the European Bank for Reconstruction and Development, the Energy Community Secretariat, Poland's National Fund for Environment Protection and Water Management, and the College of Europe in Natolin (European Investment Bank, 2021[60]). As of July 2021, however, the Government of Ukraine did not have a national policy or strategy to promote just transition across coal regions and lacked public policies to respond to the needs of coal miners.

**Box 8.5. Just Transition in the Donetsk Region: The 7C4SD initiative**

In May 2019, several coal mining towns in Ukraine joined efforts with NGOs and a regional Chamber of Commerce and Industry to create a Platform for Sustainable Development of Coal Towns in the Donetsk Region. The goal of the Platform is to communicate specific needs of local governments and communities in developing and implementing policies related to coal transition. The selected communities (including Dobropillia, Myrnohrad, Novohrodivka, Pokrovsk, Selydove, Toretsk and Vuhledar) have been affected by armed conflict and receive between 40% to 80% of their budget from coal companies. The representatives of the Platform have also become members of the Co-ordination Centre for Transformation of Coal Regions, through which they can communicate their initiatives to the central government.

Source: (European Commission, 2020[61])

### *Human rights in Ukraine's energy sector*

#### *Overview of human rights issues in Ukraine*

Further to the National Strategy on Human Rights mentioned above, Ukraine has ratified major international instruments on human rights, consisting of the Universal Declaration of Human Rights and ILO standards. It has also created an office for Ukrainian Parliament Commissioner for Human Rights to ensure the observance of human rights and freedoms, while providing citizens with an opportunity to appeal in case of infringements. While these developments have presented positive steps, Ukraine has continued to experience human rights challenges, which can also be affiliated with Ukraine's energy sector. Although the constitution guarantees freedom of speech and expression, journalists and civil society activists continue facing threats, intimidation and violence. Moreover, numerous rights, including freedom of expression, assembly and association remain restricted in the non-government controlled areas. Notably, outspoken critics and minorities (including members of the Crimean Tatar community) in these areas have been subject to intimidation, harassment and politically motivated arrests. Further challenges are faced by internally displaced persons, who are vulnerable forced labour and exploitation (OECD, 2021[2]).

#### *Human rights challenges in energy companies operating in non-government controlled territories*

More than 90% of coal resources in Ukraine are located in the Donetsk coal basin, while nearly half of the country's coal supply previously came from Donetsk and Luhansk (the Donbass). However, following the 2013-2014 Euromaidan protests and Russia's occupation of Crimea, armed groups seized control of parts of the Donbass region. The eruption of an armed conflict with Russian-backed separatists in the East of Ukraine further exacerbated economic conditions of the region and resulted in seizure of assets, damaged public infrastructure and loss of individual and corporate property (OHCHR, 2019[62]). These challenges resulted in supply chain disruptions in Ukraine's energy sector. While Ukraine produced 65 million tonnes of coal in 2014, its output amounted to 33.3 million tonnes by 2018, which introduced challenges with regard to Ukraine's energy security (OECD, 2019[26]). Some of the coal mines in the East halted or reduced operations – for example, out of seven mines located in the Toretsk city situated in the Donbass, only two, the Tsentralna and the Toretska mines, are still operational (NBC news, 2021[63]).

This situation significantly impacted the workers in the Donbass. Further to facing irregular employment and significant reduction (and, at times, absence) of wages, active combat has contributed to the loss of electricity and damages to mines and plants, which have posed safety risks. Notably, shelling has resulted in mine collapses, emergency power outages and shutdowns of ventilator systems, and difficulties in evacuating miners working underground. Workers often lack protective gear and face moratoria on inspections, while having limited opportunities to defend their rights due to severe restrictions on freedom of expression and assembly. In parallel, the region has also witnessed illegal coal mining and forced labour, with a monthly coal supply to government-controlled areas amounting to approximately 600,000 tonnes. (However, since coal transit ended between the government and non-government controlled territories in 2017, coal supplies from the latter have been redirected towards other economies. Also see Box 8.6 regarding the OECD *Due Diligence Guidance for Responsible Supply Chains of Minerals from Conflict-Affected and High-Risk Areas*) (OECD, 2021[2]) (OHCHR, 2019[62]). Further to coal mines, other companies engaged in coal production industry associations, mine construction departments and machine-building have experienced challenges in their operations, though there is limited information regarding their activities (ILO, 2018[56]).

The Office of the High Commissioner of Human Rights has also identified that retirees of extractive and energy companies residing in the Donbass have limited access to pensions and social security benefits. In particular, those looking to obtain pensions are required to regularly travel to government-controlled territories, which provides a challenge for those facing health and mobility issues (Human Rights Watch, 2021[64]).

**Box 8.6. OECD Due Diligence Guidance for Responsible Supply Chains of Minerals from Conflict-Affected and High-Risk Areas**

The *OECD Due Diligence Guidance for Responsible Supply Chains of Minerals from Conflict-Affected and High-Risk Areas* provides a framework to help companies sourcing from or directly operating in conflict-affected areas prevent or mitigate adverse impacts, including financing conflict or fuelling, facilitating or exacerbating conditions of conflict. The framework includes the following steps:

1. *Establish strong company management systems.* Companies are expected to (i) adopt and clearly communicate their policies to their suppliers, which should incorporate the standards against which due diligence is conducted; (ii) structure internal management to establish due diligence; (iii) establish systems of transparency and controls over the supply chain; (iv) strengthen company's engagement with suppliers, with a view to improving due diligence performance; (v) establish a company-level (or industry-wide) grievance mechanism.
2. *Identify and assess risks in the supply chain.* Companies are expected to (i) identify risks in the supply chain and (ii) assess risks of adverse impacts in light of the standards of their supply chain policy (consistent with Annex II recommendations).
3. *Design and implement a strategy to respond to identified risks.* Companies are expected to (i) report findings of supply chain risk assessment to relevant senior management within the company; (ii) devised and adopt a risk management plan; (iii) implement a risk management plan, and monitor and track performance of risk mitigation efforts; (iv) undertake additional fact and risk assessments requiring mitigation, or in case of change in circumstances.
4. *Carry out independent third-party audit of supply chain due diligence at identified points in the supply chain.* Companies should have due diligence practices identified by independent third parties, which may be verified by an independent institutionalised mechanism.
5. *Report on supply chain due diligence.* Companies should publicly disclose and report on their supply chain due diligence policies and practices, and may do so through their annual or sustainability reports.

Source: (OECD, 2016[65])

### *Women's employment in Ukraine's energy sector*

In 2005, a Law "On ensuring equal rights and opportunities for women and men" was introduced in Ukraine, which aims to avoid gender-based discrimination, including in the energy sector. However, Gender Inequality Index positions Ukraine 52$^{nd}$ out of 162 countries. As in many countries, Ukraine's energy sector continues to witness a gender wage gap and limited participation of women. This partly stems from lack of women obtaining tertiary education in Science, Technology, Engineering and Mathematics (STEM), as they represent less than one-third among the total number of graduates.[5] However, according to a 2019 study, one-third of women encountered discrimination in the workplace, while 19% stated that they were denied employment due to their gender and 23% stated that they earned less than men. A comparison of average monthly wages of men and women revealed that while the average gender wage gap in Ukraine's labour market is approximately 25%, the gap is wider (approx. 40%) in the mining sector and slightly narrower in the supply of power, gas, steam and air conditioning (approx. 20%) (BOELL, 2019[66]) (BOELL, 2019[67]).

## Outlook and policy recommendations

Despite progress in recent years, Ukraine should continue efforts in improving RBC framework across areas, including social and environmental protection, disclosure, and anti-corruption within its energy sector. Further to attracting quality investments and meeting international commitments, stronger RBC policy framework can enable energy companies to mitigate adverse RBC impacts throughout their operations, supply chains and business relationships, and contribute to sustainable development. Specific recommendations are as follows:

- **Further streamline the existing policy frameworks on RBC and ensure applicability to Ukraine's energy sector.** Over the years, Ukraine has adopted RBC-related policies, including the Concept on CSR and the National Strategy on Human Rights, which introduced provisions related to business and human rights. However, further steps are needed to streamline these policies and ensure alignment with the *OECD Guidelines for Multinational Enterprises* and related guidance, while continuing efforts to develop a national action plan on business and human rights. Moreover, RBC policies should be translated within legal and regulatory frameworks applicable to Ukraine's energy sector and efforts should be made to ensure their implementation.
- **Ensure protections and enforcement to prevent RBC-related infringements in the energy sector.** This includes strengthening human and labour rights protections, particularly in addressing challenges in the state-owned coal sector, preventing discrimination against women and vulnerable groups, and encouraging just transition. Further efforts are needed to improve environmental protection, paying attention to air pollution and emissions, and low energy efficiency, as well as engaging in climate action. Furthermore, moratoria on inspections should be removed.
- **Encourage energy companies to carry out due diligence to address and mitigate RBC-related risks throughout their operations, as well as in their supply chains and business relationships.** Although a number of companies have started embedding RBC due diligence frameworks, practices should be encouraged on a broader scale. In particular, efforts should be made to align with the OECD *Due Diligence Guidance for Responsible Supply Chains of Minerals from Conflict-Affected and High-Risk Areas* for companies operating or engaged in the coal sector.
- **Strengthen anti-corruption efforts in the energy sector.** In particular, Ukraine should ensure that anti-corruption institutions, such as SAPO, NABU and the High Anti-Corruption Court are sufficiently empowered, staffed and resourced to carry out investigations. In parallel, anti-corruption regulations and requirements should be further streamlined to avoid potential conflicts and ensure enforcement. In parallel, both state-owned and private companies should be expected to implement high standards of disclosure and transparency, and develop risk management systems, while improving internal controls, ethics and compliance measures.
- **Enforce transparency and disclosure in the energy sector, and strengthen non-financial reporting requirements** so that companies disclose information on human rights, environment protection, labour rights and risk mitigation, among other areas. Further efforts are needed to implement laws and regulations, and ensure compliance with EITI requirements.
- **Strengthen the role of Ukraine's National Contact Point.** The NCP can play a key role in promoting the OECD MNE Guidelines and in raising awareness among energy companies, civil society organisations and trade unions to promote RBC practices. The NCP can also act as an effective non-judicial grievance mechanism with which stakeholders in the energy sector can engage.

## Notes

[1] Further to the cross-sectoral OECD Due Diligence Guidance for Responsible Business Conduct, sector-specific instruments include: OECD Due Diligence Guidance for Responsible Supply Chains of Minerals from Conflict-Affected and High-Risk Areas minerals; the OECD-FAO Guidance on Responsible Agricultural Supply Chains; the Due Diligence Guidance for Meaningful Stakeholder Engagement in the Extractive Sector; the OECD Due Diligence Guidance for Responsible Supply Chains in the Garment and Footwear Sector; and the OECD Due Diligence Guidance for Responsible Corporate Lending and Securities Underwriting.

[2] See *Ten Human Rights priorities for the power and utilities sector* available at https://www.bsr.org/en/our-insights/primers/10-human-rights-priorities-power-and-utilities-sector and *Renewable Energy & Human Rights Benchmark* available at https://www.business-humanrights.org/en/from-us/briefings/renewable-energy-human-rights-benchmark/

[3] See https://www.ua.undp.org/content/ukraine/en/home/presscenter/articles/2021/ukraines-government-approves-action-plan-for-new-national-human-rights-strategy.html.

[4] More specifically, these include the International Covenant on Civil and Political Rights, International Covenant on Economic, Social and Cultural Rights, International Convention on the Elimination of All Forms of Racial Discrimination, Convention on the Elimination of all Forms of Discrimination Against Women, Convention against Torture and Other Cruel, Inhuman or Degrading Treatment or Punishment, Convention on the Rights of the Child, Convention on the Rights of Persons with Disabilities, core International Labour Organisation (ILO) Conventions, European Convention on Human Rights and Fundamental Freedoms.

[5] According to (BOELL, 2019[66]), on a global level, women take up 20% of jobs in the energy sector, though represent 1% in senior management positions.

## References

Bankwatch Network (2020), *Ukraine's dangerous air pollution problem in desperate need of solutions*, https://bankwatch.org/blog/ukraine-s-dangerous-air-pollution-problem-in-desperate-need-of-solutions. [45]

BOELL (2020), *European Green Deal and the contest against corruption: what is at stake in Ukraine?, Heinrich Boell Stiftung: Gunda Werner Institute*, https://ua.boell.org/en/2020/09/29/european-green-deal-and-contest-against-corruption-what-stake-ukraine. [34]

BOELL (2019), *Women and Men in the Ukrainian Energy Sector: Equal Rights and Opportunities or a Sector of Discrimination?*, Heinrich Boell Stiftung: Gunda Werner Institute, https://www.gwi-boell.de/en/2019/07/22/women-and-men-ukrainian-energy-sector-equal-rights-and-opportunities-or-sector. [67]

BOELL (2019), *Women in Ukraine's Energy Sector*, https://ua.boell.org/uk/2019/06/13/zhinki-ta-choloviki-v-energetichnomu-sektori-ukrayini-0. [66]

Centre for Economic Strategy (2020), *Lack of trust in judiciary majority obstacle to foreign investment in Ukraine*, https://ces.org.ua/en/lack-of-trust-in-judiciary-major-obstacle-to-foreign-investment-in-ukraine/. [17]

Centrenergo (2019), *Environmental protection activities*, http://www.centrenergo.com/en/env-protection/. [33]

CGPA (2020), *Ukraine Company Transparency Index 2019, Corporate Governance Professional Association*, https://cgpa.com.ua/en/novini/index/. [54]

Chatham House (2018), *Are Ukraine's Anti-corruption Reforms Working?*, https://www.chathamhouse.org/sites/default/files/publications/research/2018-11-19-ukraine-anti-corruption-reforms-lough-dubrovskiy.pdf. [16]

Danish Institute for Human Rights (2021), *National Action Plan on Business and Human Rights*, https://globalnaps.org/country/ukraine/. [7]

DiXi Group (2018), *Infographics about the Law 6629 "on ensuring transparency in extractive industries"*, https://www.slideshare.net/ssuser4149c5/dixi-6229-brochureengstr. [51]

DTEK (2020), *Annual Report 2019*, DTEK Group, https://dtek.com/content/announces/dtek_annual-report-2019_pdf_s226_t3112.pdf. [32]

Energy Community (2016), *Case ECS 13/16: Ukraine/Environment*, https://www.energy-community.org/legal/cases/2016/case1316UA.html. [38]

Environmental Performance Index (2020), *Yale Environmental Performance Index Ukraine*, https://epi.yale.edu/epi-country-report/UKR. [44]

EU4Climate (2020), *Climate policy development and advancing cooperation with the EU in Ukraine*, https://eu4climate.eu/wp-content/uploads/countries/EU4Climate-UKRAINE.pdf. [50]

EUEA (2018), *Environmental Impact Assessment (EIA) for wind and solar projects in Ukraine - European-Ukrainian Energy Agency*, https://euea-energyagency.org/en/news/euea-latest-accomplishments/environmental-impact-assessment-eia-for-wind-solar-projects-in-ukraine/. [42]

European Business Association (2020), *Government has legalised the development of CSR for the first time in Ukraine*, https://eba.com.ua/en/vpershe-v-ukrayini-uryad-legalizuvav-rozvytok-ksv-napryamku/. [11]

European Commission (2020), *Just Transition Platform Meeting - coal regions in transition virtual week 16-19 November 2020*, https://ec.europa.eu/info/events/just-transition-platform-meeting-16-19-november-2020_en. [61]

European Investment Bank (2021), *EIB records high investments in Ukraine in 2020: over €1 billion for infrastructure, environment, innovation and post-COVID-19 recovery*, https://www.eib.org/en/press/all/2021-042-eib-records-high-investments-in-ukraine-in-2020-over-eur1-billion-for-infrastructure-environment-innovation-and-post-covid-19-recovery#. [60]

Extractive Industries Transparency Initiative (2021), *Board decision on the second validation of Ukraine*, https://eiti.org/scorecard-pdf?filter%5Bcountry%5D=26&filter%5Byear%5D=2020. [53]

Extractive Industries Transparency Initiative (2020), *Ukraine 2019 Annual Progress Report*, https://eiti.org/publication-types-public/annual-progress-report. [47]

Extractive Industries Transparency Initiative (2019), *Ukraine's revolution against corruption and hidden ownership*, https://eiti.org/blog/ukraines-revolution-against-corruption-hidden-ownership. [14]

Extractive Industries Transparency Initiative (2018), *Ukraine passes extractive industries transparency law based on best practice from EITI and EU*, https://eiti.org/news/ukraine-transprarency-law. [52]

Flaker, M., B. Sergi and F. Teichmann (2021), "Extractive industries, corruption and potential solutions: the case of Ukraine", *Resources Policy*, Vol. 69/4, http://dx.doi.org/10.1016/j.resourpol.2020.101844. [15]

Government of Ukraine (2021), *Decree of the President of Ukraine N. 119-2021 about the National Strategy in the field of human rights*, https://www.president.gov.ua/documents/1192021-37537. [6]

Government of Ukraine (2021), *More than 2 billion hryvnias of losses were calculated by the inspection agency for environmental violations during 2020*, https://www.dei.gov.ua/posts/1343. [49]

Government of Ukraine (2021), *Unified register for environmental impact assessment*, http://eia.menr.gov.ua/. [40]

Government of Ukraine (2020), *Anti-corruption strategy*, https://nazk.gov.ua/en/anti-corruption-strategy/. [19]

Government of Ukraine (2020), *NABU exposed corrupt scheme of causing UAH 51 million damages to coal mining state enterprise*, https://nabu.gov.ua/en/novyny/nabu-exposed-corrupt-scheme-causing-uah-51-million-damages-coal-mining-state-enterprises. [24]

Government of Ukraine (2020), *Order on approval of the Concept for the implementation of state policy in the field of promoting the development of socially responsible business in Ukraine for the period up to 2030 (No. 66-r)*, Cabinet of Ministers of Ukraine, https://zakon.rada.gov.ua/laws/show/66-2020-%D1%80#Text. [10]

Government of Ukraine (2020), *Ukraine's greenhouse gas inventory*. [31]

Government of Ukraine (2018), *Our mission and functions*, https://eng.dei.gov.ua/. [46]

Government of Ukraine (2017), *On approval of the Energy Strategy of Ukraine for the period up to 2035 "Security, energy efficiency, competitiveness"*, Cabinet of Ministers of Ukraine, https://www.kmu.gov.ua/ua/npas/250250456. [12]

Government of Ukraine (2015), *National Action Plan on Human Rights*, https://www.coe.int/t/commissioner/source/NAP/Ukraine-National-Action-Plan-on-Human-Rights.pdf. [4]

Human Rights Watch (2021), *Ukraine Events of 2020*, https://www.hrw.org/world-report/2021/country-chapters/ukraine#. [64]

ILO (2018), *Occupational safety and health in the mining industry in Ukraine*, International Labour Organization, https://www.ilo.org/wcmsp5/groups/public/---europe/---ro-geneva/---sro-budapest/documents/publication/wcms_670764.pdf. [56]

IndustriAll (2020), *Ukrainian energy unions demand dialogue for Just Transition*, http://www.industriall-union.org/ukrainian-energy-unions-demand-dialogue-for-just-transition. [59]

Industriall Global Union (2020), *Ukrainian coal miners win after 11-day protest*, Industriall Global Union, http://www.industriall-union.org/ukrainian-coal-miners-win-after-11-day-protest. [58]

International Finance Corporation (2017), *Environmental, Health, and Safety Guidelines for Onshore Oil and Gas Development.* [28]

International Finance Corporation (2008), *Environmental, Health, and Safety Guidelines for Thermal Power Plants*, https://www.ifc.org/wps/wcm/connect/9ec08f40-9bc9-4c6b-9445-b3aed5c9afad/Thermal+Power+Guideline+2017+clean.pdf?MOD=AJPERES&CVID=lNwcJZX. [29]

International Monetary fund (2020), *Ukraine: request for stand-by arrangement-press release; Staff Report; and Statement by the Executive Director of Ukraine*, https://www.imf.org/en/Publications/CR/Issues/2020/06/10/Ukraine-Request-for-Stand-by-Arrangement-Press-Release-Staff-Report-and-Statement-by-the-49501. [20]

International Renaissance Foundation (2020), *European Green Deal: opportunities and threats to Ukraine*, https://www.irf.ua/wp-content/uploads/2020/09/web_european-green-deal_2020_en.pdf. [35]

NABU (2021), *NABU investigation into the fuel and energy sector*, https://nabu.gov.ua/open-office/biblio/infographics/rozsliduvannya-nabu-v-galuzi-pek. [13]

NABU (2020), *4 persons were given notices of suspicion of UAH 14.33 million funds embezzlement allocated on coal mines*, https://nabu.gov.ua/en/novyny/4-persons-were-given-notices-suspicion-uah-1433-million-funds-embezzlement-allocated-coal. [25]

Naftogaz (2020), *Annual Report 2019*, Naftogaz Group, http://www.naftogaz.com/files/Zvity/Naftogaz_2019_EN.pdf. [23]

NBC news (2021), *Ukraine's war-torn Donbas region is on the verge of environmental disaster*, https://www.nbcnews.com/news/world/ukraine-s-war-torn-donbas-region-verge-environmental-disaster-n1266372. [63]

OECD (2021), *OECD Review of the Corporate Governance of State-Owned Enterprises: Ukraine*, https://www.oecd.org/corporate/soe-review-ukraine.htm (accessed on 12 May 2021). [18]

OECD (2021), *Responsible Business Conduct and Due Diligence Practices in Ukraine's Energy Companies*, http://mneguidelines.oecd.org/responsible-business-conduct-due-diligence-practices-in-ukraine-energy-sector.htm. [2]

OECD (2020), *Annual Report on the OECD Guidelines for Multinational Enterprises 2020: Update on National Contact Point Activity*, http://mneguidelines.oecd.org/2020-Annual-Report-MNE-Guidelines-EN.pdf. [3]

OECD (2019), *Responsible business: Key messages from international instruments, UN OHCHR, OECD, EU, ILO*, https://mneguidelines.oecd.org/Brochure-responsible-business-key-messages-from-international-instruments.pdf. [1]

OECD (2019), *Snapshot of Ukraine's Energy Sector: Institutions, Governance and Policy Framework*, https://www.oecd.org/eurasia/competitiveness-programme/eastern-partners/Snapshot-of-Ukraines-Energy-Sector-EN.pdf. [26]

OECD (2016), *OECD Due Diligence Guidance for Responsible Supply Chains of Minerals from Conflict-Affected and High-Risk Areas: Third Edition*, OECD Publishing, Paris, https://dx.doi.org/10.1787/9789264252479-en. [65]

OHCHR (2019), *Report on the human rights situation in Ukraine 16 August to 15 November 2019*, https://reliefweb.int/report/ukraine/report-human-rights-situation-ukraine-16-august-15-november-2019-enruuk. [62]

State Statistics Service of Ukraine (2019), *Statistical Yearbook 2018*, http://ukrstat.gov.ua/druk/publicat/kat_u/2019/zb/11/Zb_dovk_2018.pdf. [43]

State Statistics Service of Ukraine (n.d.), *Statistical Yearbook 2018*, http://ukrstat.gov.ua/druk/publicat/kat_u/2019/zb/11/Zb_dovk_2018.pdf. [37]

STATISTA (2020), *Ukraine: installed power system capacity 2020, by plant type*, https://www.statista.com/statistics/1219982/ukraine-power-system-capacity-by-plant-type/. [30]

Synyutka, N. (2019), "Digitalisation of public procurement: the case study of Ukraine", *Annales Universitatis*, Vol. 3, pp. 61-71, http://dx.doi.org/10.17951/h.2019.53.3.61-71. [21]

Ukrainian Helsinki Human Rights Union (2020), *Evaluation of implementation of the National Human Rights Strategy (2016-2019)*, https://www.ua.undp.org/content/ukraine/en/home/library/democratic_governance/the-national-human-rights-strategy-assessment.html. [8]

Ukrenergo (2019), "Ukrenergo 2019 Sustainability Report", https://ua.energy/wp-content/uploads/2020/09/Ukrenergo_Sustainability-Report_2019.pdf. [22]

Ukrinform (2021), *Zelensky enacts National Human Rights Strategy*, https://www.ukrinform.net/rubric-society/3214900-zelensky-enacts-national-human-rights-strategy.html. [5]

Ukrinform (2020), *Ukraine preparing political agreement to join European Green Deal*, https://www.ukrinform.net/rubric-economy/3155719-ukraine-preparing-political-agreement-to-join-european-green-deal.html. [36]

US Department of State (2020), *2020 Investment Climate Statement of Ukraine*, https://2017-2021.state.gov/reports/2020-investment-climate-statements/ukraine/index.html. [57]

Vasil Kisil & Partners (2020), *State Ecological Inspection of Ukraine Launches a Major Assault on Polluting Factories: What Is Important to Know for Those Who Now Face State Environmental Examination*, https://www.lexology.com/library/detail.aspx?g=4bd139e6-d609-4478-bba4-6b562e2ed89e. [48]

Verkhovna Rada (2017), *Law of Ukraine on environmental impact assessment (2059-VIII)*, Verkhovna Rada of Ukraine, https://zakon.rada.gov.ua/laws/show/2059-19#Text. [39]

Verkhovna Rada of Ukraine (2020), *Amendments to the Law of Ukraine "On Environmental Impact Assessment" to Prevent the Occurrence and Spread of Coronavirus*, https://www.rada.gov.ua/news/Novyny/194390.html. [41]

Verkhovna Rada of Ukraine (1999), *Law on Mining*, https://zakon.rada.gov.ua/laws/show/1127-14#top. [55]

World Bank (2016), *Ukraine country environmental analysis*, https://openknowledge.worldbank.org/bitstream/handle/10986/24971/Ukraine000Coun0ironmental0analysis.pdf?sequence=4&isAllowed=y. [27]

Yaroslav Mudryi National Law University (2019), *Business and Human Rights: National Baseline Assessment*, https://legalforum.nlu.edu.ua/wp-content/uploads/2019/06/executive-summary.pdf. [9]

www.ingramcontent.com/pod-product-compliance
Ingram Content Group UK Ltd.
Pitfield, Milton Keynes, MK11 3LW, UK
UKHW051502290926
15471UKWH00008B/1358

9 789264 729971